THE NEW AVENGERS
SECRETS & LIES

Writer: **Brian Michael Bendis**

New Avengers #11-13
Penciler: **David Finch**
Inker: **Danny Miki**
Colorist: **Frank D'Armata**
Letterers: **Richard Starkings & Comicraft's Albert Deschesne**

Giant-Size Spider-Woman #1
Penciler: **Rick Mays**
Inker: **Jason Martin**
Colorist: **Rob Schwager**
Letterer: **Dave Sharpe**

New Avengers #14-15
Artist: **Frank Cho**
Colorist: **Jason Keith**
Letterers: **Richard Starkings & Comicraft's Albert Deschesne**

Covers: **David Finch, Andrea DiVito & Frank Cho**

Assistant Editors: **Molly Lazer & Aubrey Sitterson**
Associate Editor: **Andy Schmidt**
Editor: **Tom Brevoort**

Collection Editor: **Jennifer Grünwald** • Editorial Assistants: **James Emmett & Joe Hochstein**
Assistant Editors: **Alex Starbuck & Nelson Ribeiro** • Editor, Special Projects: **Mark D. Beazley**
Senior Editor, Special Projects: **Jeff Youngquist** • Senior Vice President of Sales: **David Gabriel**
SVP of Brand Planning & Communications: **Michael Pasciullo**

Editor in Chief: **Axel Alonso** • Chief Creative Officer: **Joe Quesada**
Publisher: **Dan Buckley** • Executive Producer: **Alan Fine**

NEW AVENGERS VOL. 3: SECRETS & LIES. Contains material originally published in magazine form as NEW AVENGERS #11-15 and GIANT-SIZE SPIDER-WOMAN #1. Fourth printing 2011. ISBN# 978-0-7851-1706-3. Published by MARVEL WORLDWIDE, INC., a subsidiary of MARVEL ENTERTAINMENT, LLC. OFFICE OF PUBLICATION: 135 West 50th Street, New York, NY 10020. Copyright © 2005 and 2006 Marvel Characters, Inc. All rights reserved. $14.99 per copy in the U.S. and $16.99 in Canada (GST #R127032852); Canadian Agreement #40668537. All characters featured in this issue and the distinctive names and likenesses thereof, and all related indicia are trademarks of Marvel Characters, Inc. No similarity between any of the names, characters, persons, and/or institutions in this magazine with those of any living or dead person or institution is intended, and any such similarity which may exist is purely coincidental. **Printed in the U.S.A.** ALAN FINE, EVP - Office of the President, Marvel Worldwide, Inc. and EVP & CMO Marvel Characters B.V.; DAN BUCKLEY, Publisher & President - Print, Animation & Digital Divisions; JOE QUESADA, Chief Creative Officer; JIM SOKOLOWSKI, Chief Operating Officer; DAVID BOGART, SVP of Business Affairs & Talent Management; TOM BREVOORT, SVP of Publishing; C.B. CEBULSKI, SVP of Creator & Content Development; DAVID GABRIEL, SVP of Publishing Sales & Circulation; MICHAEL PASCIULLO, SVP of Brand Planning & Communications; JIM O'KEEFE, VP of Operations & Logistics; DAN CARR, Executive Director of Publishing Technology; SUSAN CRESPI, Editorial Operations Manager; ALEX MORALES, Publishing Operations Manager; STAN LEE, Chairman Emeritus. For information regarding advertising in Marvel Comics or on Marvel.com, please contact John Dokes, SVP Integrated Sales and Marketing, at jdokes@marvel.com. For Marvel subscription inquiries, please call 800-217-9158. **Manufactured between 8/29/11 and 9/20/11 by QUAD/GRAPHICS, DUBUQUE, IA, USA.**

7 6 5 4

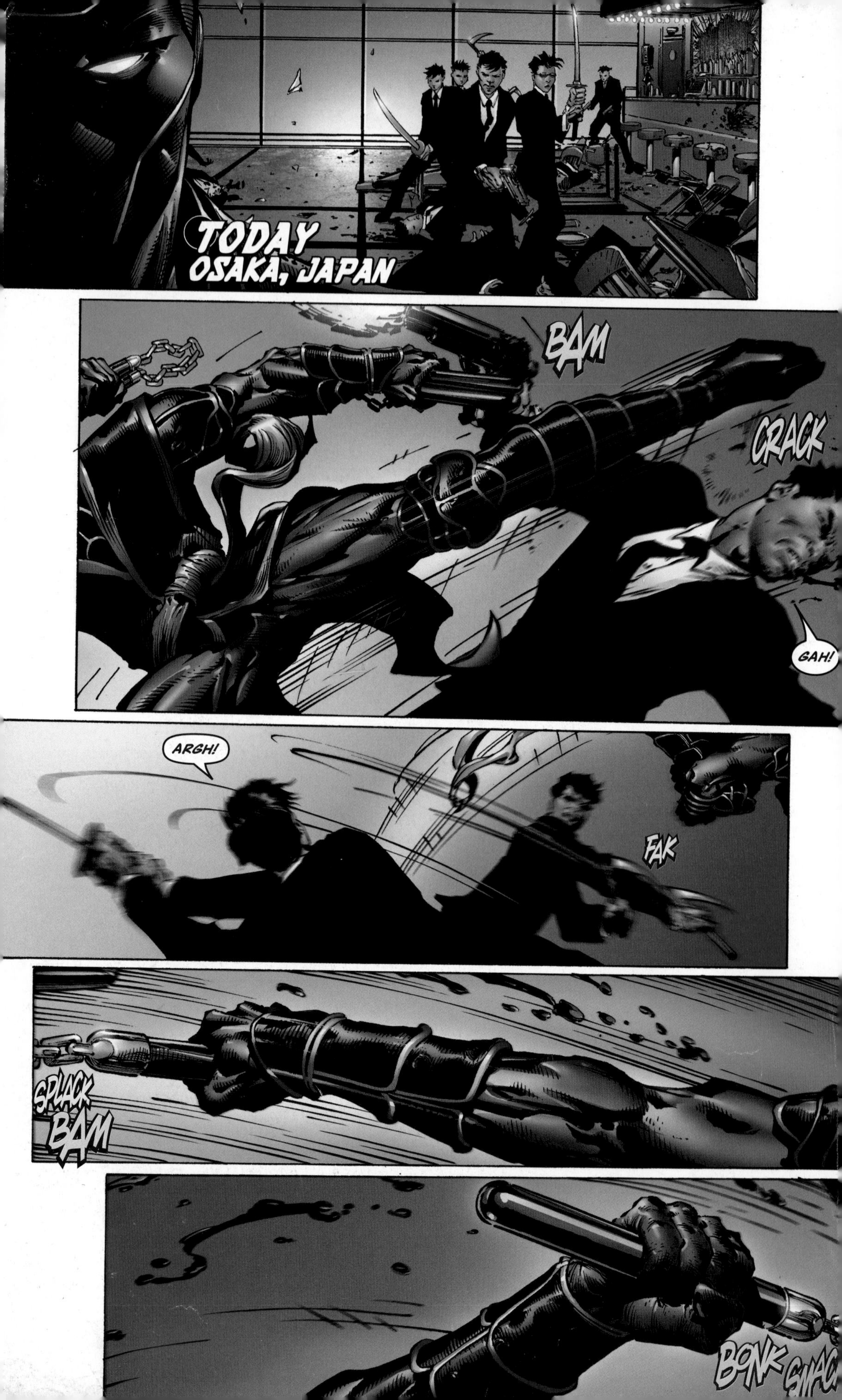
TODAY
OSAKA, JAPAN
BAM
CRACK
GAH!
ARGH!
FAK
SPLACK
BAM
BONK

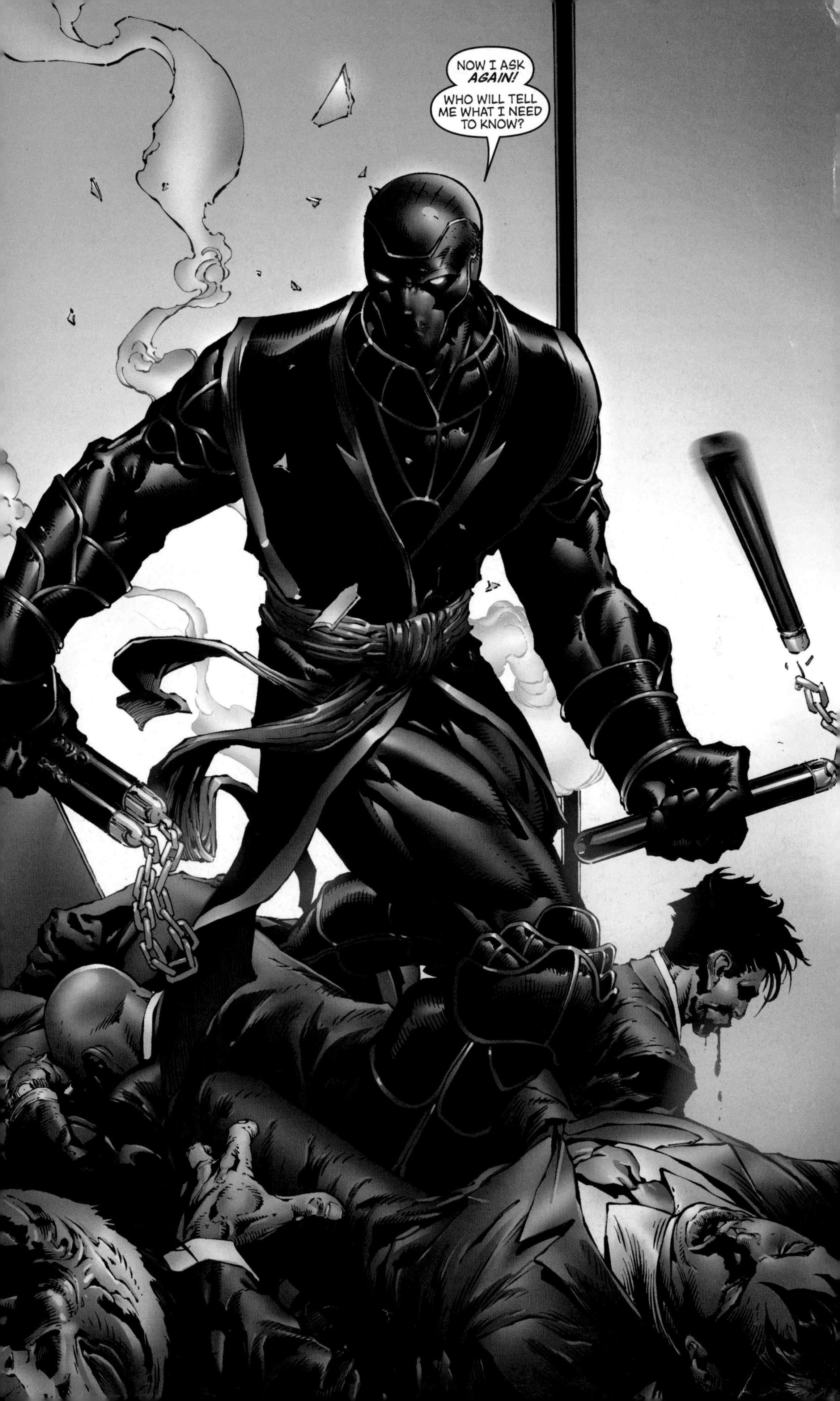
NOW I ASK **AGAIN!**
WHO WILL TELL ME WHAT I NEED TO KNOW?

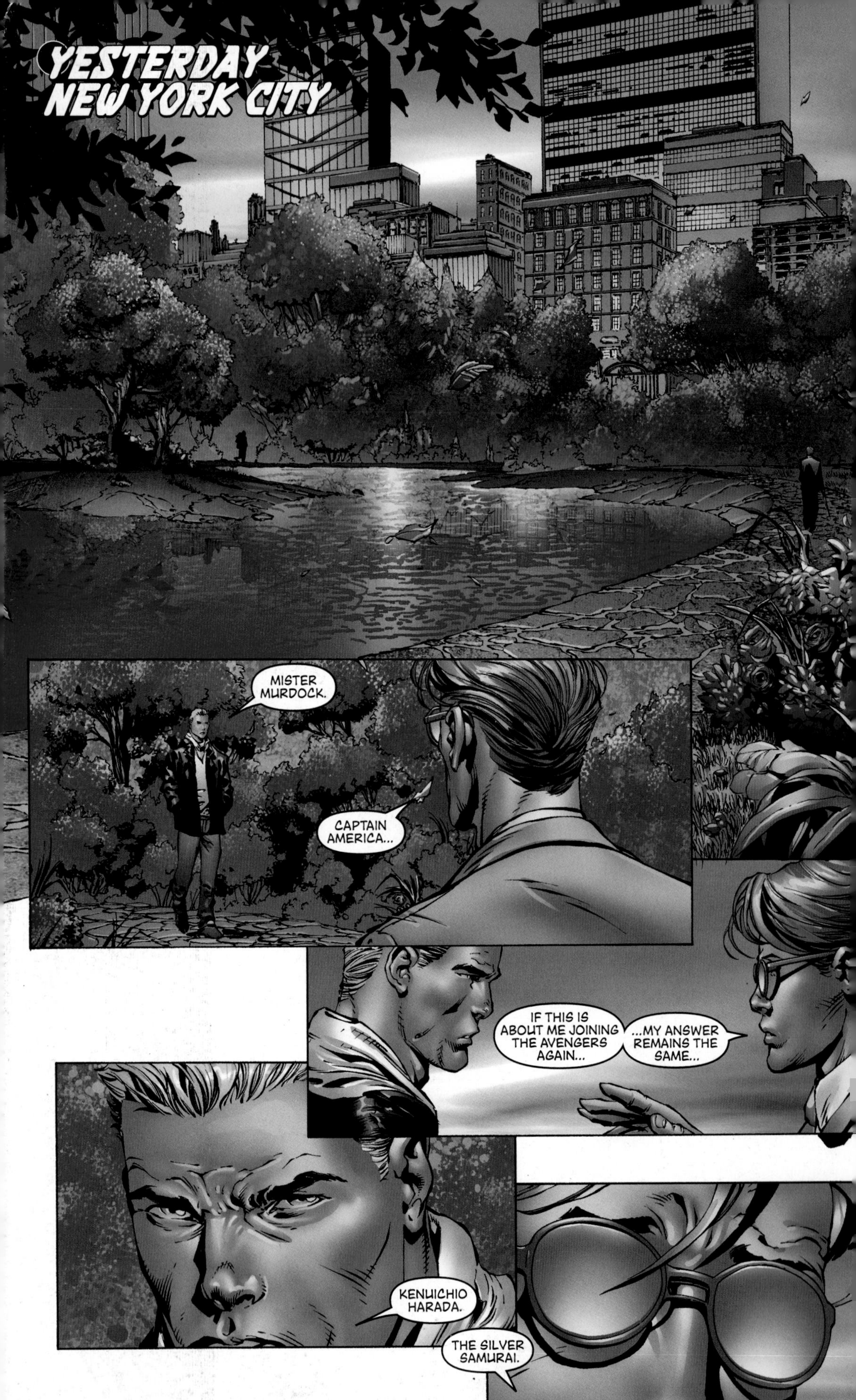
YESTERDAY NEW YORK CITY
MISTER MURDOCK.
CAPTAIN AMERICA...
IF THIS IS ABOUT ME JOINING THE AVENGERS AGAIN...
...MY ANSWER REMAINS THE SAME...
KENUICHIO HARADA.
THE SILVER SAMURAI.

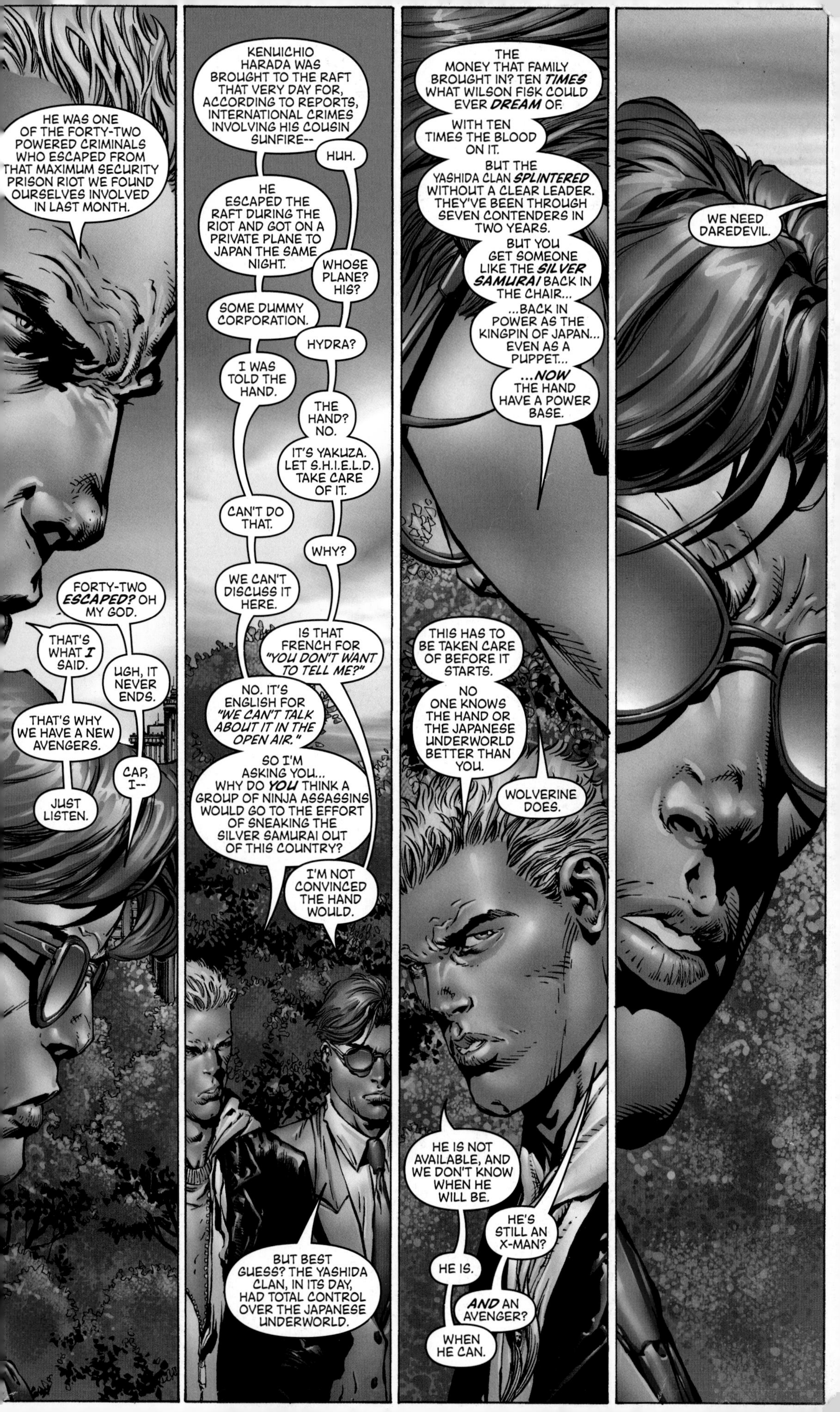
HE WAS ONE OF THE FORTY-TWO POWERED CRIMINALS WHO ESCAPED FROM THAT MAXIMUM SECURITY PRISON RIOT WE FOUND OURSELVES INVOLVED IN LAST MONTH.
FORTY-TWO ESCAPED? OH MY GOD.
THAT'S WHAT I SAID.
UGH, IT NEVER ENDS.
THAT'S WHY WE HAVE A NEW AVENGERS.
CAP, I--
JUST LISTEN.
KENUICHIO HARADA WAS BROUGHT TO THE RAFT THAT VERY DAY FOR, ACCORDING TO REPORTS, INTERNATIONAL CRIMES INVOLVING HIS COUSIN SUNFIRE--
HUH.
HE ESCAPED THE RAFT DURING THE RIOT AND GOT ON A PRIVATE PLANE TO JAPAN THE SAME NIGHT.
WHOSE PLANE? HIS?
SOME DUMMY CORPORATION.
HYDRA?
I WAS TOLD THE HAND.
THE HAND? NO.
IT'S YAKUZA. LET S.H.I.E.L.D. TAKE CARE OF IT.
CAN'T DO THAT.
WHY?
WE CAN'T DISCUSS IT HERE.
IS THAT FRENCH FOR "YOU DON'T WANT TO TELL ME?"
NO. IT'S ENGLISH FOR "WE CAN'T TALK ABOUT IT IN THE OPEN AIR."
SO I'M ASKING YOU... WHY DO YOU THINK A GROUP OF NINJA ASSASSINS WOULD GO TO THE EFFORT OF SNEAKING THE SILVER SAMURAI OUT OF THIS COUNTRY?
I'M NOT CONVINCED THE HAND WOULD.
BUT BEST GUESS? THE YASHIDA CLAN, IN ITS DAY, HAD TOTAL CONTROL OVER THE JAPANESE UNDERWORLD.
THE MONEY THAT FAMILY BROUGHT IN? TEN TIMES WHAT WILSON FISK COULD EVER DREAM OF.
WITH TEN TIMES THE BLOOD ON IT.
BUT THE YASHIDA CLAN SPLINTERED WITHOUT A CLEAR LEADER. THEY'VE BEEN THROUGH SEVEN CONTENDERS IN TWO YEARS.
BUT YOU GET SOMEONE LIKE THE SILVER SAMURAI BACK IN THE CHAIR...
...BACK IN POWER AS THE KINGPIN OF JAPAN... EVEN AS A PUPPET...
...NOW THE HAND HAVE A POWER BASE.
THIS HAS TO BE TAKEN CARE OF BEFORE IT STARTS.
NO ONE KNOWS THE HAND OR THE JAPANESE UNDERWORLD BETTER THAN YOU.
WOLVERINE DOES.
HE IS NOT AVAILABLE, AND WE DON'T KNOW WHEN HE WILL BE.
HE'S STILL AN X-MAN?
HE IS.
AND AN AVENGER?
WHEN HE CAN.
WE NEED DAREDEVIL.

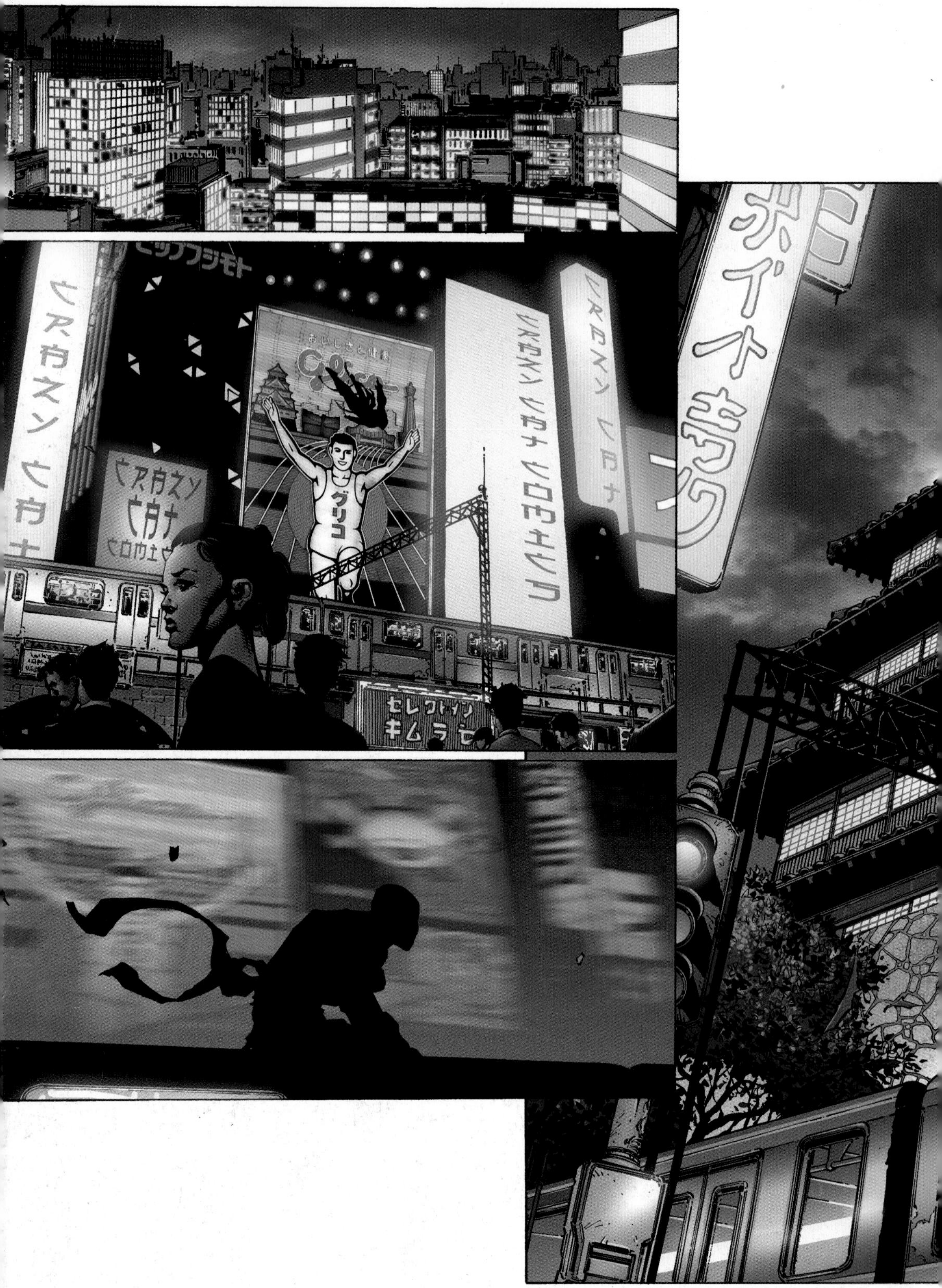

おいしさと健康
グリコ

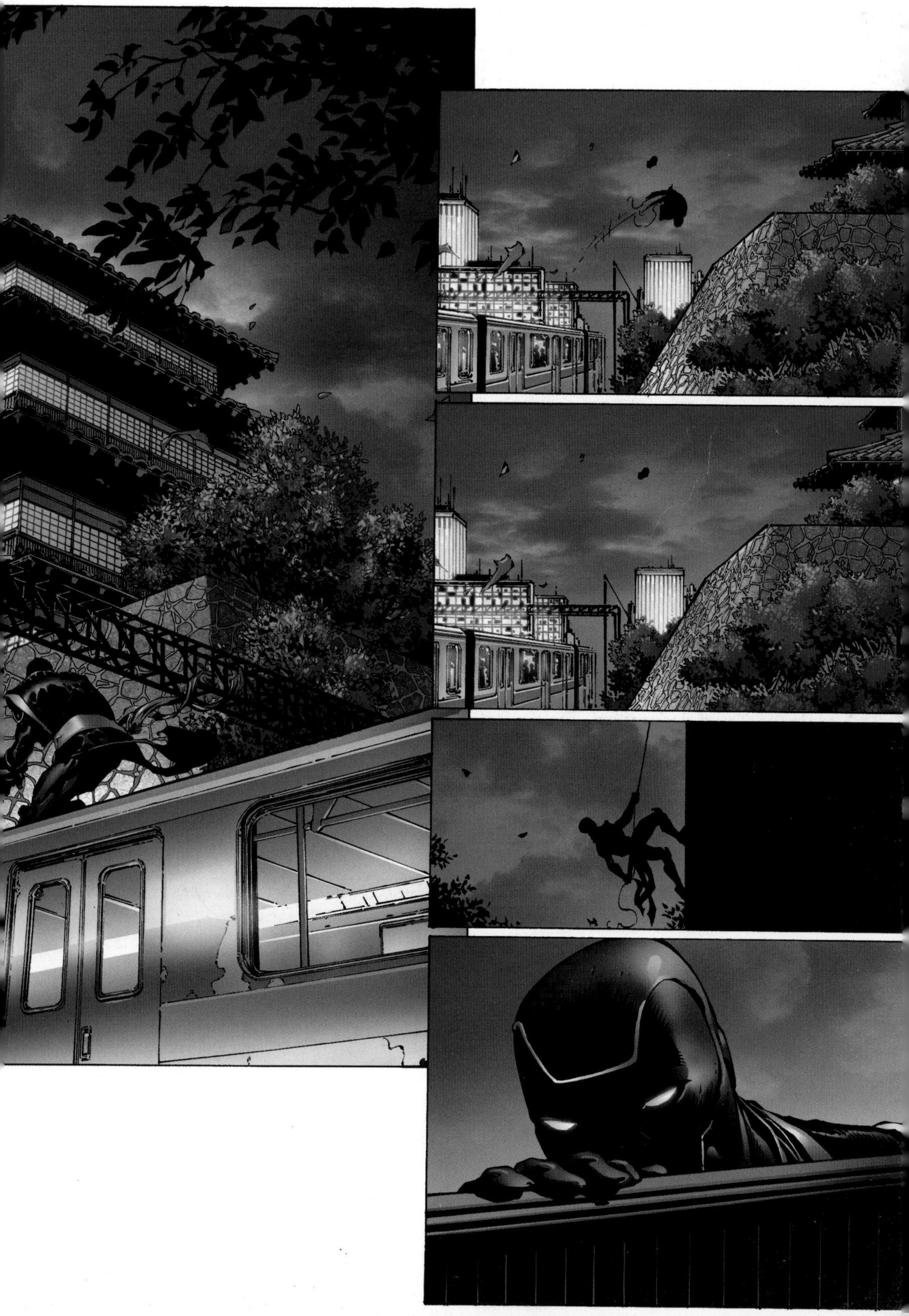

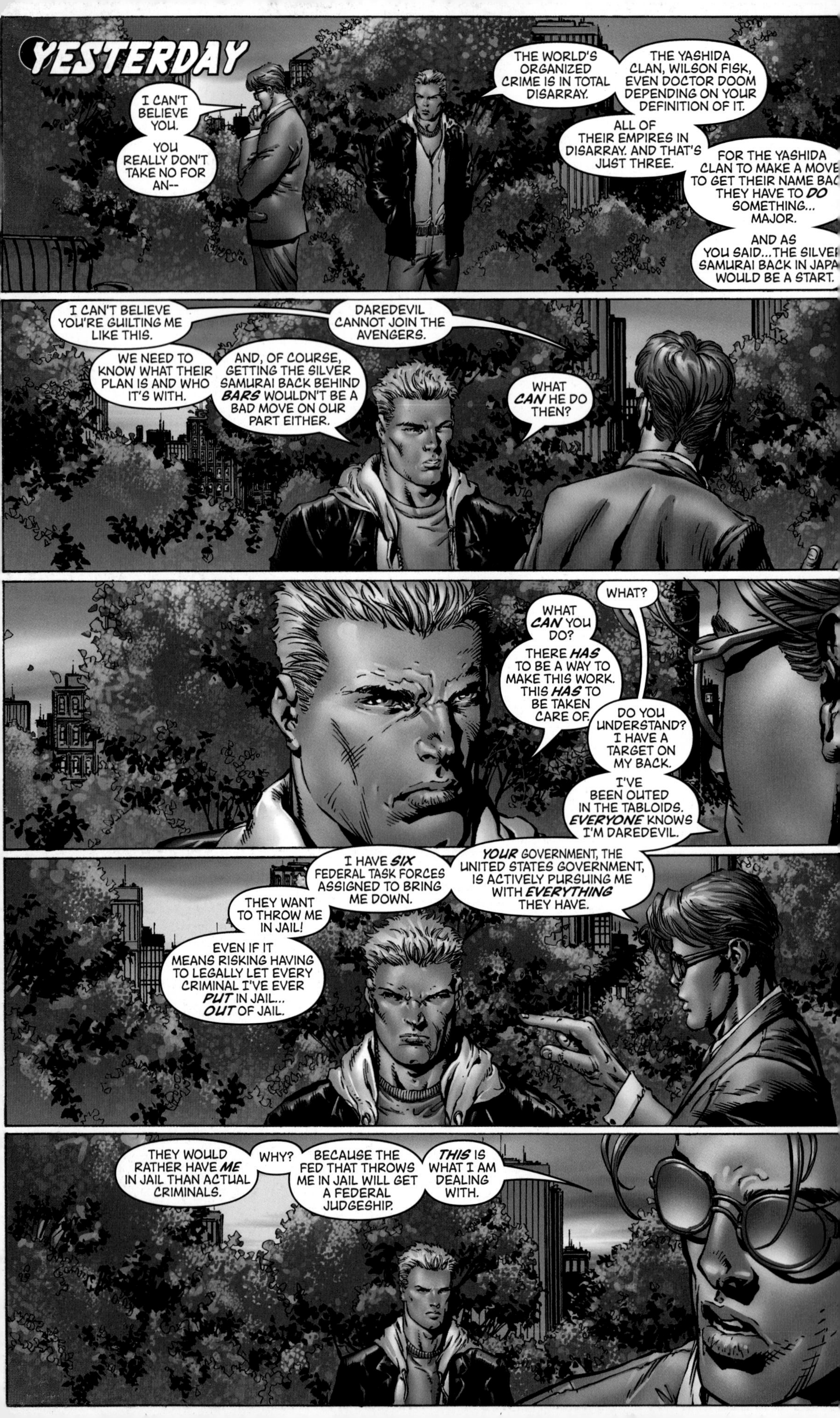
YESTERDAY
I CAN'T BELIEVE YOU.
YOU REALLY DON'T TAKE NO FOR AN--
THE WORLD'S ORGANIZED CRIME IS IN TOTAL DISARRAY.
THE YASHIDA CLAN, WILSON FISK, EVEN DOCTOR DOOM DEPENDING ON YOUR DEFINITION OF IT.
ALL OF THEIR EMPIRES IN DISARRAY. AND THAT'S JUST THREE.
FOR THE YASHIDA CLAN TO MAKE A MOVE TO GET THEIR NAME BAC THEY HAVE TO DO SOMETHING... MAJOR.
AND AS YOU SAID... THE SILVEI SAMURAI BACK IN JAPA WOULD BE A START.
I CAN'T BELIEVE YOU'RE GUILTING ME LIKE THIS.
DAREDEVIL CANNOT JOIN THE AVENGERS.
WE NEED TO KNOW WHAT THEIR PLAN IS AND WHO IT'S WITH.
AND, OF COURSE, GETTING THE SILVER SAMURAI BACK BEHIND BARS WOULDN'T BE A BAD MOVE ON OUR PART EITHER.
WHAT CAN HE DO THEN?
WHAT?
WHAT CAN YOU DO?
THERE HAS TO BE A WAY TO MAKE THIS WORK. THIS HAS TO BE TAKEN CARE OF.
DO YOU UNDERSTAND? I HAVE A TARGET ON MY BACK.
I'VE BEEN OUTED IN THE TABLOIDS. EVERYONE KNOWS I'M DAREDEVIL.
YOUR GOVERNMENT, THE UNITED STATES GOVERNMENT, IS ACTIVELY PURSUING ME WITH EVERYTHING THEY HAVE.
I HAVE SIX FEDERAL TASK FORCES ASSIGNED TO BRING ME DOWN.
THEY WANT TO THROW ME IN JAIL!
EVEN IF IT MEANS RISKING HAVING TO LEGALLY LET EVERY CRIMINAL I'VE EVER PUT IN JAIL... OUT OF JAIL.
THEY WOULD RATHER HAVE ME IN JAIL THAN ACTUAL CRIMINALS.
WHY?
BECAUSE THE FED THAT THROWS ME IN JAIL WILL GET A FEDERAL JUDGESHIP.
THIS IS WHAT I AM DEALING WITH.

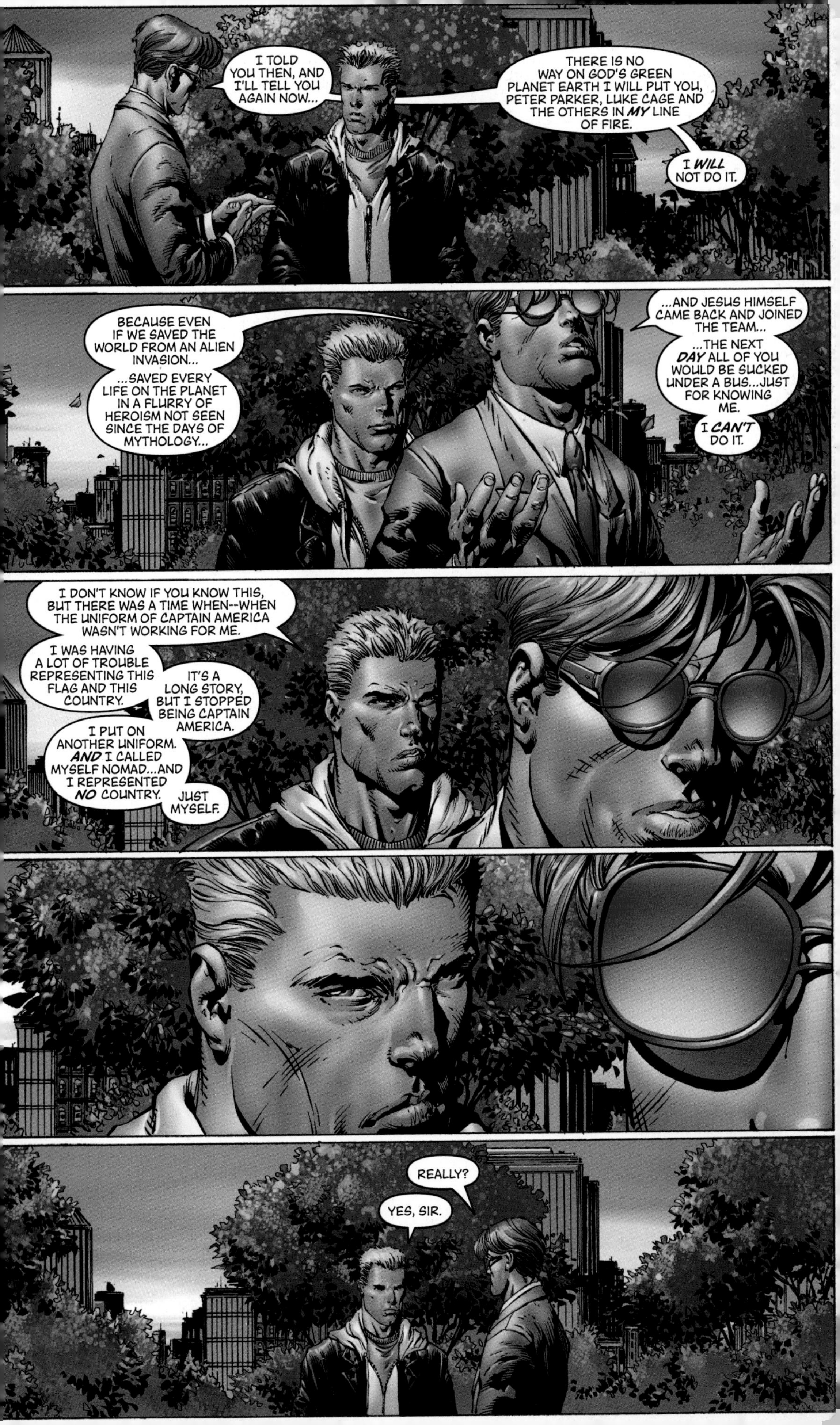
I TOLD YOU THEN, AND I'LL TELL YOU AGAIN NOW...
THERE IS NO WAY ON GOD'S GREEN PLANET EARTH I WILL PUT YOU, PETER PARKER, LUKE CAGE AND THE OTHERS IN ***MY*** LINE OF FIRE.
I ***WILL*** NOT DO IT.
BECAUSE EVEN IF WE SAVED THE WORLD FROM AN ALIEN INVASION...
...SAVED EVERY LIFE ON THE PLANET IN A FLURRY OF HEROISM NOT SEEN SINCE THE DAYS OF MYTHOLOGY...
...AND JESUS HIMSELF CAME BACK AND JOINED THE TEAM...
...THE NEXT ***DAY*** ALL OF YOU WOULD BE SUCKED UNDER A BUS...JUST FOR KNOWING ME.
I ***CAN'T*** DO IT.
I DON'T KNOW IF YOU KNOW THIS, BUT THERE WAS A TIME WHEN--WHEN THE UNIFORM OF CAPTAIN AMERICA WASN'T WORKING FOR ME.
I WAS HAVING A LOT OF TROUBLE REPRESENTING THIS FLAG AND THIS COUNTRY.
IT'S A LONG STORY, BUT I STOPPED BEING CAPTAIN AMERICA.
I PUT ON ANOTHER UNIFORM. ***AND*** I CALLED MYSELF NOMAD...AND I REPRESENTED ***NO*** COUNTRY.
JUST MYSELF.
REALLY?
YES, SIR.

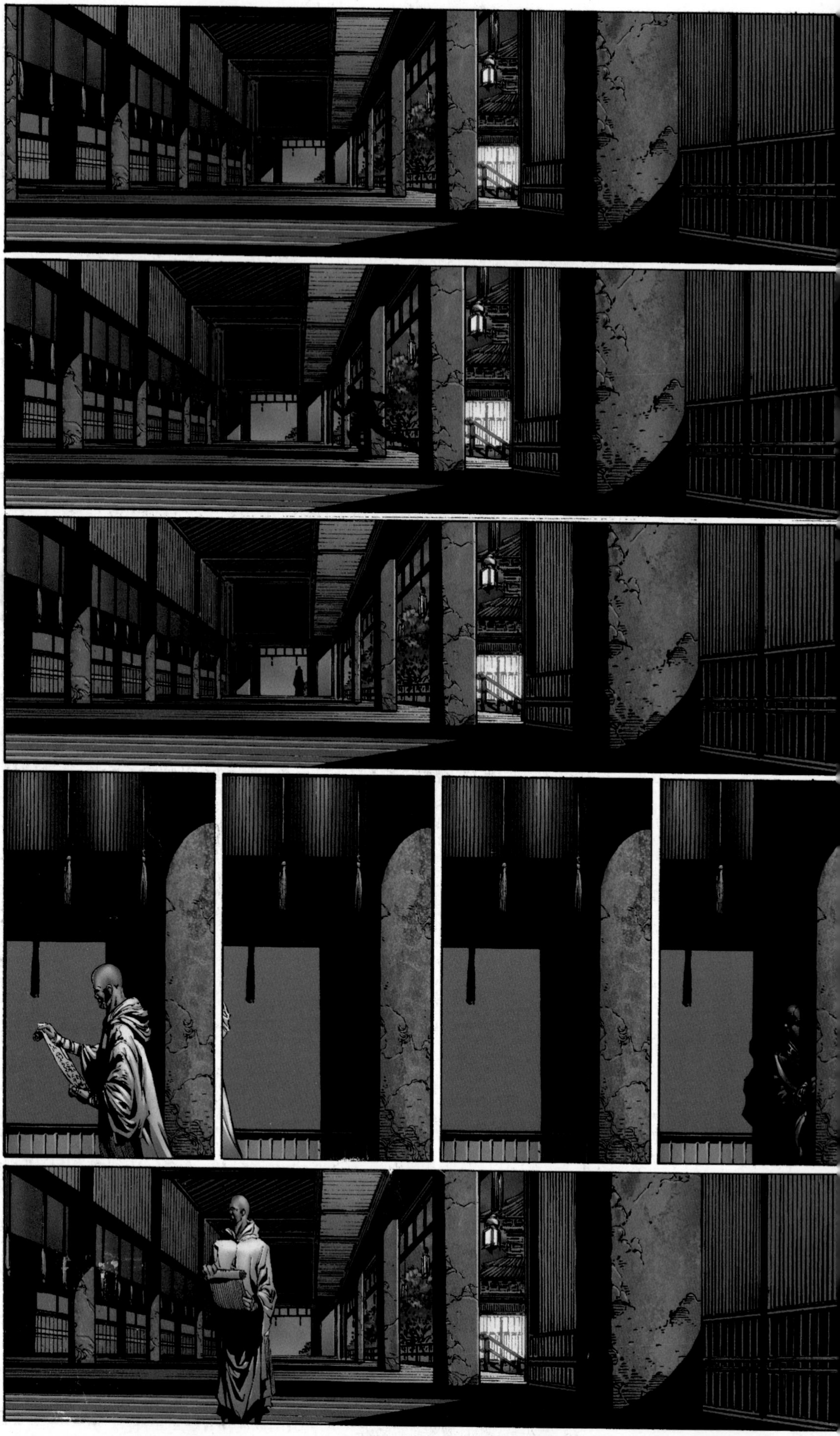

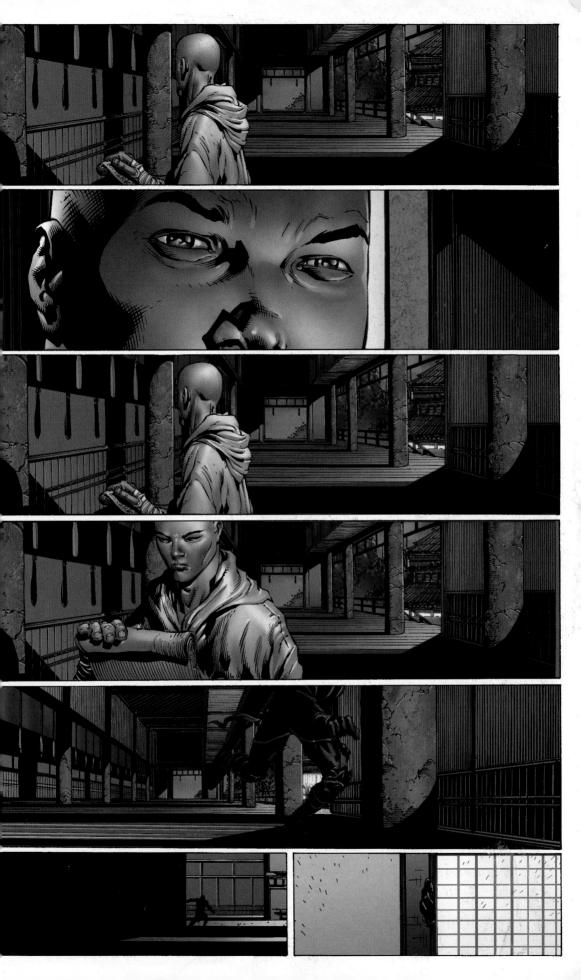

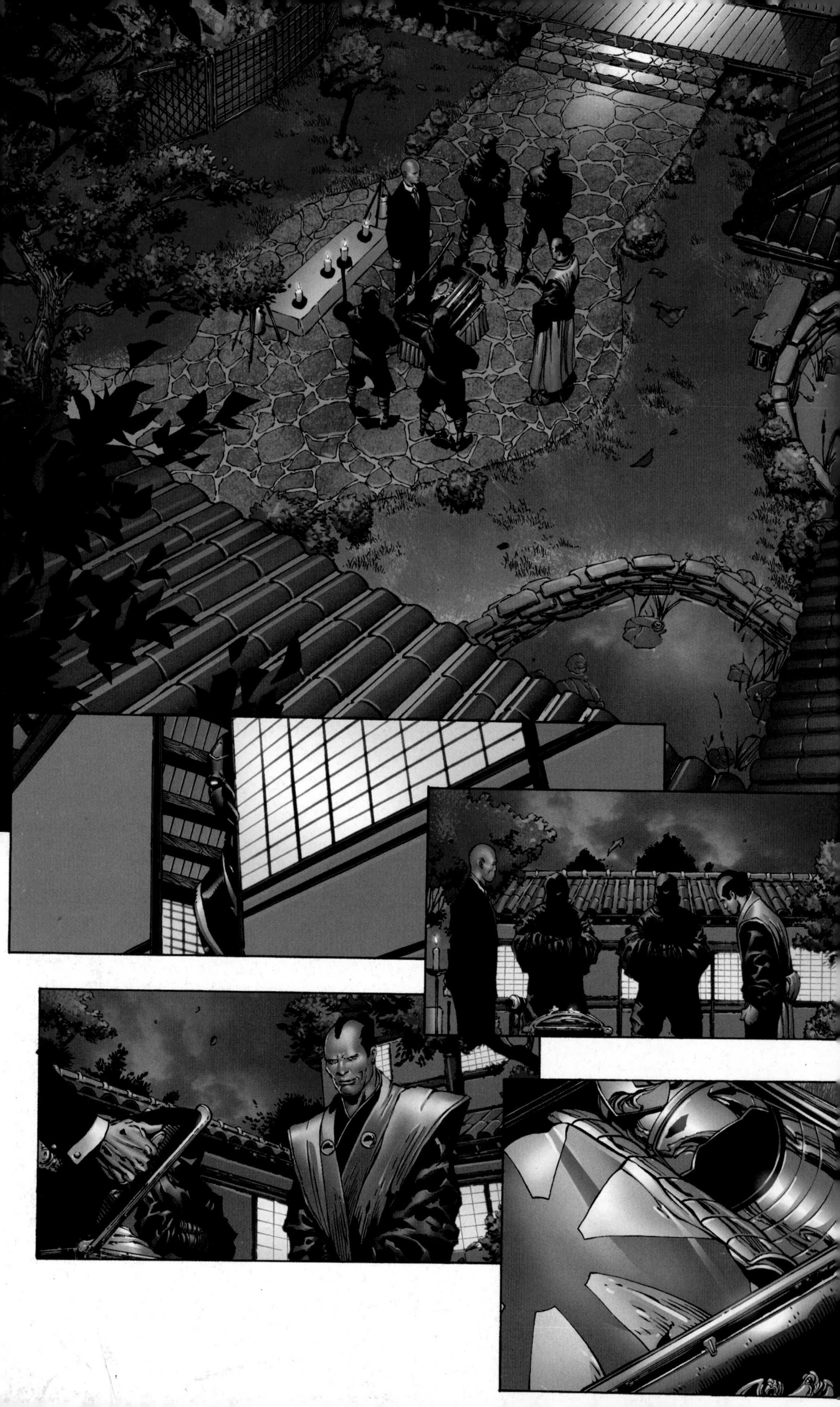

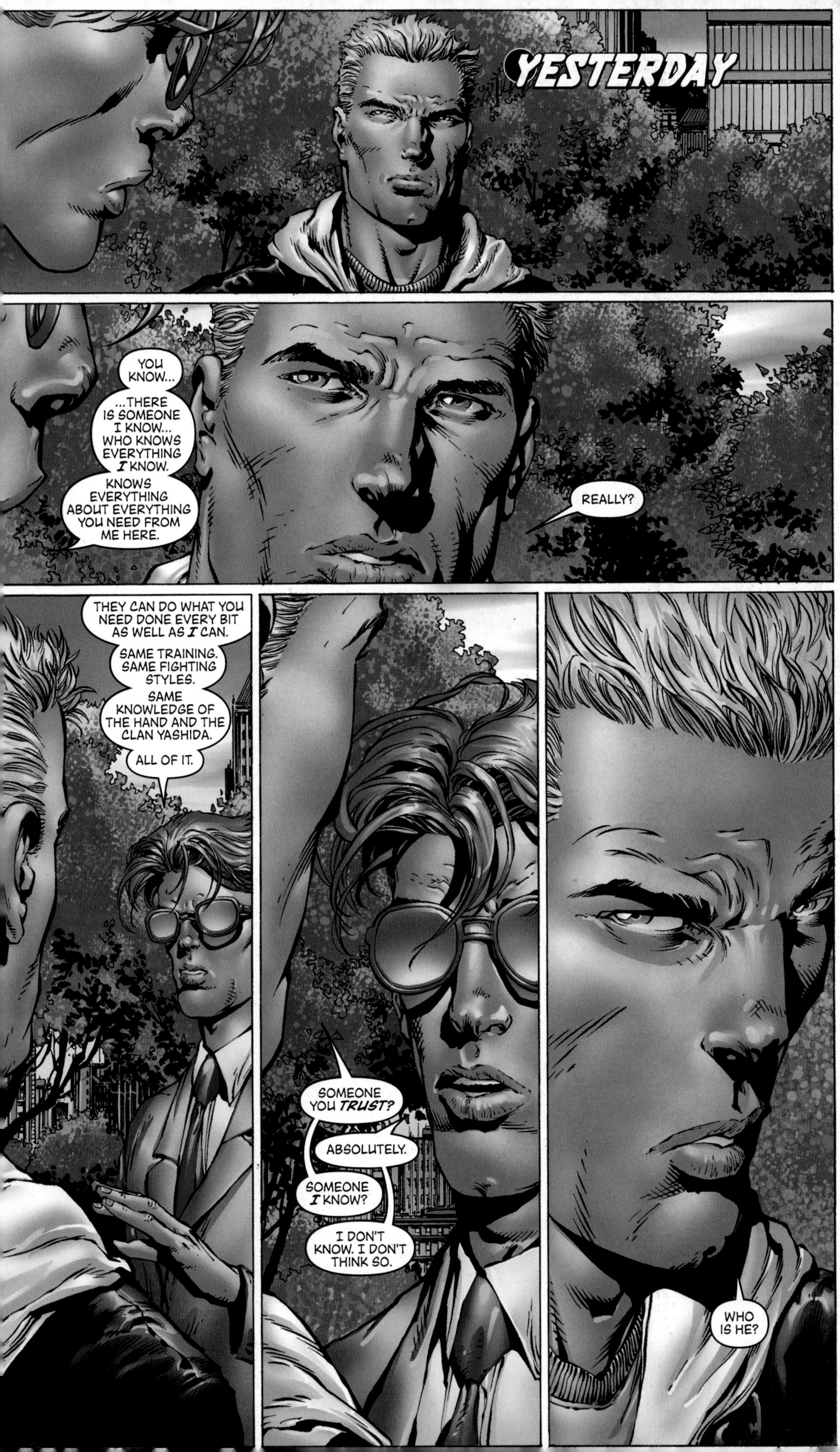
YESTERDAY
YOU KNOW...
...THERE IS SOMEONE I KNOW... WHO KNOWS EVERYTHING I KNOW.
KNOWS EVERYTHING ABOUT EVERYTHING YOU NEED FROM ME HERE.
REALLY?
THEY CAN DO WHAT YOU NEED DONE EVERY BIT AS WELL AS I CAN.
SAME TRAINING. SAME FIGHTING STYLES.
SAME KNOWLEDGE OF THE HAND AND THE CLAN YASHIDA.
ALL OF IT.
SOMEONE YOU TRUST?
ABSOLUTELY.
SOMEONE I KNOW?
I DON'T KNOW. I DON'T THINK SO.
WHO IS HE?

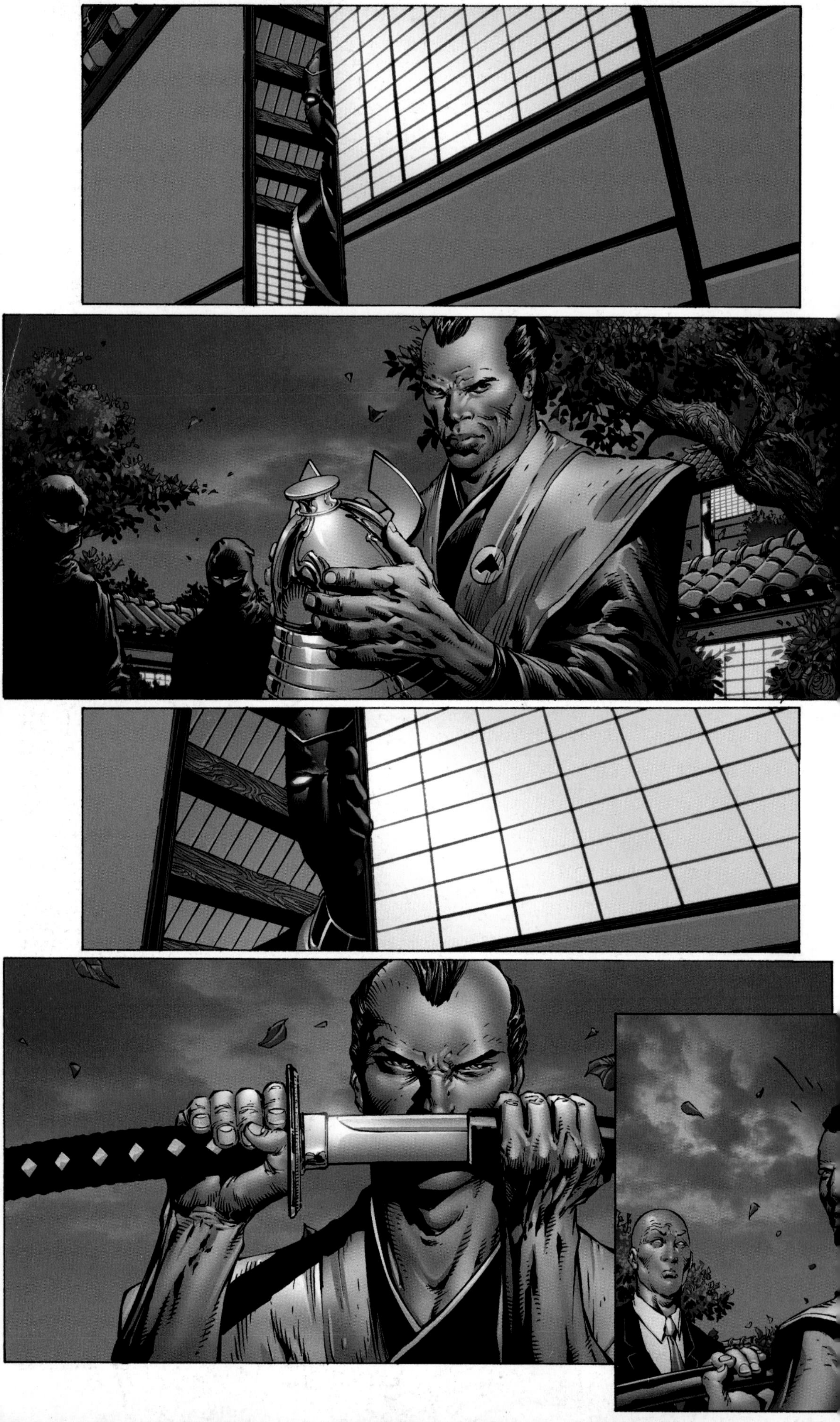

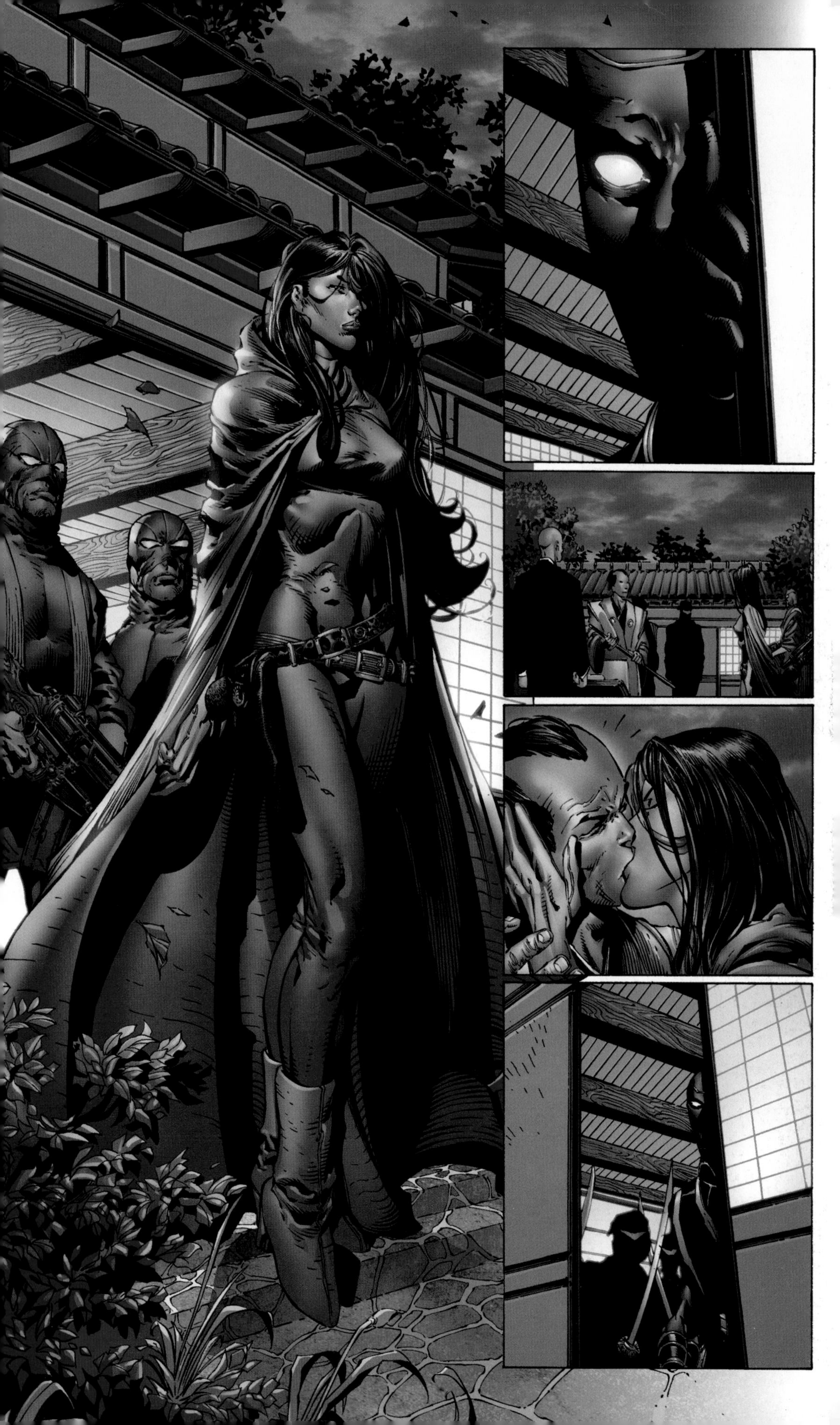

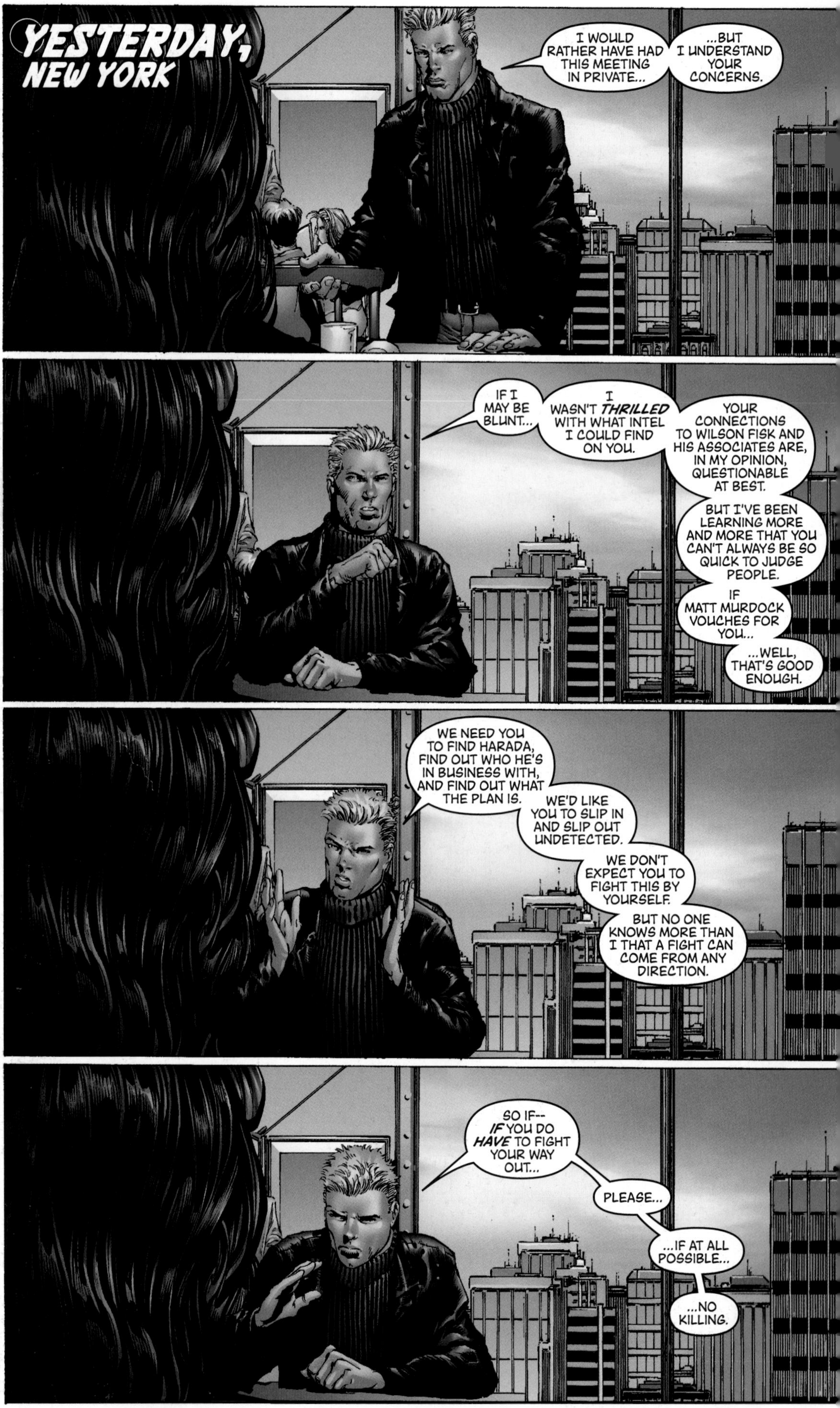
YESTERDAY, NEW YORK
I WOULD RATHER HAVE HAD THIS MEETING IN PRIVATE...
...BUT I UNDERSTAND YOUR CONCERNS.
IF I MAY BE BLUNT...
I WASN'T THRILLED WITH WHAT INTEL I COULD FIND ON YOU.
YOUR CONNECTIONS TO WILSON FISK AND HIS ASSOCIATES ARE, IN MY OPINION, QUESTIONABLE AT BEST.
BUT I'VE BEEN LEARNING MORE AND MORE THAT YOU CAN'T ALWAYS BE SO QUICK TO JUDGE PEOPLE.
IF MATT MURDOCK VOUCHES FOR YOU...
...WELL, THAT'S GOOD ENOUGH.
WE NEED YOU TO FIND HARADA, FIND OUT WHO HE'S IN BUSINESS WITH, AND FIND OUT WHAT THE PLAN IS.
WE'D LIKE YOU TO SLIP IN AND SLIP OUT UNDETECTED.
WE DON'T EXPECT YOU TO FIGHT THIS BY YOURSELF.
BUT NO ONE KNOWS MORE THAN I THAT A FIGHT CAN COME FROM ANY DIRECTION.
SO IF-- IF YOU DO HAVE TO FIGHT YOUR WAY OUT...
PLEASE...
...IF AT ALL POSSIBLE...
...NO KILLING.

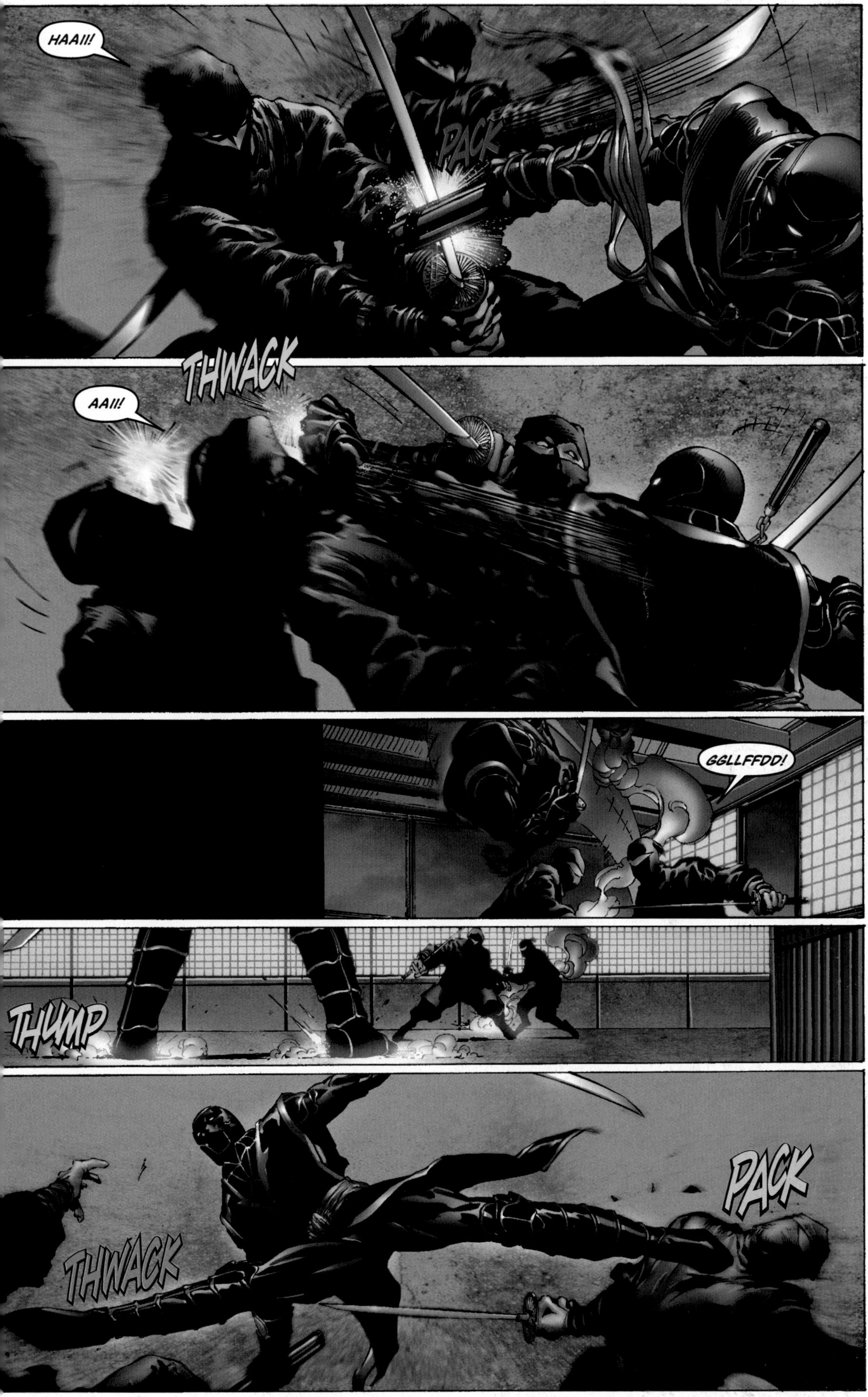
HAAII!
PACK
THWACK
AAII!
GGLLFFDD!
THUMP
PACK
THWACK

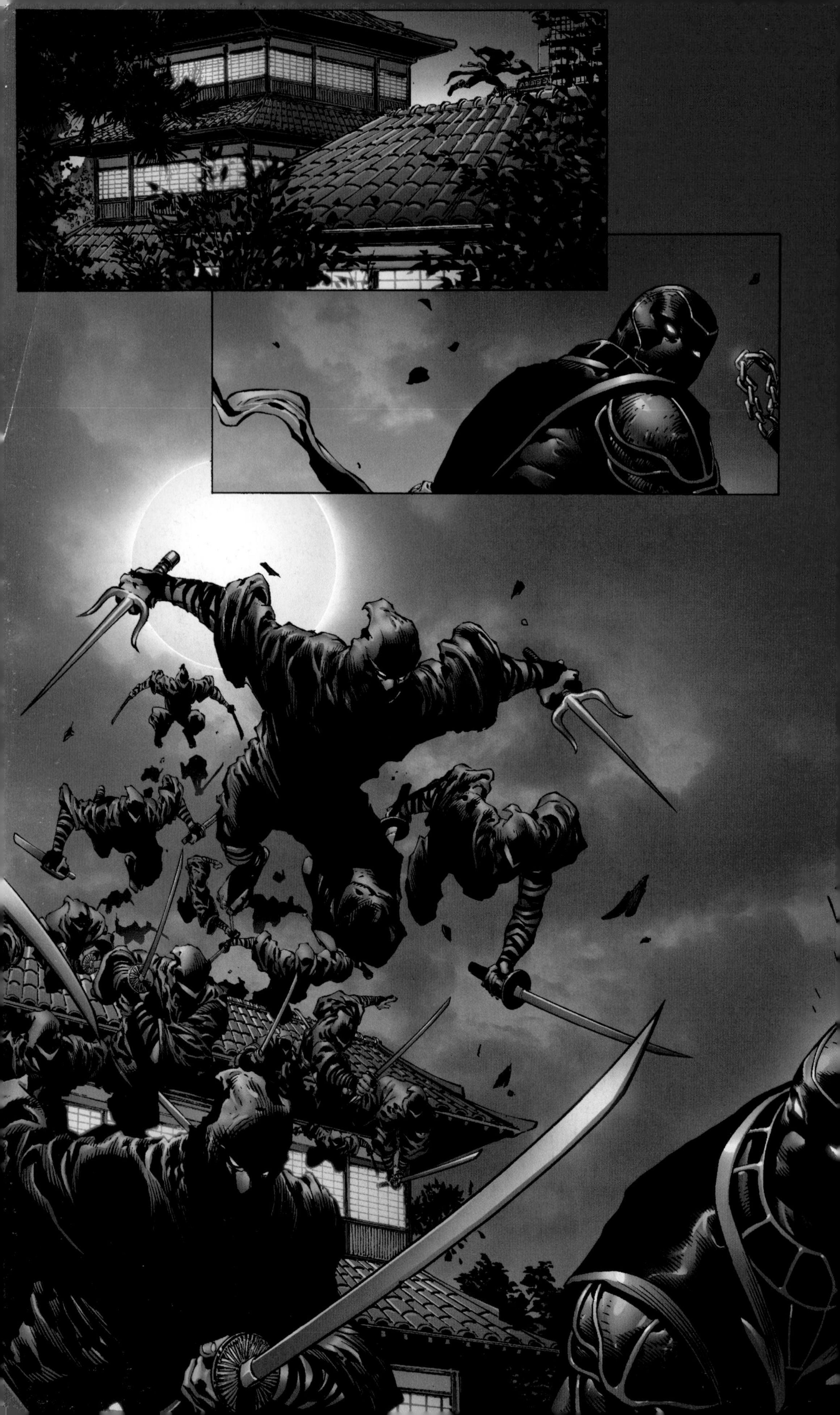

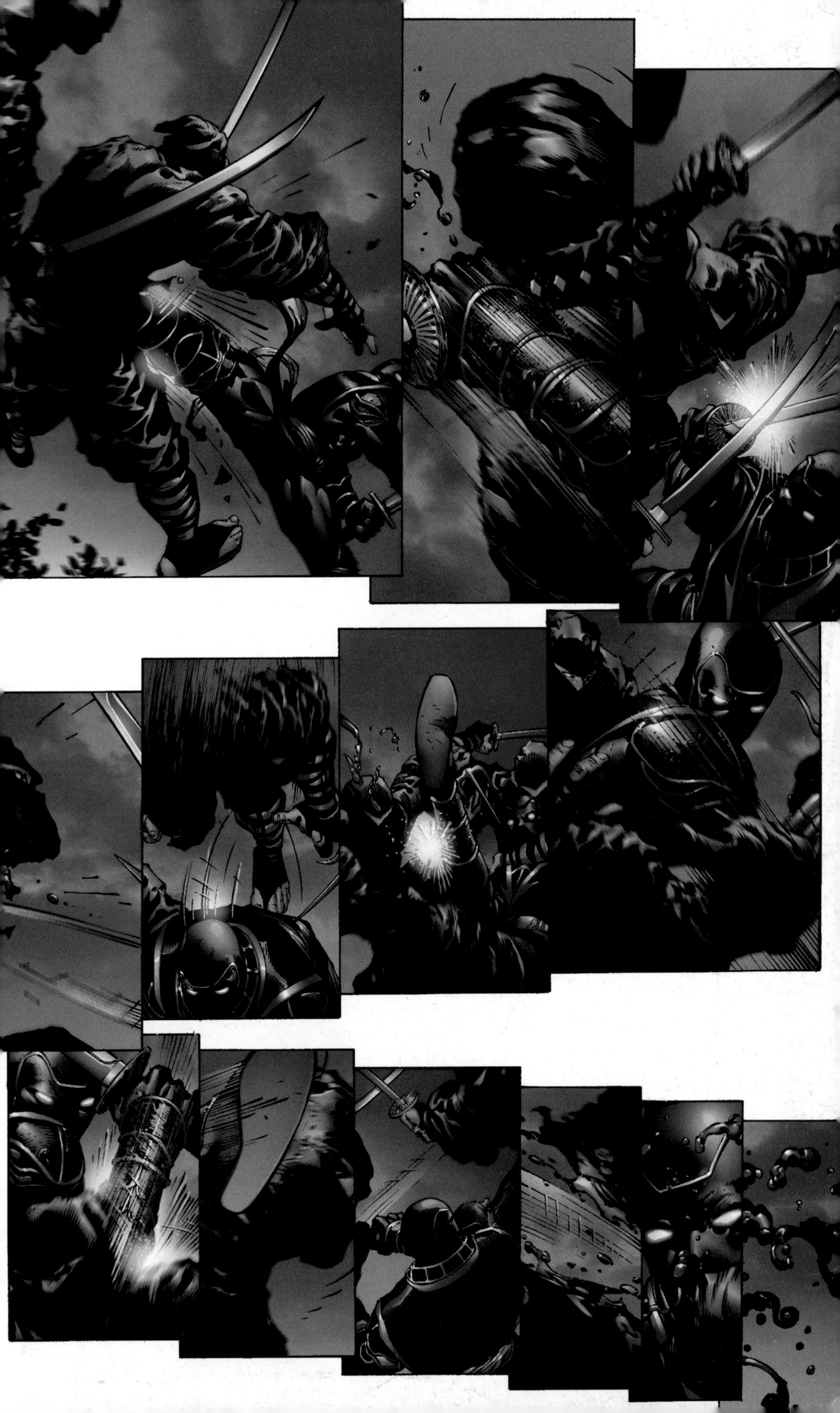

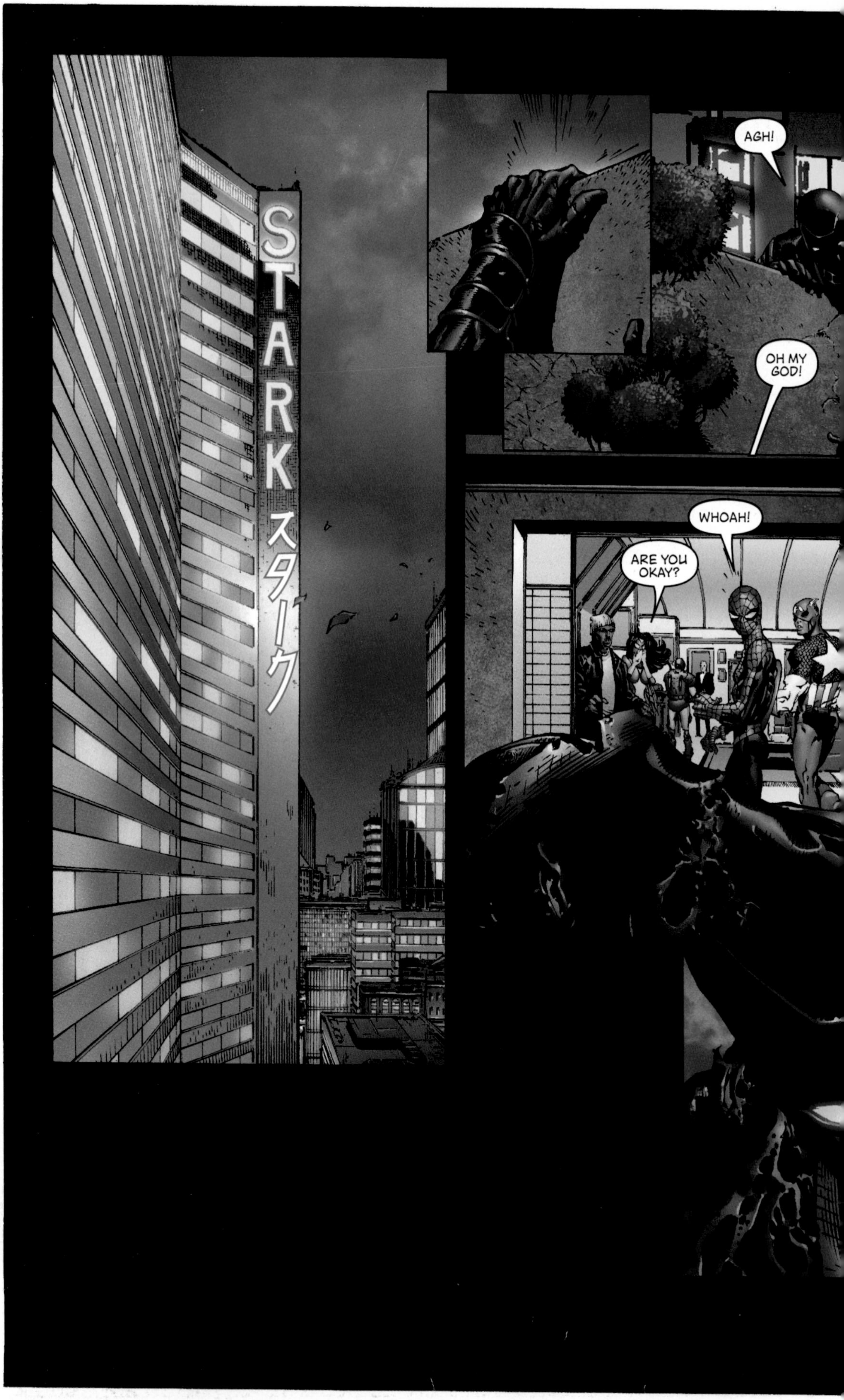
STARK スターク
AGH!
OH MY GOD!
WHOAH!
ARE YOU OKAY?

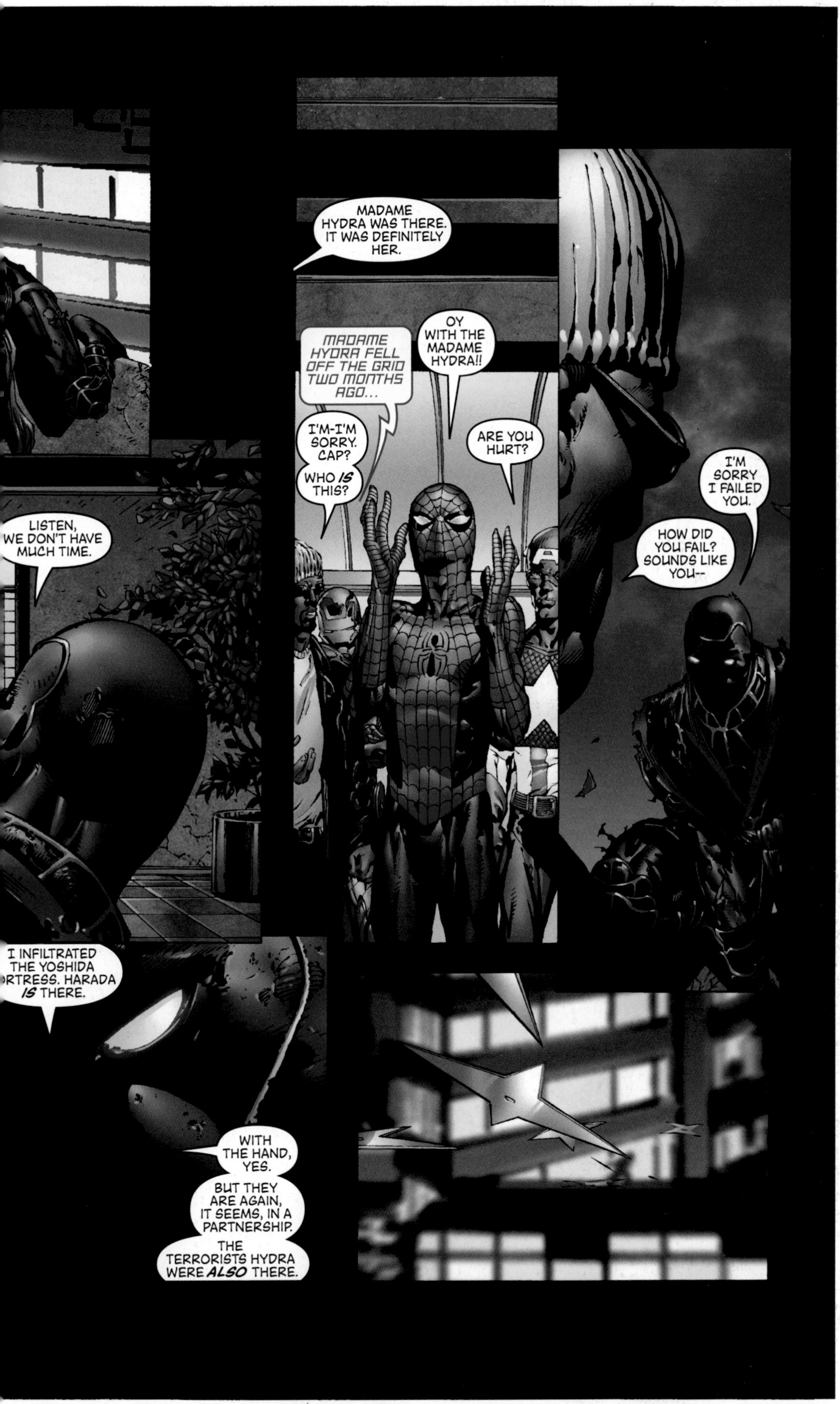
LISTEN, WE DON'T HAVE MUCH TIME.
I INFILTRATED THE YOSHIDA ...RTRESS. HARADA IS THERE.
WITH THE HAND, YES.
BUT THEY ARE AGAIN, IT SEEMS, IN A PARTNERSHIP.
THE TERRORISTS HYDRA WERE ALSO THERE.
MADAME HYDRA WAS THERE. IT WAS DEFINITELY HER.
MADAME HYDRA FELL OFF THE GRID TWO MONTHS AGO...
OY WITH THE MADAME HYDRA!!
I'M-I'M SORRY. CAP?
WHO IS THIS?
ARE YOU HURT?
I'M SORRY I FAILED YOU.
HOW DID YOU FAIL? SOUNDS LIKE YOU--

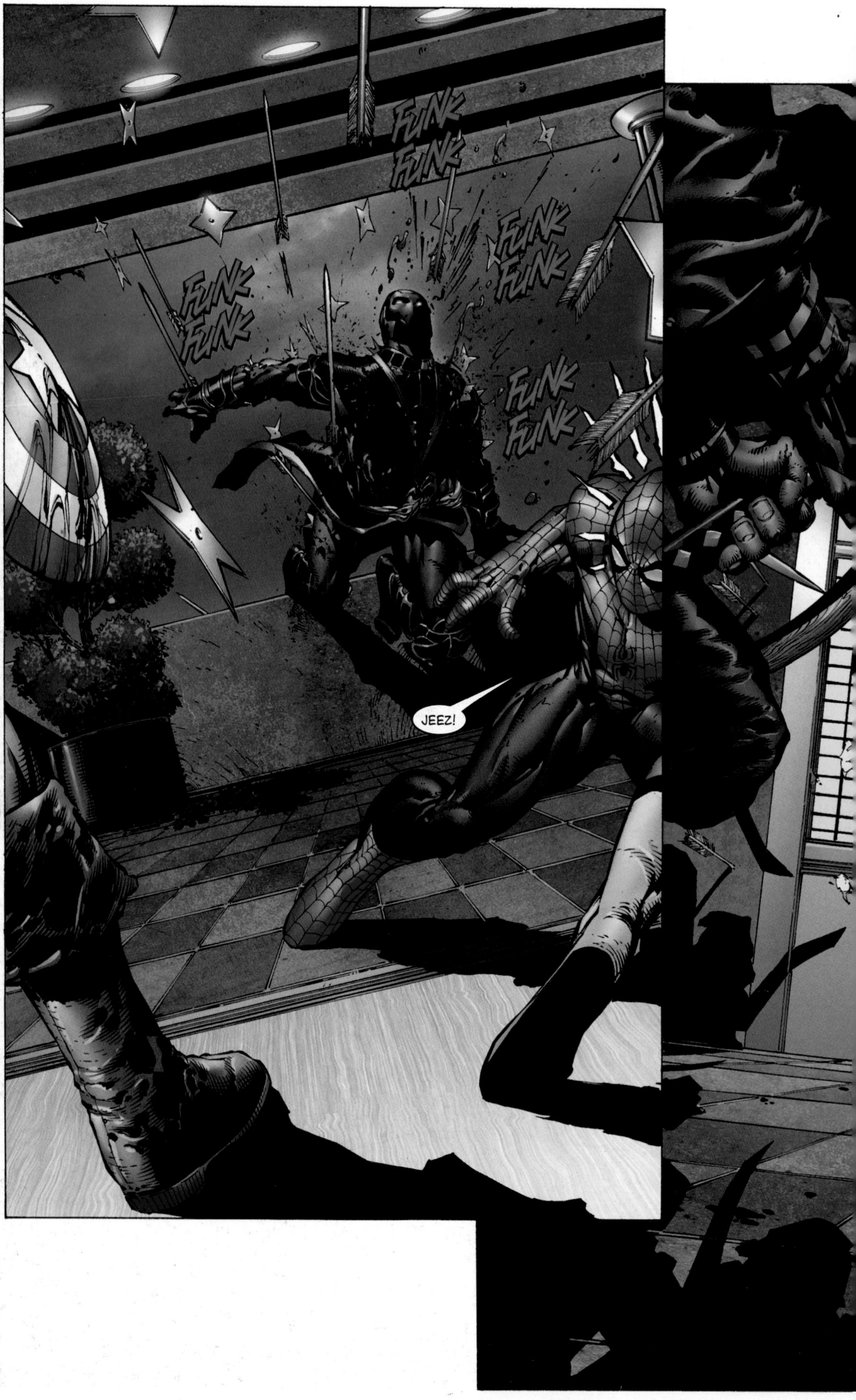
FUNK FUNK
FUNK FUNK
FUNK FUNK
FUNK FUNK
JEEZ!

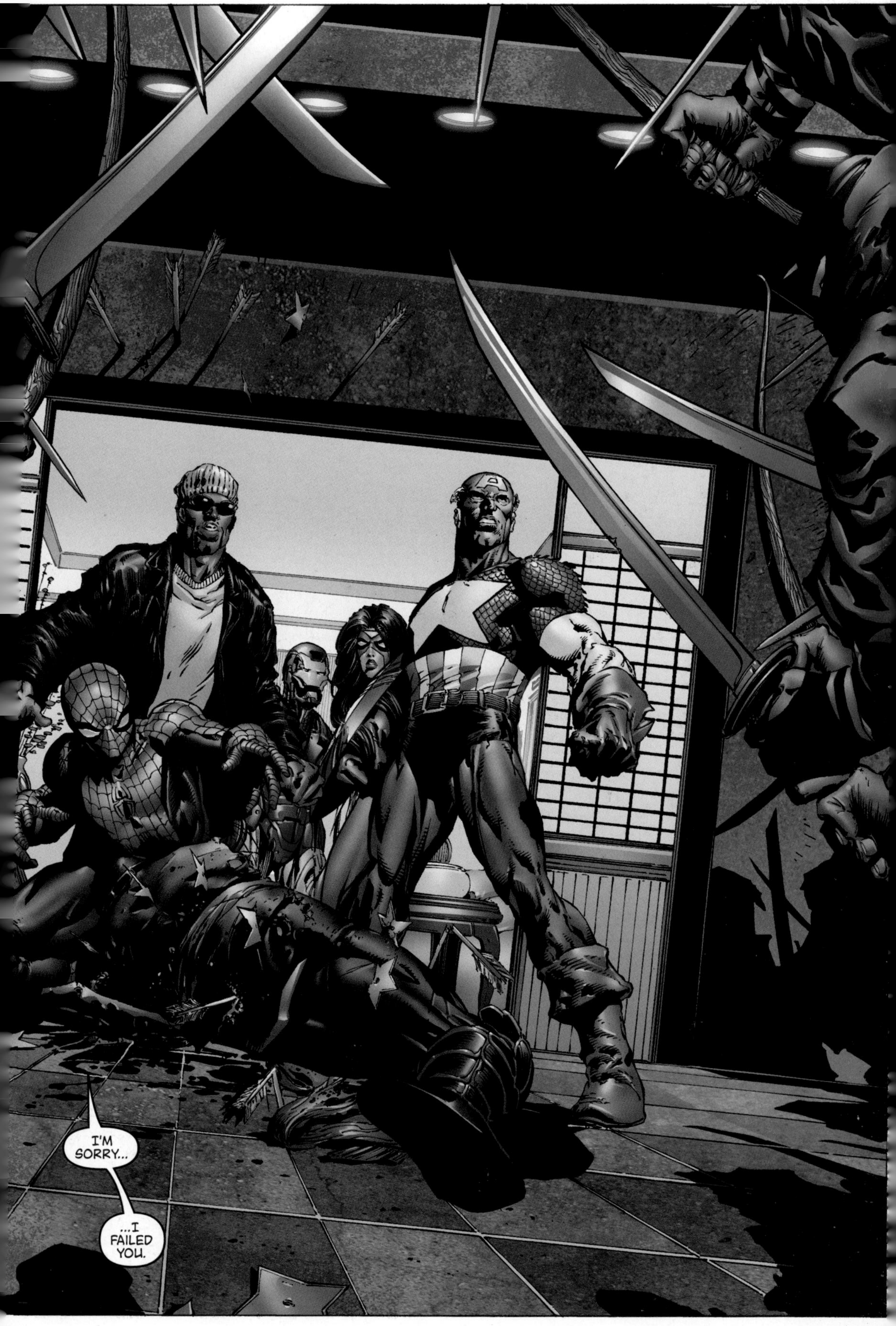
I'M SORRY...
...I FAILED YOU.

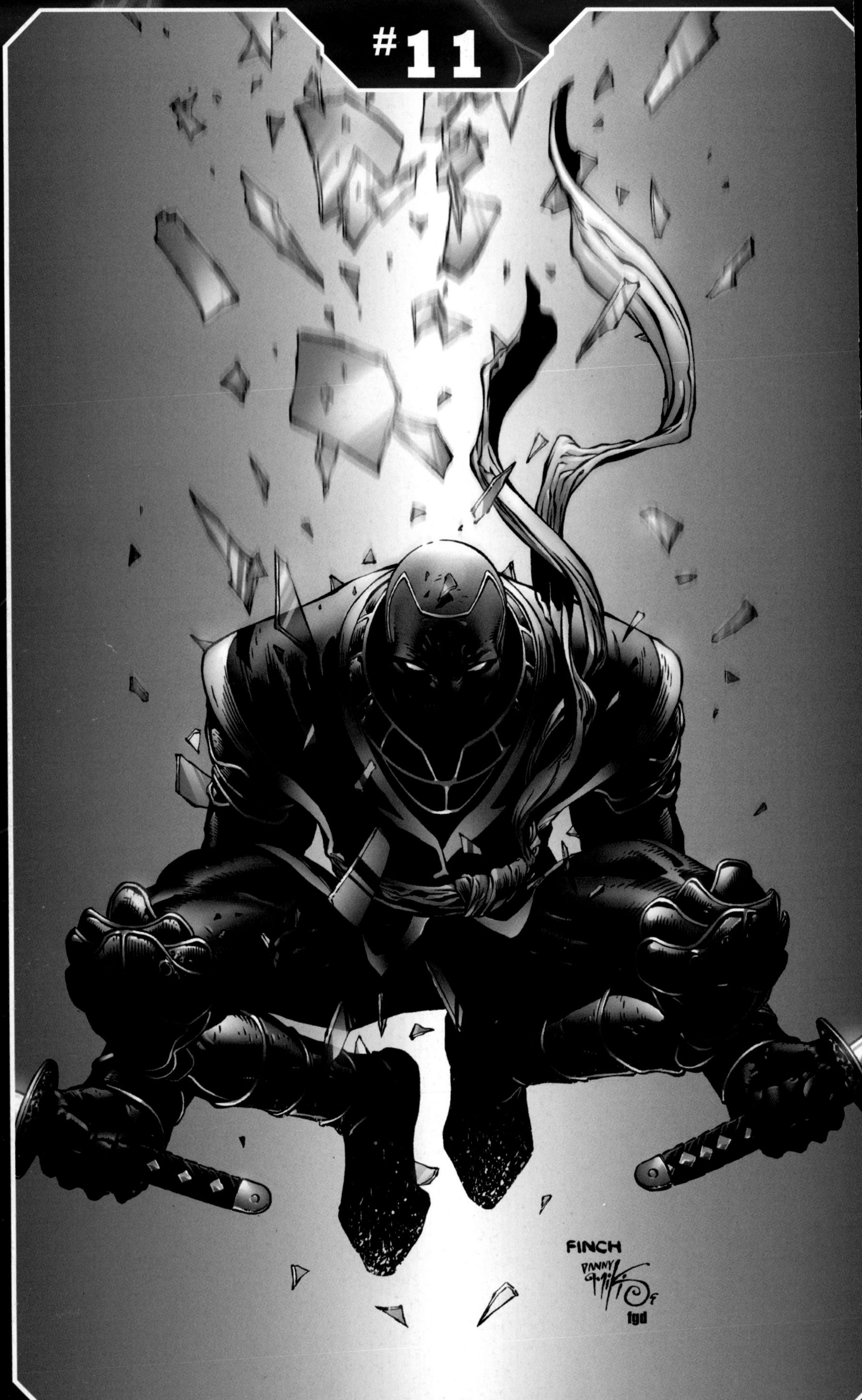
#11
FINCH
fgd

#12

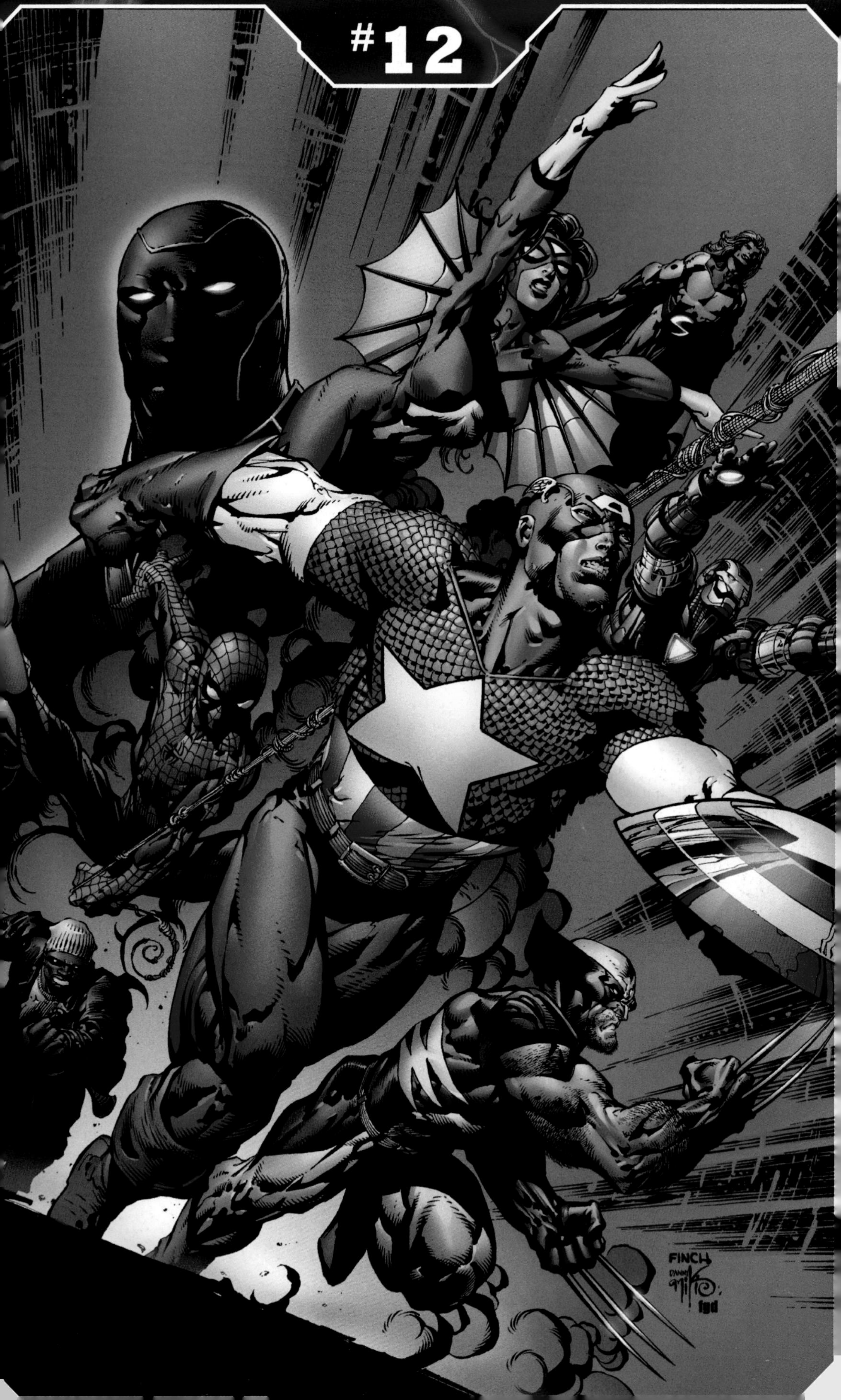
FINCH

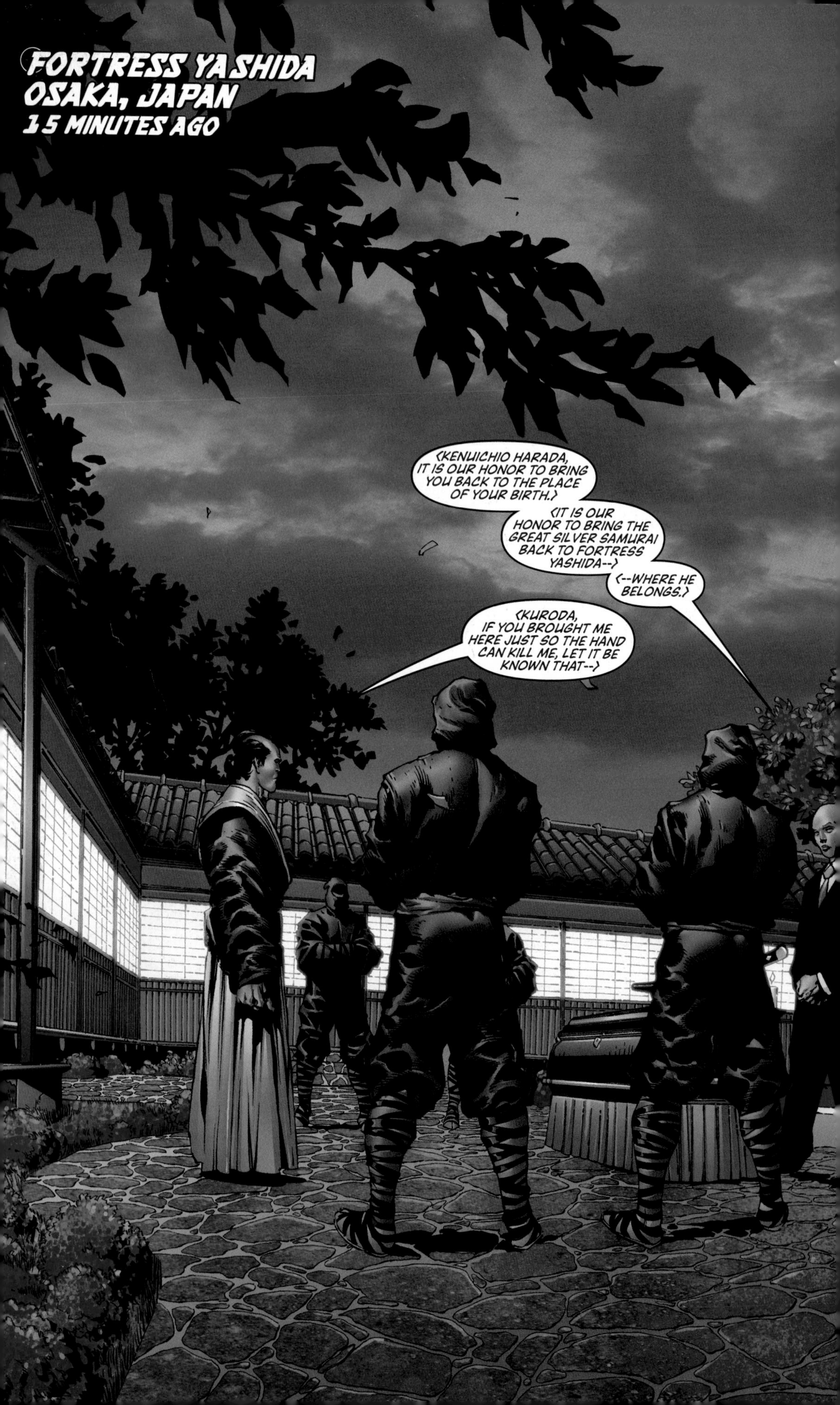
FORTRESS YASHIDA
OSAKA, JAPAN
15 MINUTES AGO
<KENUICHIO HARADA, IT IS OUR HONOR TO BRING YOU BACK TO THE PLACE OF YOUR BIRTH.>
<IT IS OUR HONOR TO BRING THE GREAT SILVER SAMURAI BACK TO FORTRESS YASHIDA-->
<--WHERE HE BELONGS.>
<KURODA, IF YOU BROUGHT ME HERE JUST SO THE HAND CAN KILL ME, LET IT BE KNOWN THAT-->

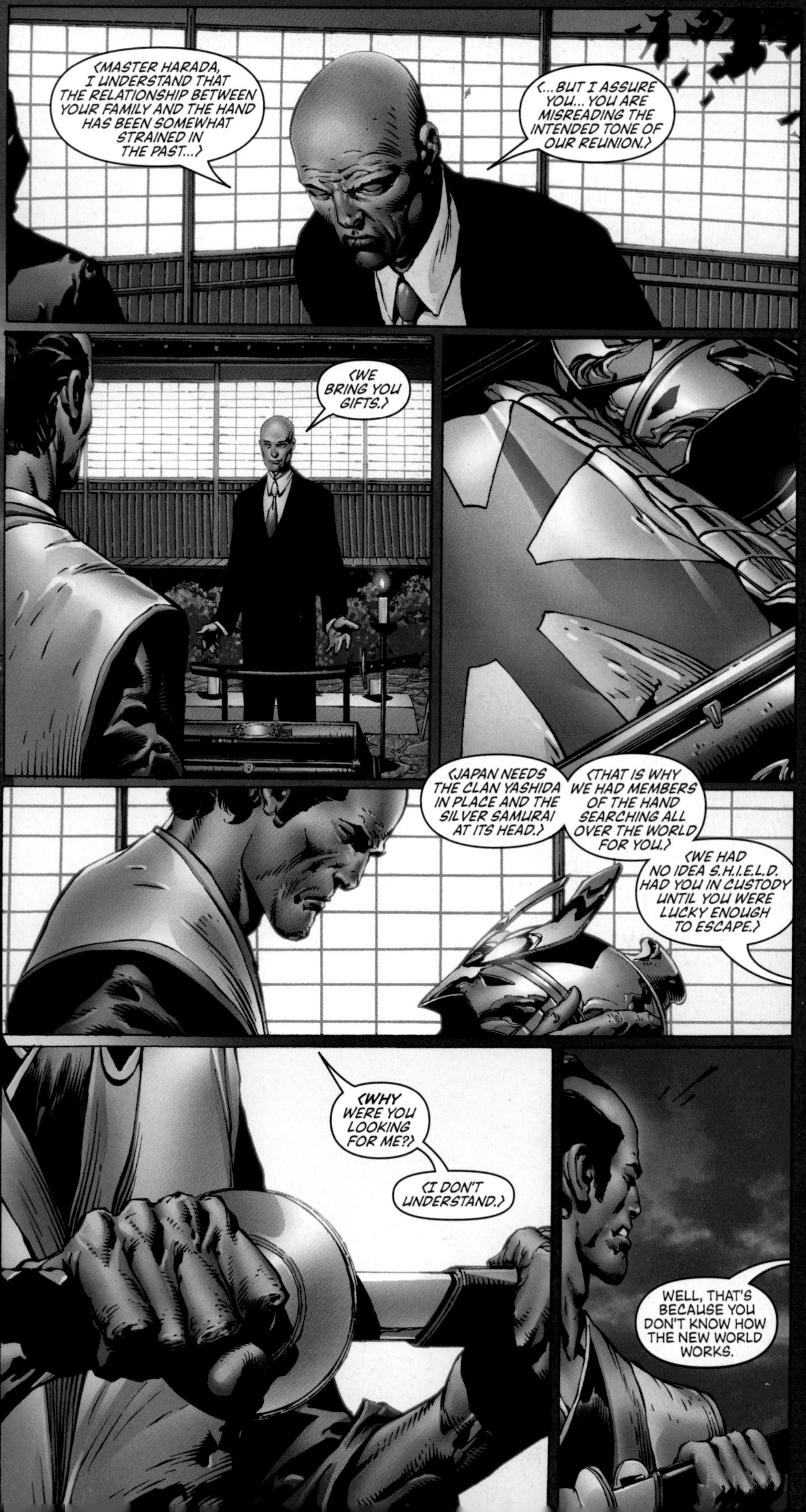

<MASTER HARADA, I UNDERSTAND THAT THE RELATIONSHIP BETWEEN YOUR FAMILY AND THE HAND HAS BEEN SOMEWHAT STRAINED IN THE PAST...>
<...BUT I ASSURE YOU... YOU ARE MISREADING THE INTENDED TONE OF OUR REUNION.>
<WE BRING YOU GIFTS.>
<JAPAN NEEDS THE CLAN YASHIDA IN PLACE AND THE SILVER SAMURAI AT ITS HEAD.>
<THAT IS WHY WE HAD MEMBERS OF THE HAND SEARCHING ALL OVER THE WORLD FOR YOU.>
<WE HAD NO IDEA S.H.I.E.L.D. HAD YOU IN CUSTODY UNTIL YOU WERE LUCKY ENOUGH TO ESCAPE.>
<WHY WERE YOU LOOKING FOR ME?>
<I DON'T UNDERSTAND.>
WELL, THAT'S BECAUSE YOU DON'T KNOW HOW THE NEW WORLD WORKS.

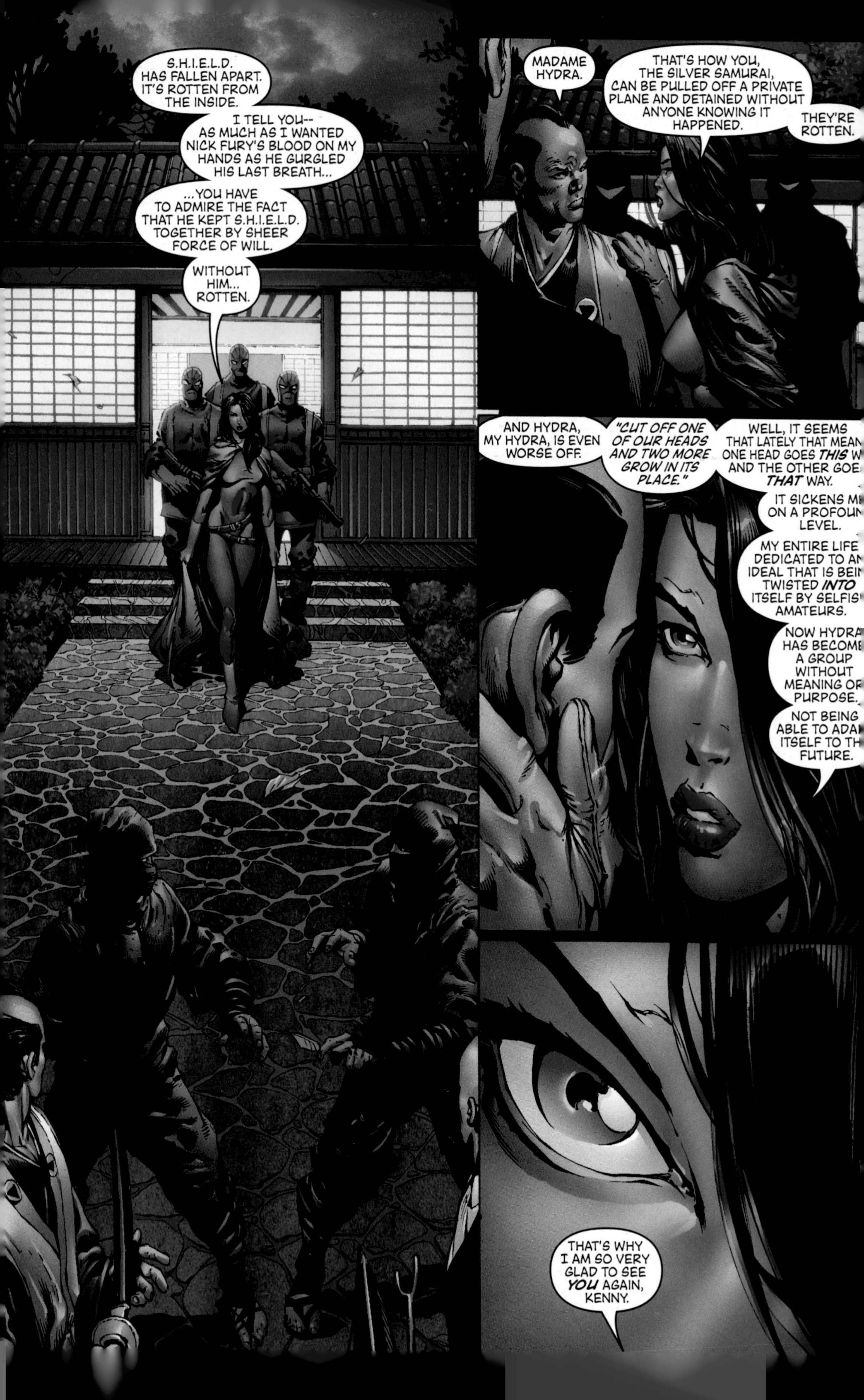
S.H.I.E.L.D. HAS FALLEN APART. IT'S ROTTEN FROM THE INSIDE.
I TELL YOU-- AS MUCH AS I WANTED NICK FURY'S BLOOD ON MY HANDS AS HE GURGLED HIS LAST BREATH...
...YOU HAVE TO ADMIRE THE FACT THAT HE KEPT S.H.I.E.L.D. TOGETHER BY SHEER FORCE OF WILL.
WITHOUT HIM... ROTTEN.
MADAME HYDRA.
THAT'S HOW YOU, THE SILVER SAMURAI, CAN BE PULLED OFF A PRIVATE PLANE AND DETAINED WITHOUT ANYONE KNOWING IT HAPPENED.
THEY'RE ROTTEN.
AND HYDRA, MY HYDRA, IS EVEN WORSE OFF.
"CUT OFF ONE OF OUR HEADS AND TWO MORE GROW IN ITS PLACE."
THAT'S WHY I AM SO VERY GLAD TO SEE YOU AGAIN, KENNY.

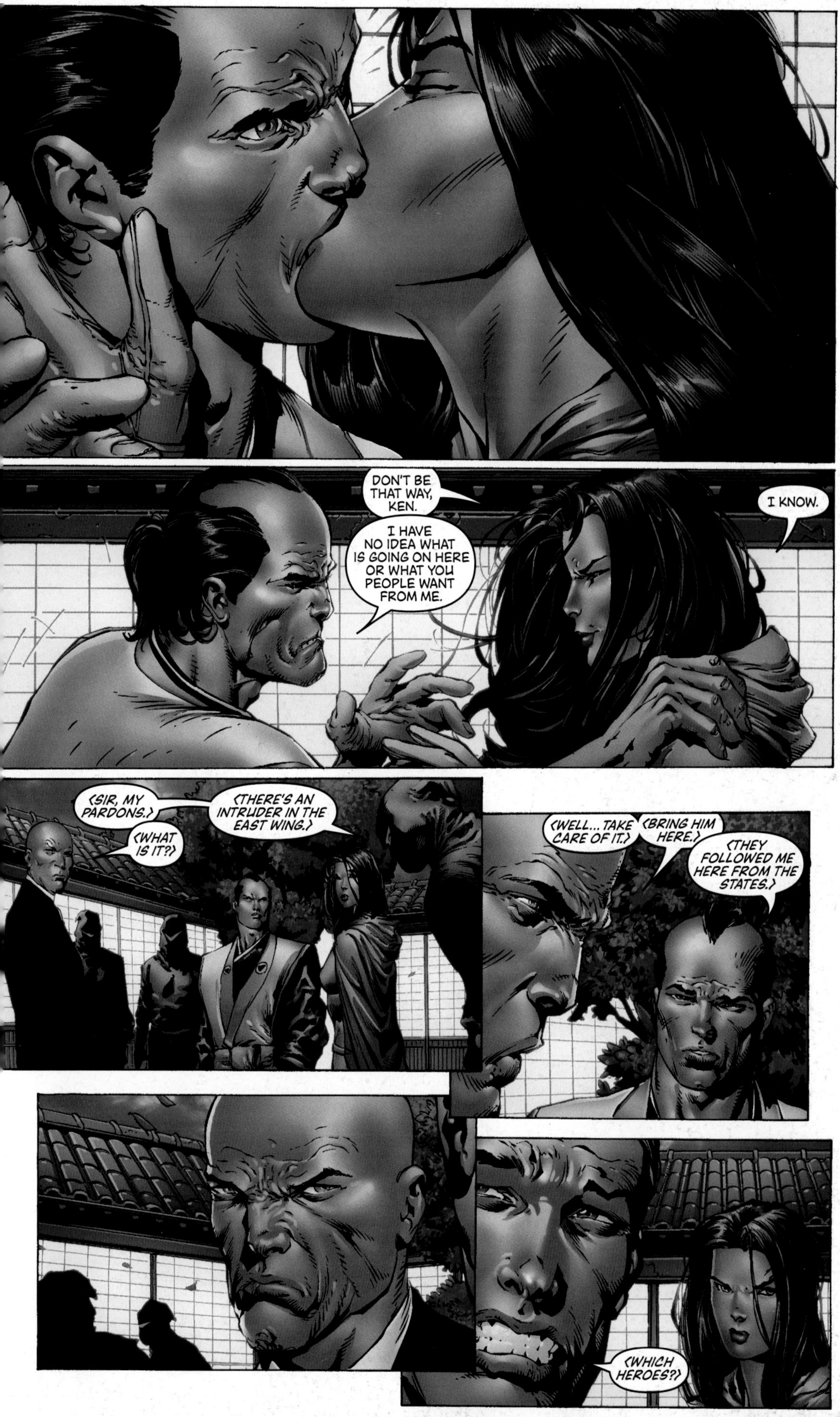
DON'T BE THAT WAY, KEN.
I HAVE NO IDEA WHAT IS GOING ON HERE OR WHAT YOU PEOPLE WANT FROM ME.
I KNOW.
<SIR, MY PARDONS.>
<WHAT IS IT?>
<THERE'S AN INTRUDER IN THE EAST WING.>
<WELL... TAKE CARE OF IT.>
<BRING HIM HERE.>
<THEY FOLLOWED ME HERE FROM THE STATES.>
<WHICH HEROES?>

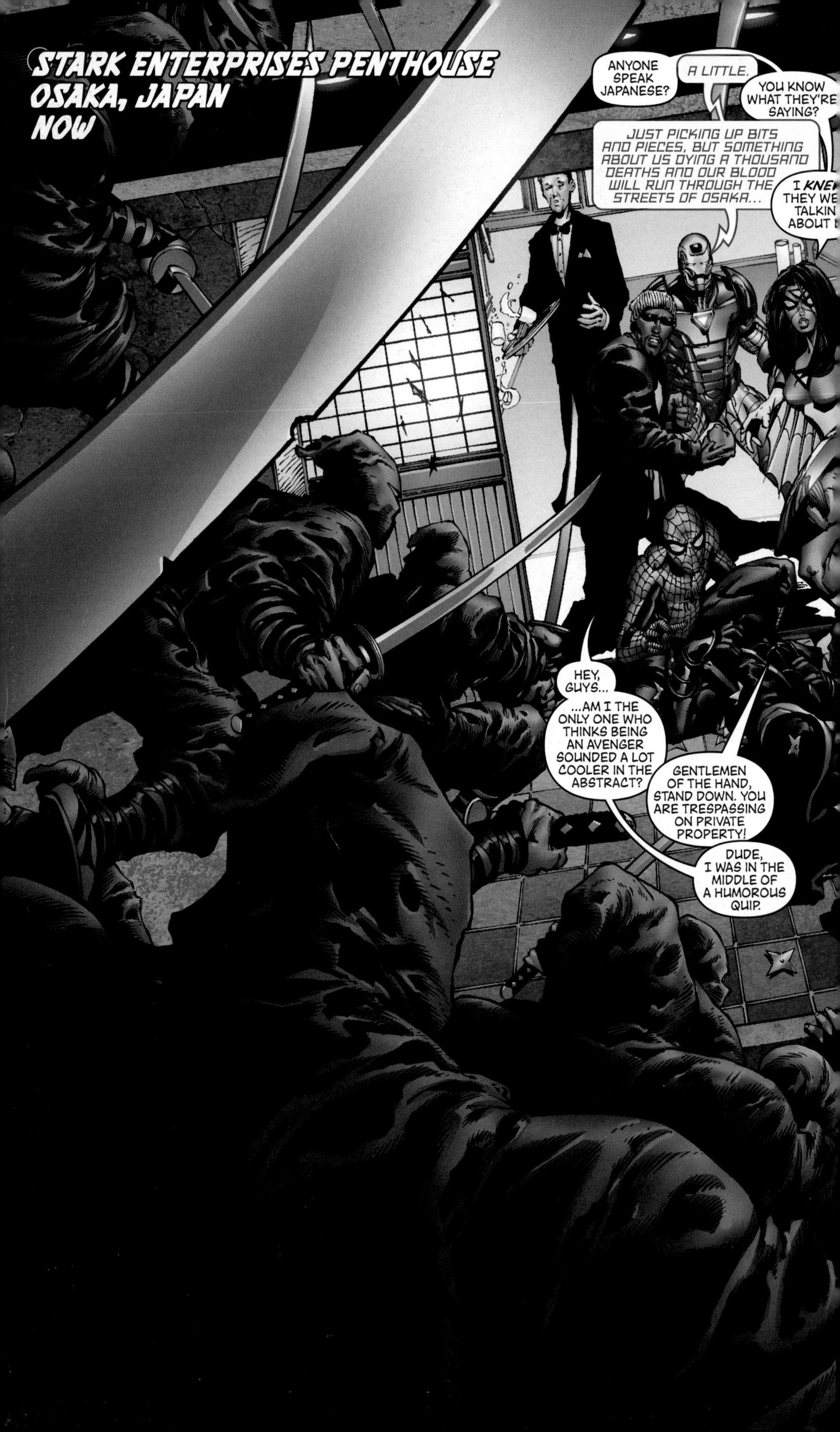
STARK ENTERPRISES PENTHOUSE
OSAKA, JAPAN
NOW
ANYONE SPEAK JAPANESE?
A LITTLE.
YOU KNOW WHAT THEY'RE SAYING?
JUST PICKING UP BITS AND PIECES, BUT SOMETHING ABOUT US DYING A THOUSAND DEATHS AND OUR BLOOD WILL RUN THROUGH THE STREETS OF OSAKA...
I KNE THEY WE TALKIN ABOUT
HEY, GUYS...
...AM I THE ONLY ONE WHO THINKS BEING AN AVENGER SOUNDED A LOT COOLER IN THE ABSTRACT?
GENTLEMEN OF THE HAND, STAND DOWN. YOU ARE TRESPASSING ON PRIVATE PROPERTY!
DUDE, I WAS IN THE MIDDLE OF A HUMOROUS QUIP.

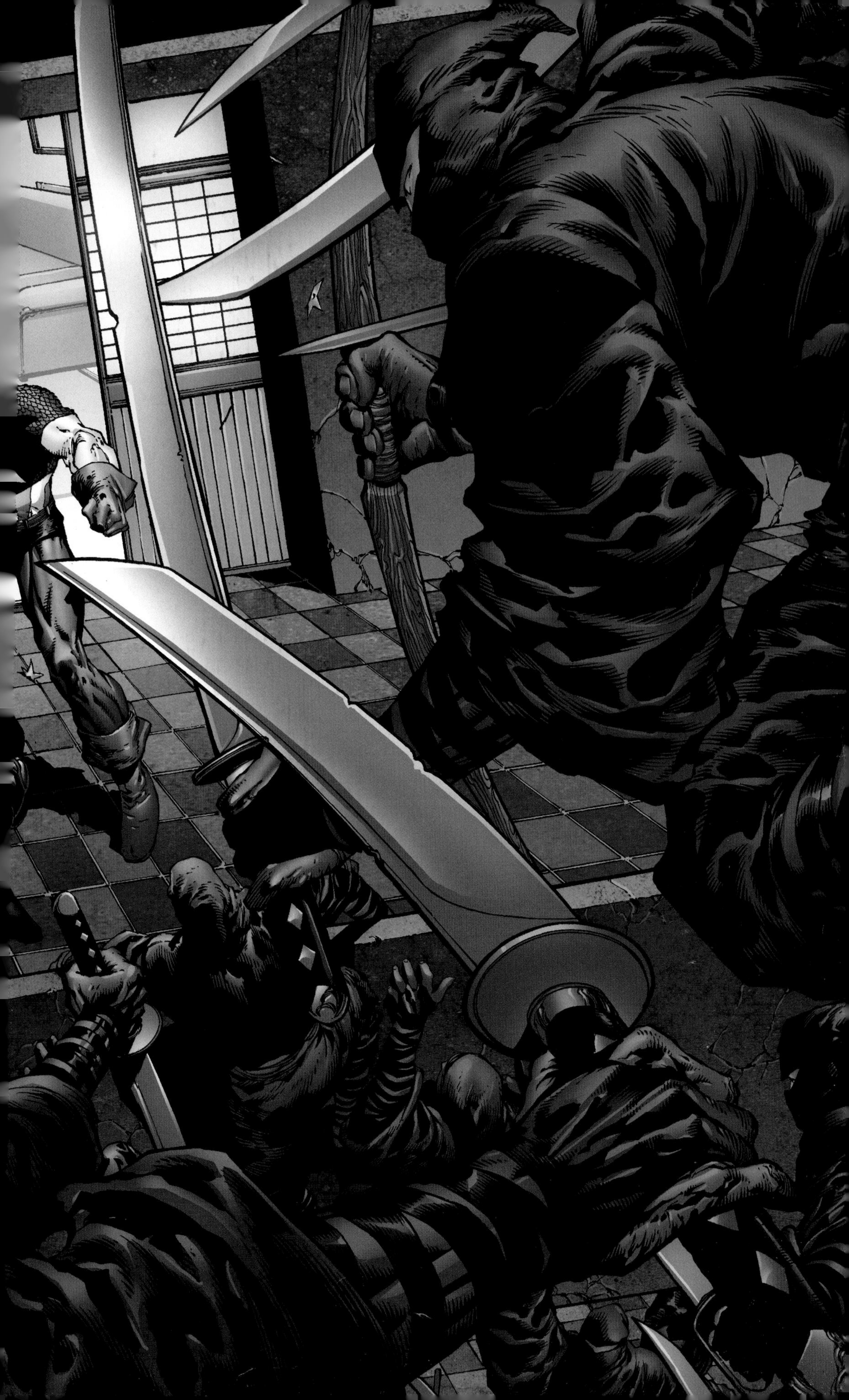

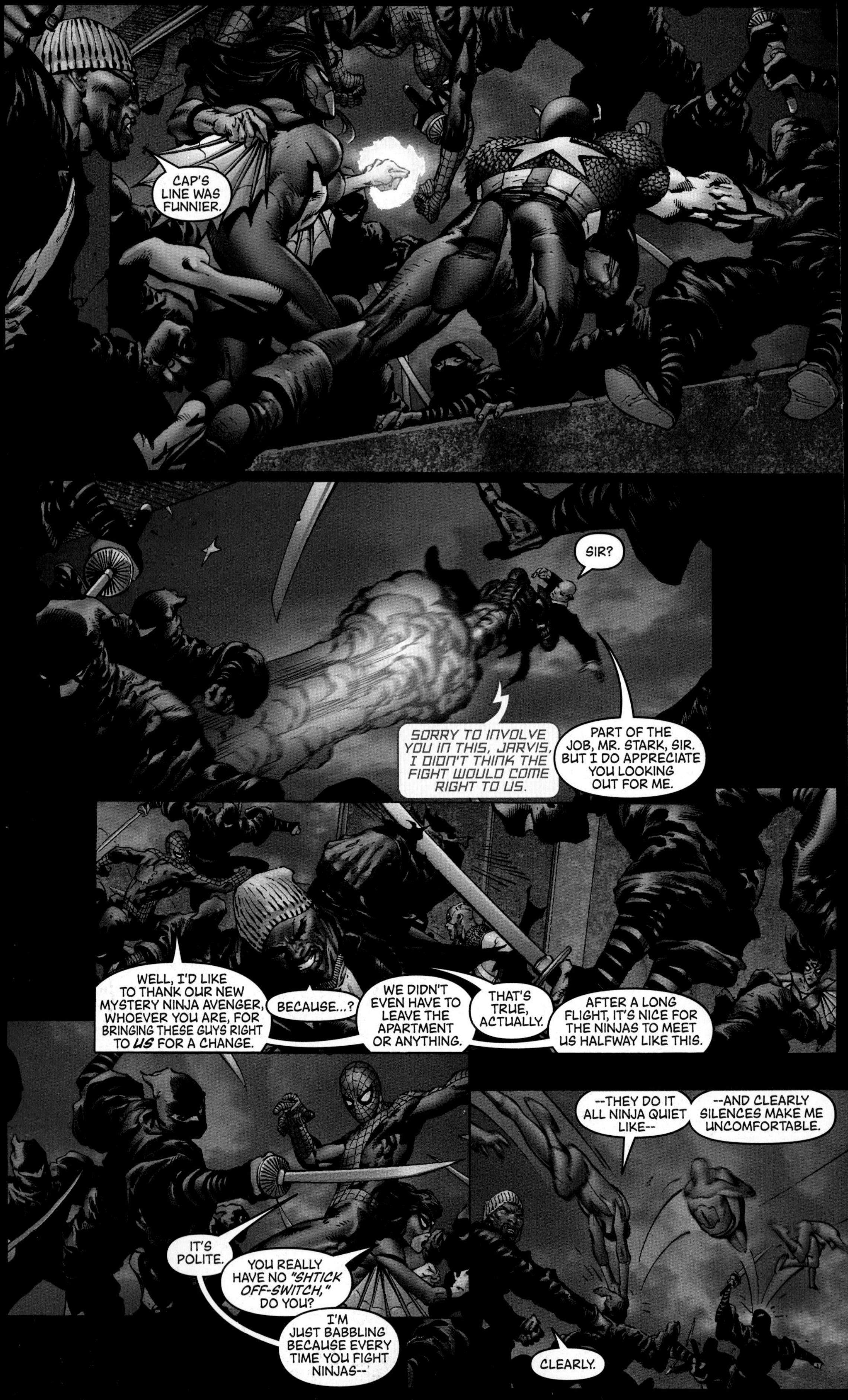
CAP'S LINE WAS FUNNIER.
SIR?
SORRY TO INVOLVE YOU IN THIS, JARVIS, I DIDN'T THINK THE FIGHT WOULD COME RIGHT TO US.
PART OF THE JOB, MR. STARK, SIR. BUT I DO APPRECIATE YOU LOOKING OUT FOR ME.
WELL, I'D LIKE TO THANK OUR NEW MYSTERY NINJA AVENGER, WHOEVER YOU ARE, FOR BRINGING THESE GUYS RIGHT TO US FOR A CHANGE.
BECAUSE...?
WE DIDN'T EVEN HAVE TO LEAVE THE APARTMENT OR ANYTHING.
THAT'S TRUE, ACTUALLY.
AFTER A LONG FLIGHT, IT'S NICE FOR THE NINJAS TO MEET US HALFWAY LIKE THIS.
IT'S POLITE.
YOU REALLY HAVE NO "SHTICK OFF-SWITCH," DO YOU?
I'M JUST BABBLING BECAUSE EVERY TIME YOU FIGHT NINJAS--
--THEY DO IT ALL NINJA QUIET LIKE--
--AND CLEARLY SILENCES MAKE ME UNCOMFORTABLE.
CLEARLY.

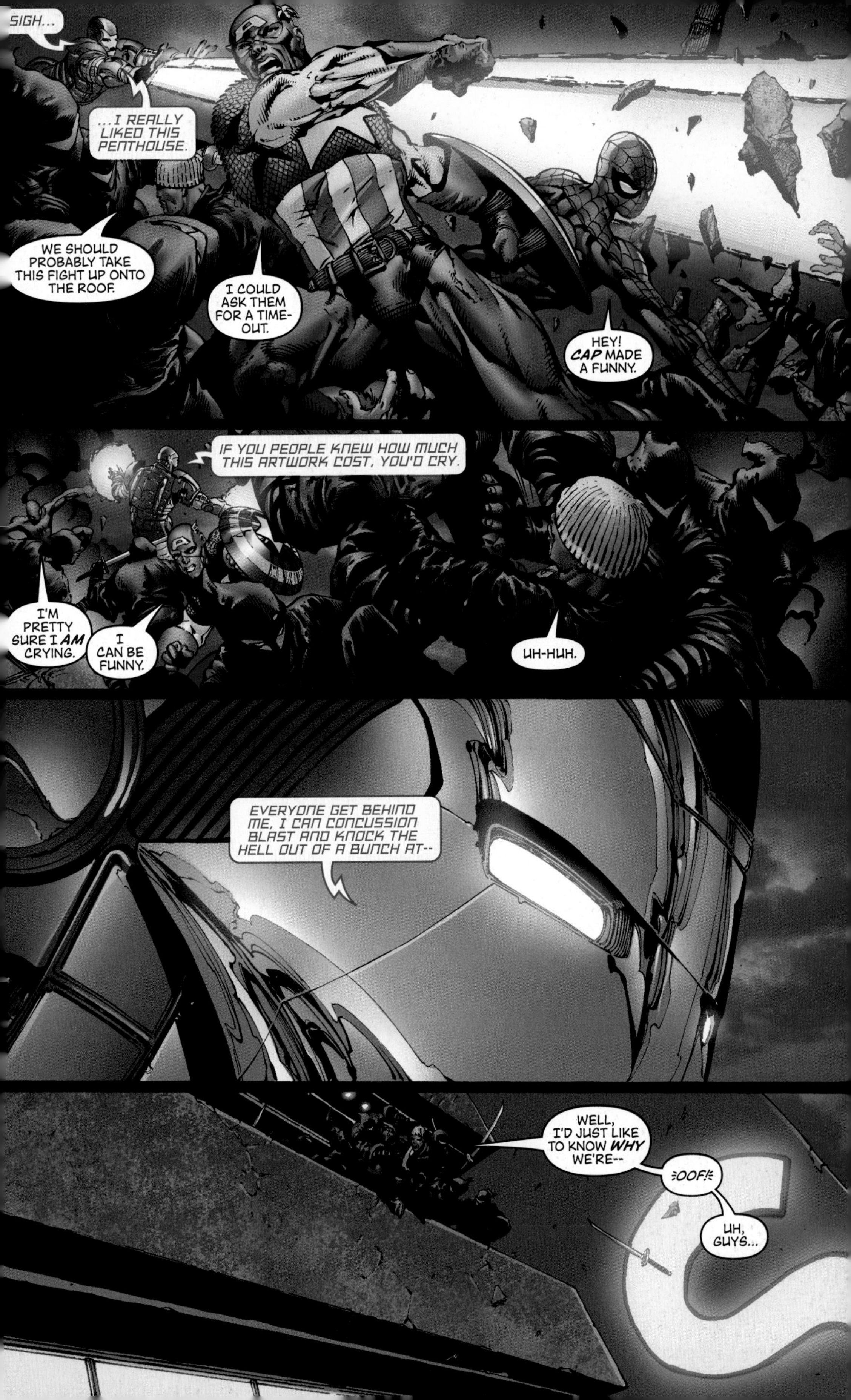
SIGH...
...I REALLY LIKED THIS PENTHOUSE.
WE SHOULD PROBABLY TAKE THIS FIGHT UP ONTO THE ROOF.
I COULD ASK THEM FOR A TIME-OUT.
HEY! CAP MADE A FUNNY.
IF YOU PEOPLE KNEW HOW MUCH THIS ARTWORK COST, YOU'D CRY.
I'M PRETTY SURE I AM CRYING.
I CAN BE FUNNY.
UH-HUH.
EVERYONE GET BEHIND ME, I CAN CONCUSSION BLAST AND KNOCK THE HELL OUT OF A BUNCH AT--
WELL, I'D JUST LIKE TO KNOW WHY WE'RE--
OOF!
UH, GUYS...

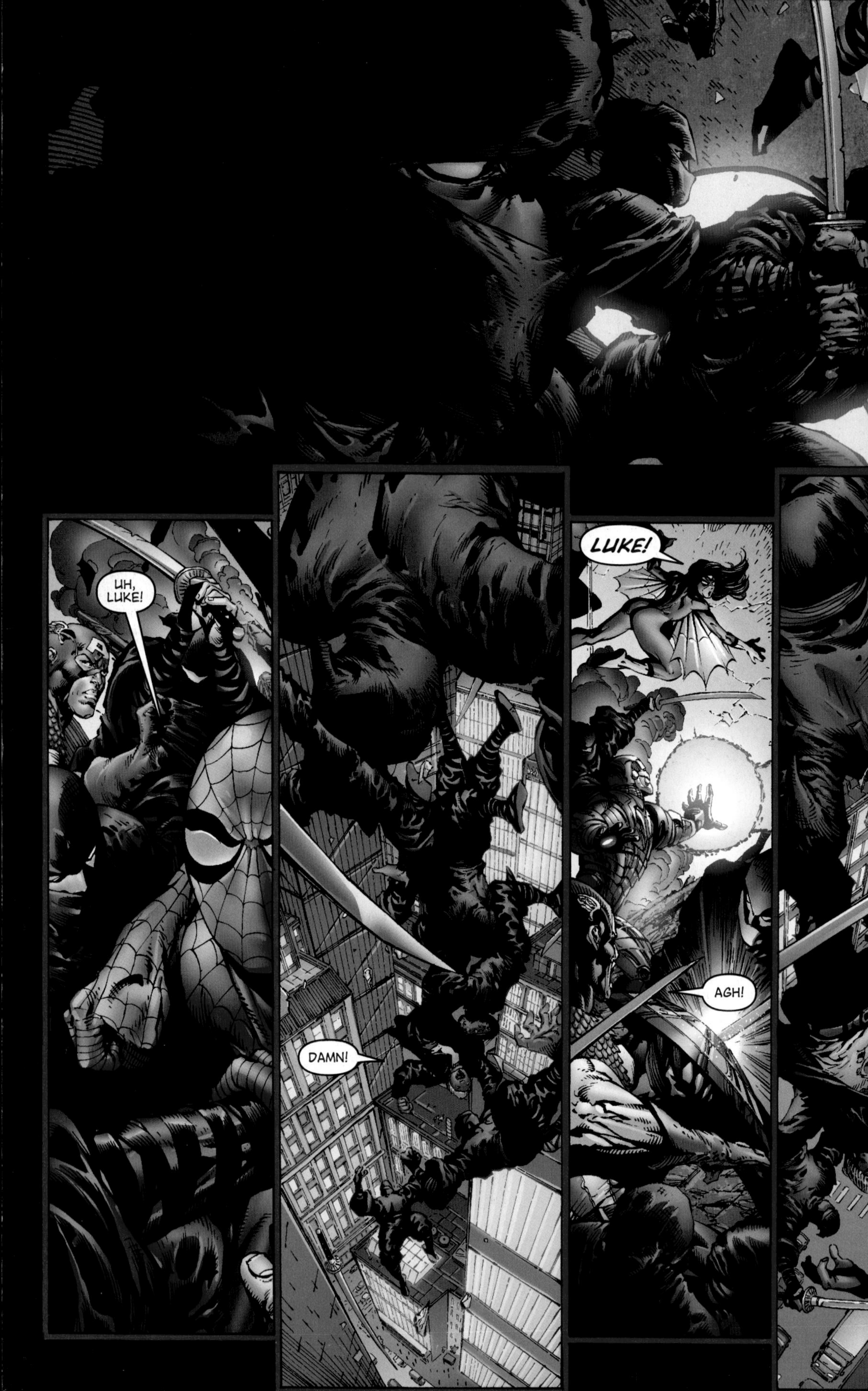
UH, LUKE!
DAMN!
LUKE!
AGH!

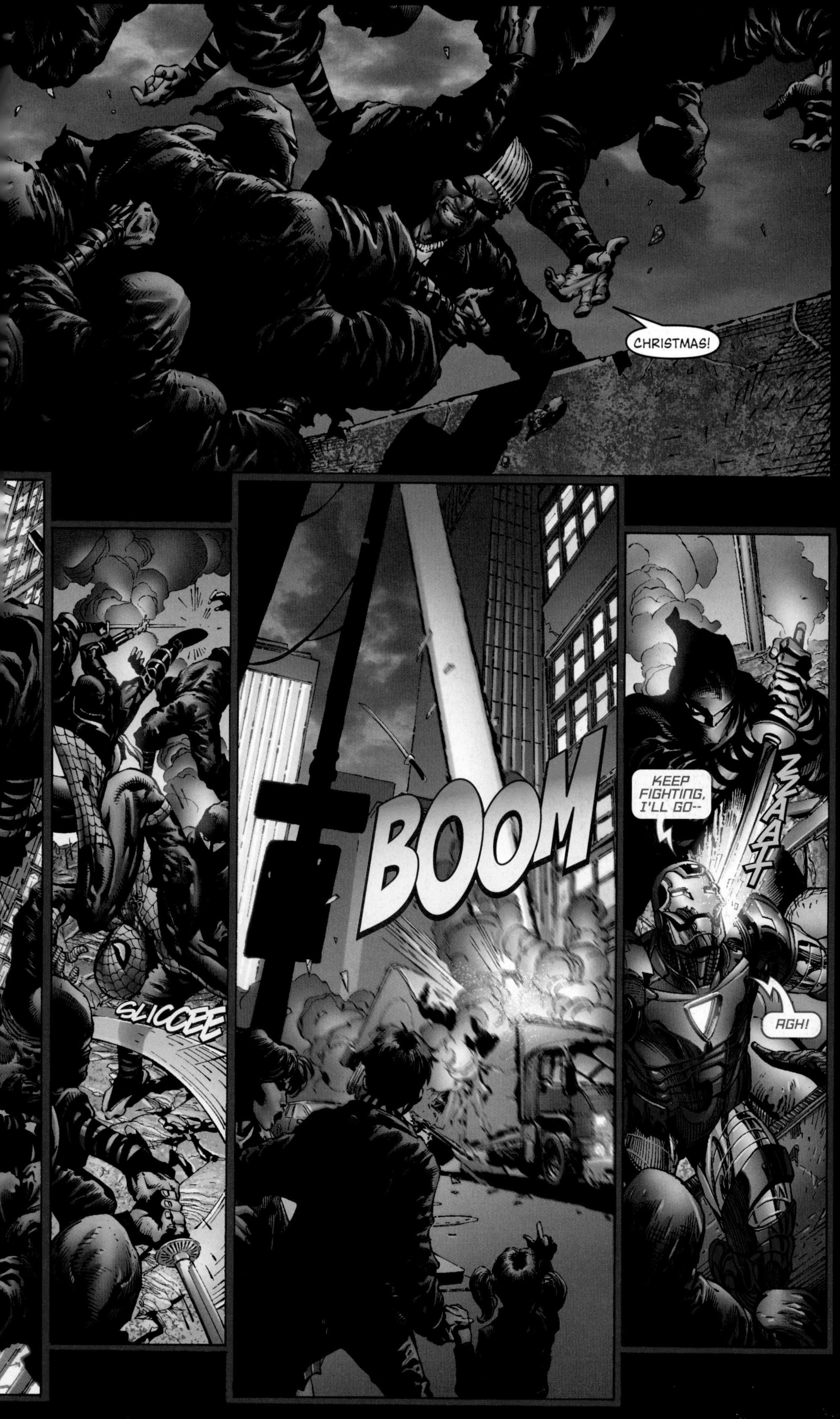
CHRISTMAS!
SLICCEE
BOOM
KEEP FIGHTING, I'LL GO--
ZZAAT
AGH!

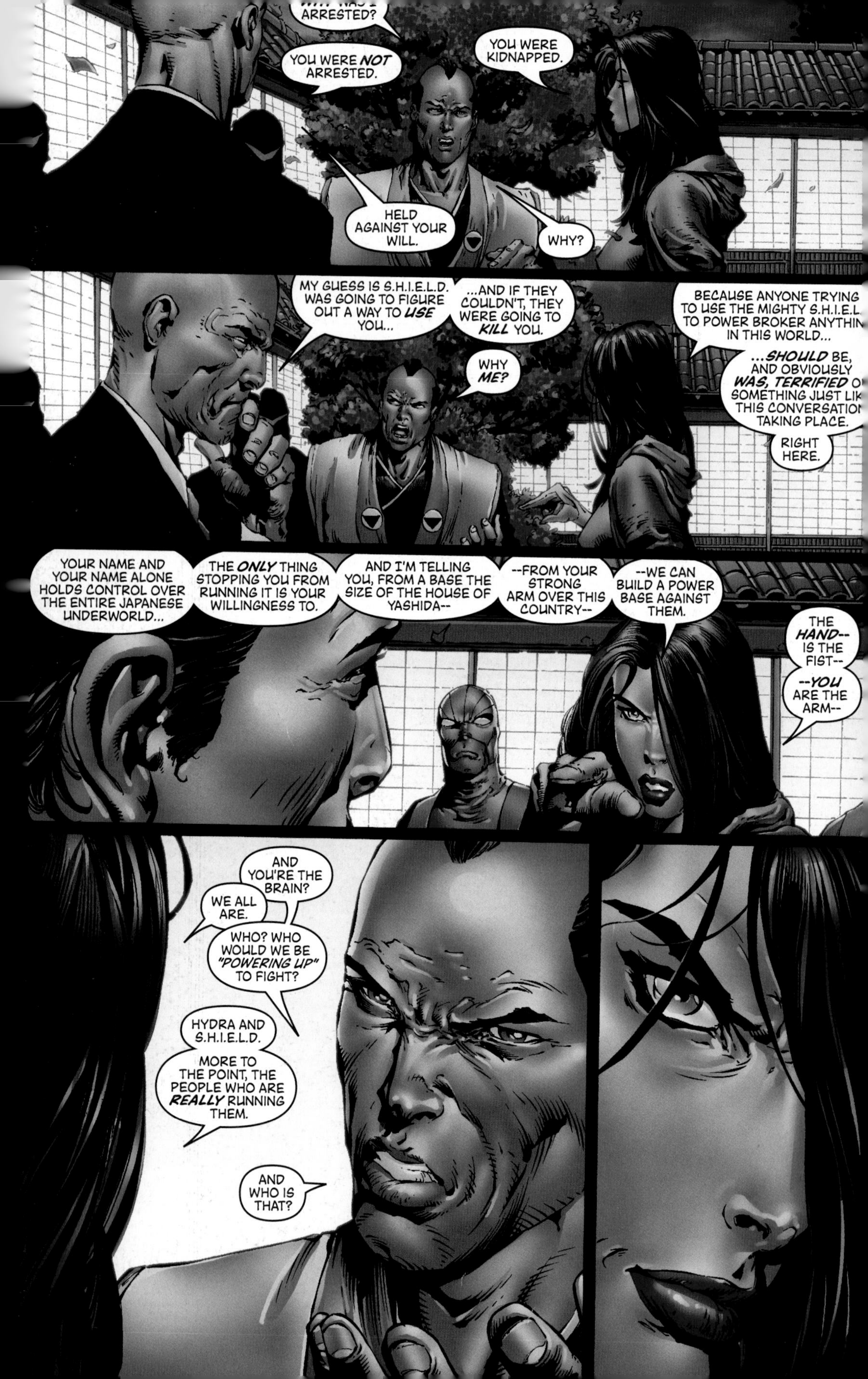
ARRESTED?
YOU WERE NOT ARRESTED.
YOU WERE KIDNAPPED.
HELD AGAINST YOUR WILL.
WHY?
MY GUESS IS S.H.I.E.L.D. WAS GOING TO FIGURE OUT A WAY TO USE YOU...
...AND IF THEY COULDN'T, THEY WERE GOING TO KILL YOU.
WHY ME?
BECAUSE ANYONE TRYING TO USE THE MIGHTY S.H.I.E.L. TO POWER BROKER ANYTHIN IN THIS WORLD...
...SHOULD BE, AND OBVIOUSLY WAS, TERRIFIED O SOMETHING JUST LIK THIS CONVERSATIO TAKING PLACE.
RIGHT HERE.
YOUR NAME AND YOUR NAME ALONE HOLDS CONTROL OVER THE ENTIRE JAPANESE UNDERWORLD...
THE ONLY THING STOPPING YOU FROM RUNNING IT IS YOUR WILLINGNESS TO.
AND I'M TELLING YOU, FROM A BASE THE SIZE OF THE HOUSE OF YASHIDA--
--FROM YOUR STRONG ARM OVER THIS COUNTRY--
--WE CAN BUILD A POWER BASE AGAINST THEM.
THE HAND-- IS THE FIST--
--YOU ARE THE ARM--
AND YOU'RE THE BRAIN?
WE ALL ARE.
WHO? WHO WOULD WE BE "POWERING UP" TO FIGHT?
HYDRA AND S.H.I.E.L.D.
MORE TO THE POINT, THE PEOPLE WHO ARE REALLY RUNNING THEM.
AND WHO IS THAT?

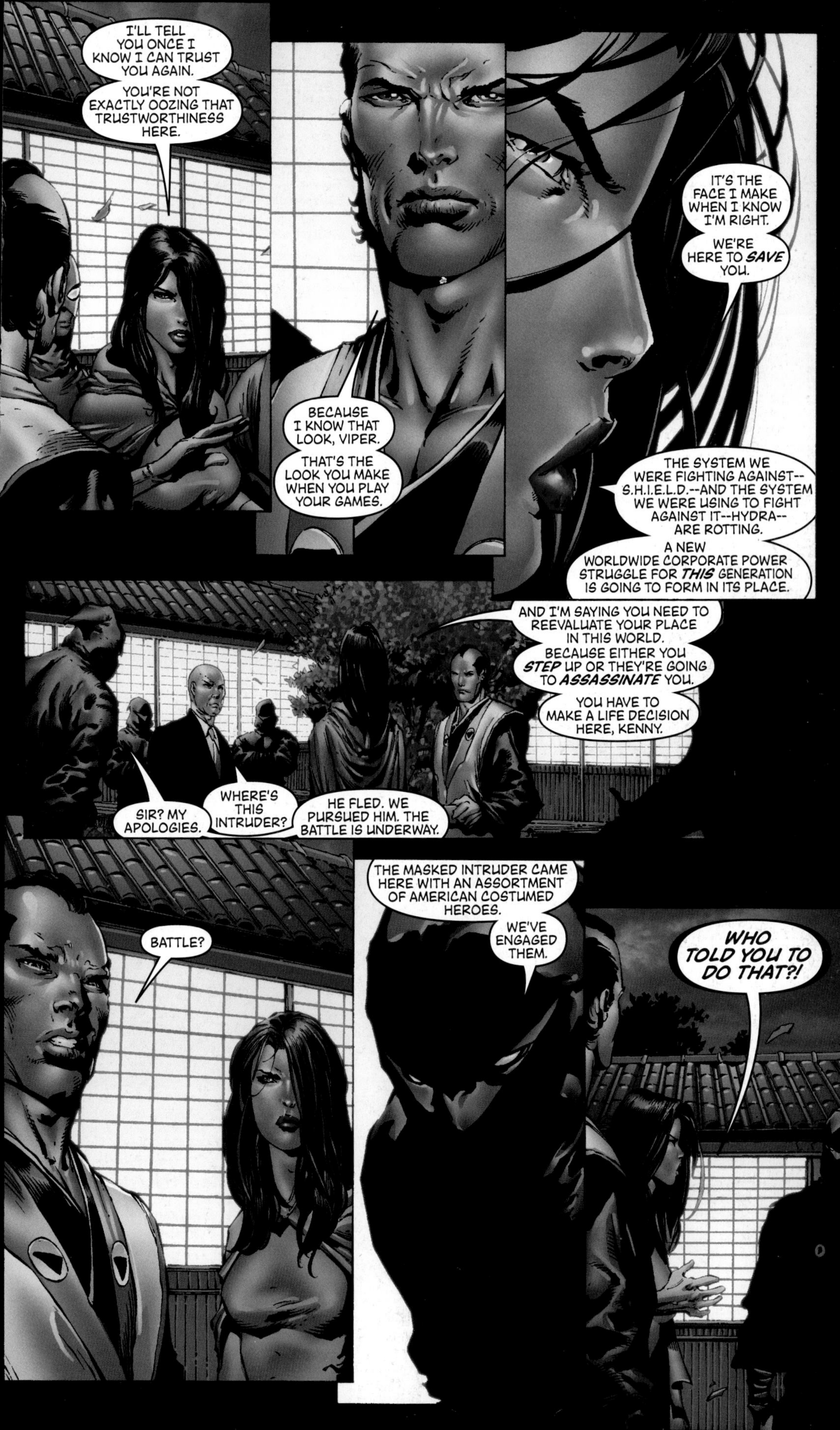

I'LL TELL YOU ONCE I KNOW I CAN TRUST YOU AGAIN.
YOU'RE NOT EXACTLY OOZING THAT TRUSTWORTHINESS HERE.
BECAUSE I KNOW THAT LOOK, VIPER.
THAT'S THE LOOK YOU MAKE WHEN YOU PLAY YOUR GAMES.
IT'S THE FACE I MAKE WHEN I KNOW I'M RIGHT.
WE'RE HERE TO SAVE YOU.
THE SYSTEM WE WERE FIGHTING AGAINST-- S.H.I.E.L.D.--AND THE SYSTEM WE WERE USING TO FIGHT AGAINST IT--HYDRA-- ARE ROTTING.
A NEW WORLDWIDE CORPORATE POWER STRUGGLE FOR THIS GENERATION IS GOING TO FORM IN ITS PLACE.
AND I'M SAYING YOU NEED TO REEVALUATE YOUR PLACE IN THIS WORLD.
BECAUSE EITHER YOU STEP UP OR THEY'RE GOING TO ASSASSINATE YOU.
YOU HAVE TO MAKE A LIFE DECISION HERE, KENNY.
SIR? MY APOLOGIES.
WHERE'S THIS INTRUDER?
HE FLED. WE PURSUED HIM. THE BATTLE IS UNDERWAY.
BATTLE?
THE MASKED INTRUDER CAME HERE WITH AN ASSORTMENT OF AMERICAN COSTUMED HEROES.
WE'VE ENGAGED THEM.
WHO TOLD YOU TO DO THAT?!

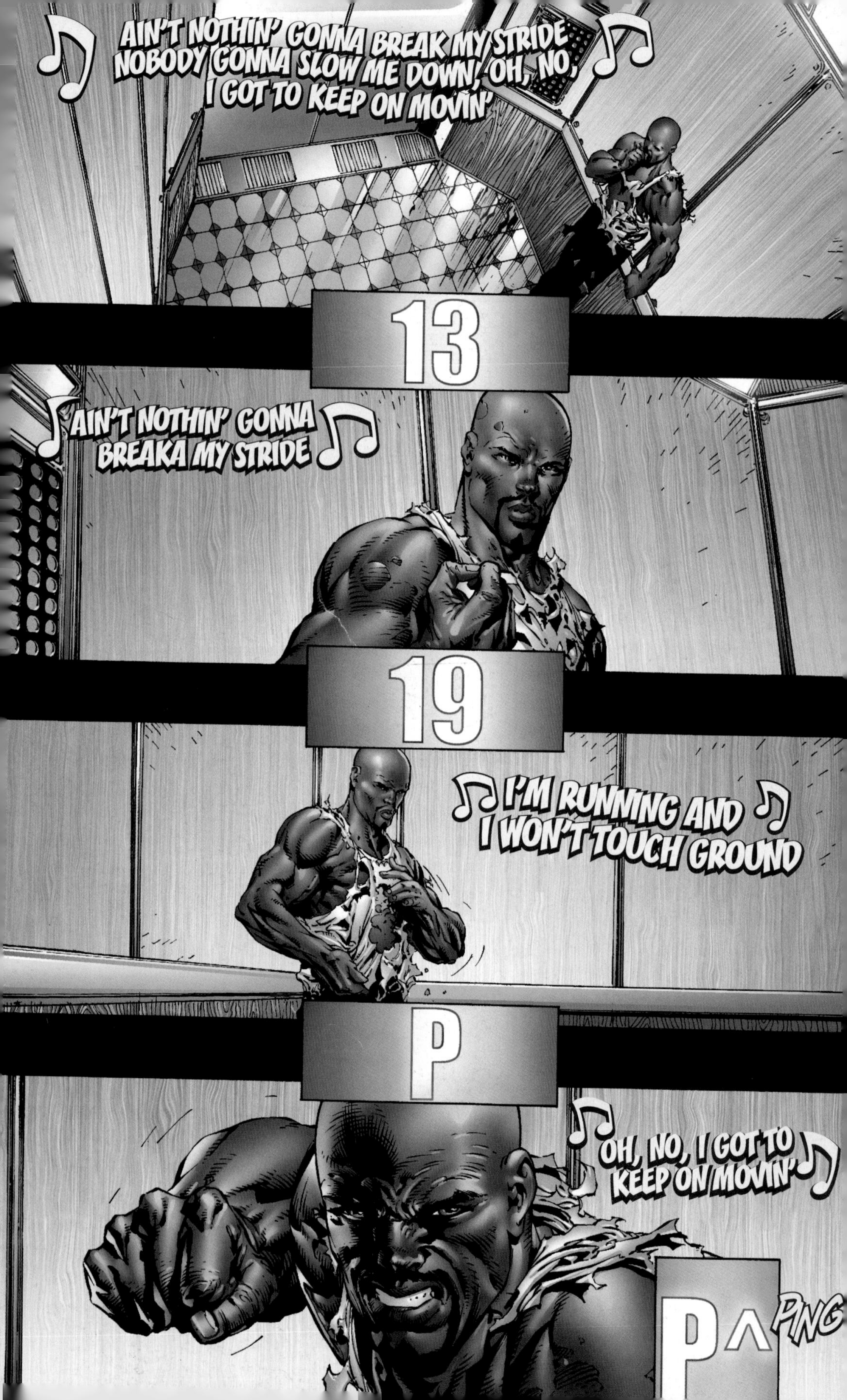
AIN'T NOTHIN' GONNA BREAK MY STRIDE
NOBODY GONNA SLOW ME DOWN, OH, NO,
I GOT TO KEEP ON MOVIN'
13
AIN'T NOTHIN' GONNA
BREAKA MY STRIDE
19
I'M RUNNING AND
I WON'T TOUCH GROUND
P
OH, NO, I GOT TO
KEEP ON MOVIN'
P
PING

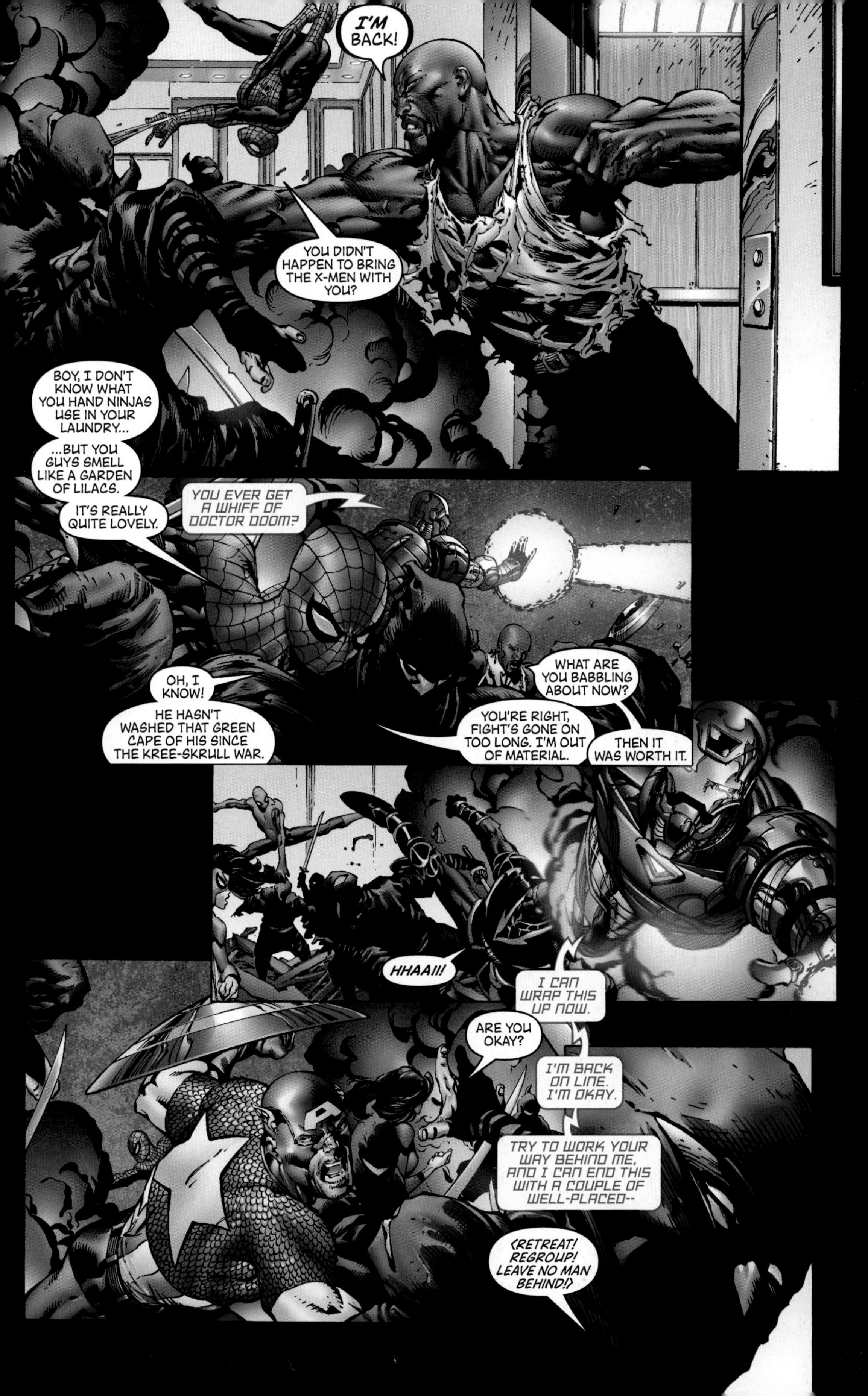
I'M BACK!
YOU DIDN'T HAPPEN TO BRING THE X-MEN WITH YOU?
BOY, I DON'T KNOW WHAT YOU HAND NINJAS USE IN YOUR LAUNDRY...
...BUT YOU GUYS SMELL LIKE A GARDEN OF LILACS.
IT'S REALLY QUITE LOVELY.
YOU EVER GET A WHIFF OF DOCTOR DOOM?
OH, I KNOW!
HE HASN'T WASHED THAT GREEN CAPE OF HIS SINCE THE KREE-SKRULL WAR.
WHAT ARE YOU BABBLING ABOUT NOW?
YOU'RE RIGHT, FIGHT'S GONE ON TOO LONG. I'M OUT OF MATERIAL.
THEN IT WAS WORTH IT.
HHAAII!
I CAN WRAP THIS UP NOW.
ARE YOU OKAY?
I'M BACK ON LINE. I'M OKAY.
TRY TO WORK YOUR WAY BEHIND ME, AND I CAN END THIS WITH A COUPLE OF WELL-PLACED--
<RETREAT! REGROUP! LEAVE NO MAN BEHIND!>

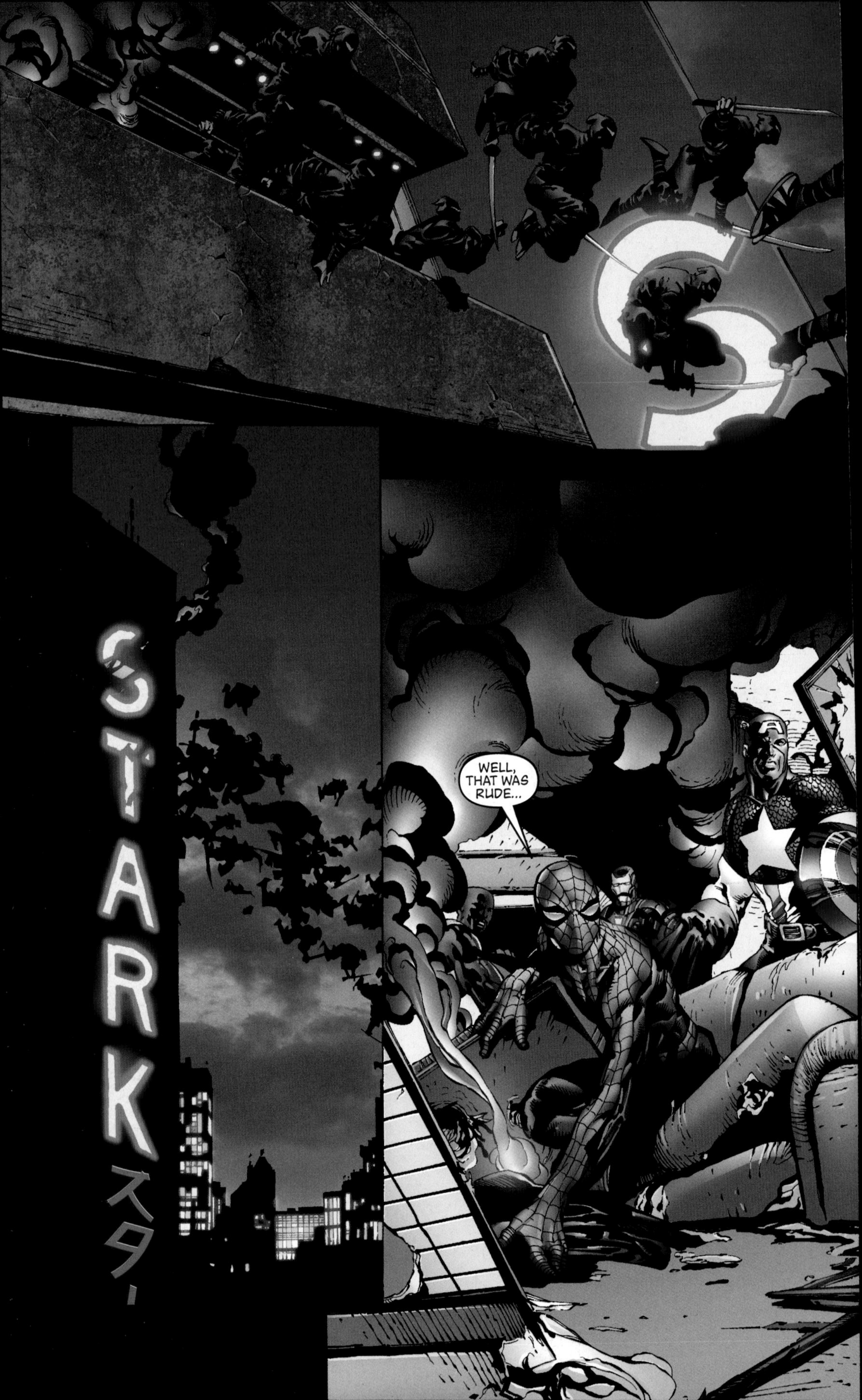
STARK スタ-
WELL, THAT WAS RUDE...

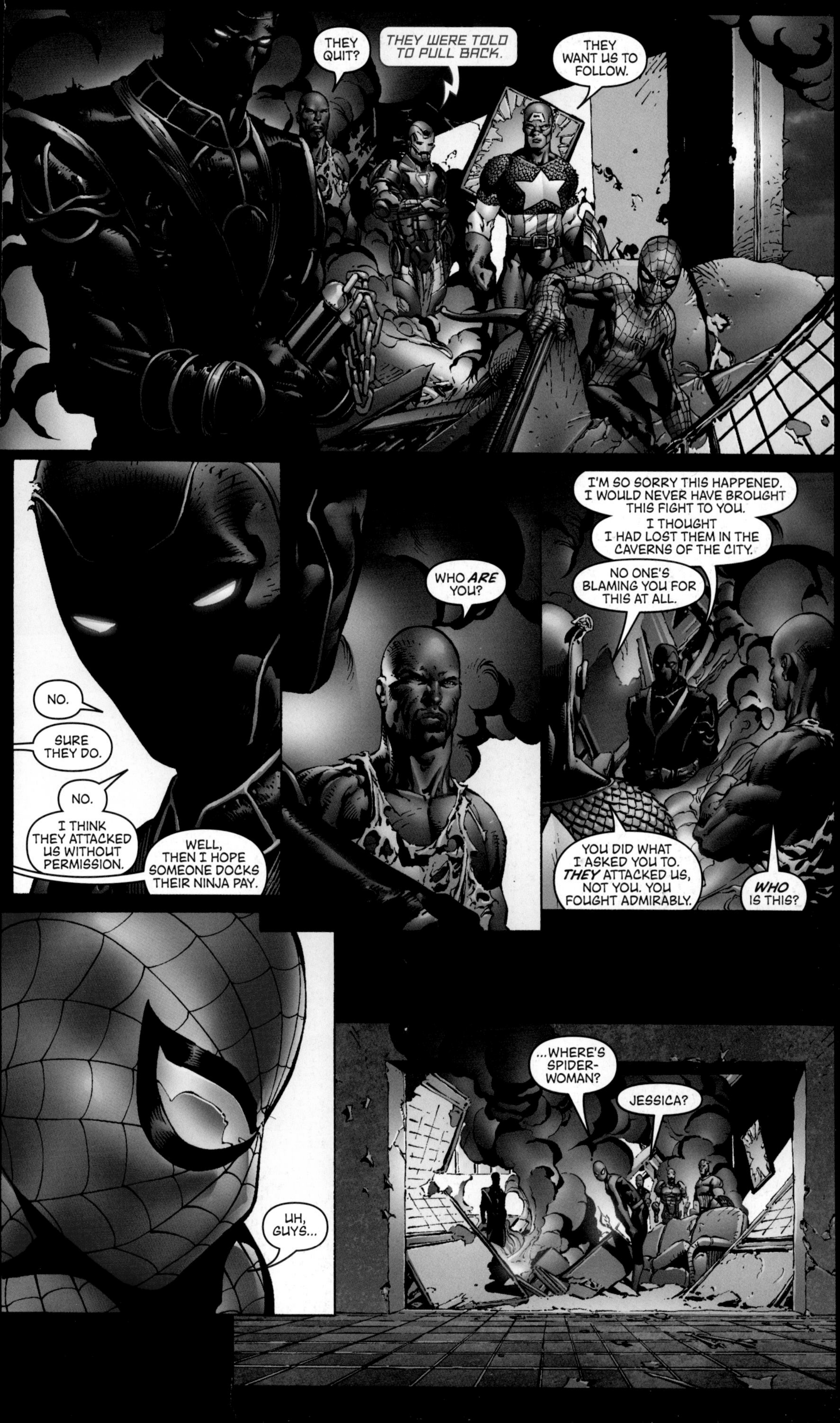
THEY QUIT?
THEY WERE TOLD TO PULL BACK.
THEY WANT US TO FOLLOW.
NO.
SURE THEY DO.
NO.
I THINK THEY ATTACKED US WITHOUT PERMISSION.
WELL, THEN I HOPE SOMEONE DOCKS THEIR NINJA PAY.
WHO ARE YOU?
I'M SO SORRY THIS HAPPENED. I WOULD NEVER HAVE BROUGHT THIS FIGHT TO YOU.
I THOUGHT I HAD LOST THEM IN THE CAVERNS OF THE CITY.
NO ONE'S BLAMING YOU FOR THIS AT ALL.
YOU DID WHAT I ASKED YOU TO. THEY ATTACKED US, NOT YOU. YOU FOUGHT ADMIRABLY.
WHO IS THIS?
UH, GUYS...
...WHERE'S SPIDER-WOMAN?
JESSICA?

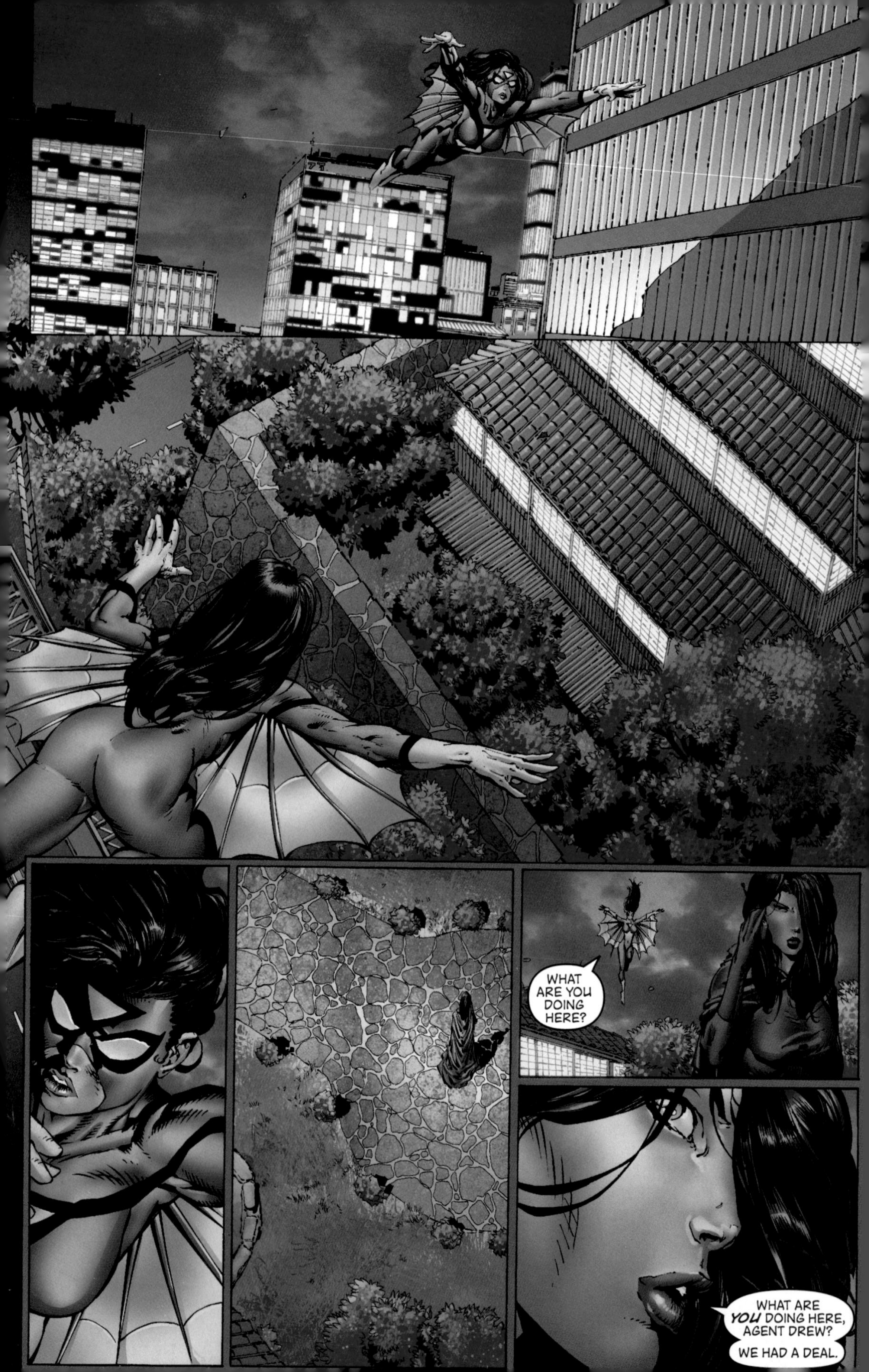
WHAT ARE YOU DOING HERE?
WHAT ARE *YOU* DOING HERE, AGENT DREW?
WE HAD A DEAL.

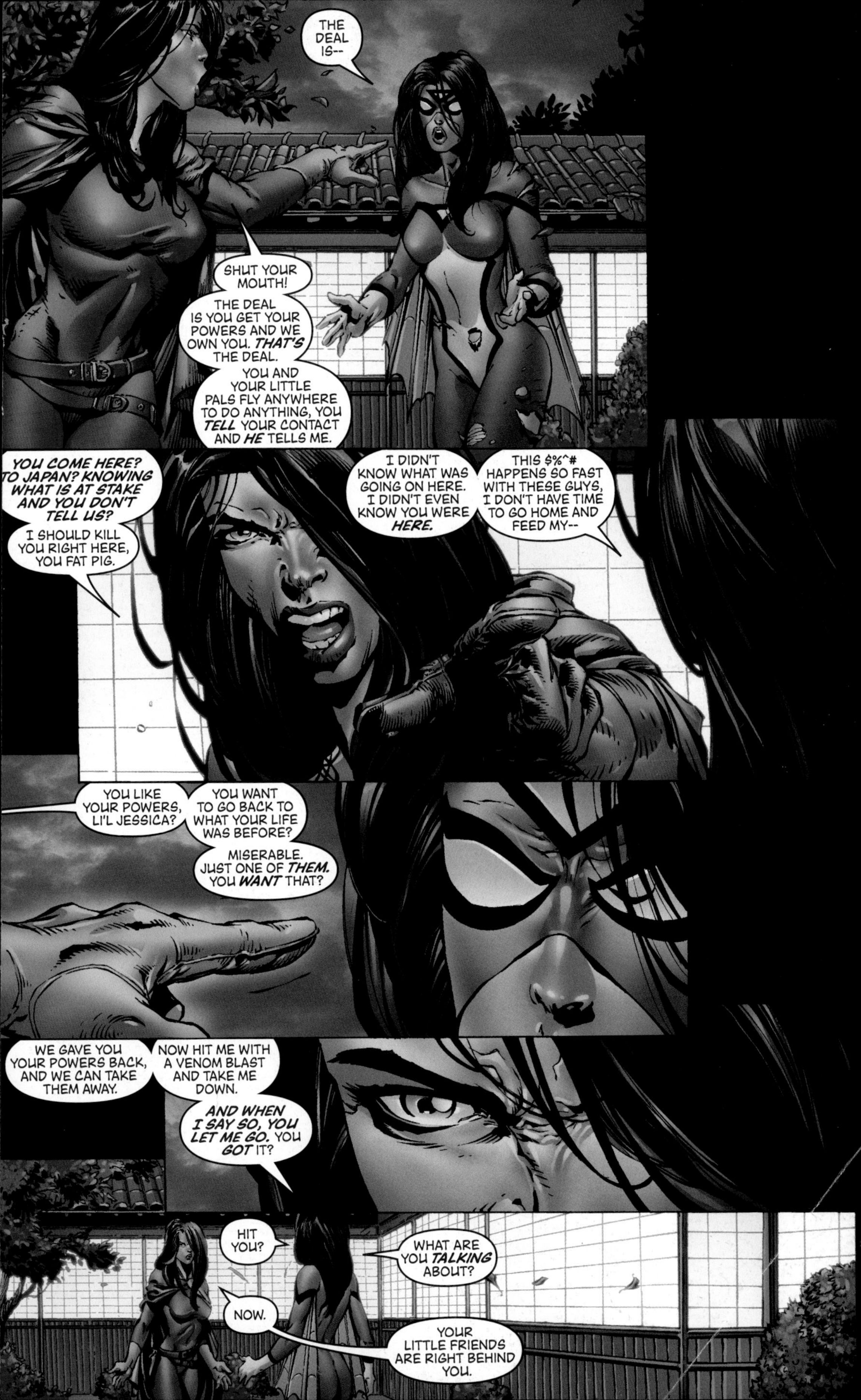

THE DEAL IS--
SHUT YOUR MOUTH!
THE DEAL IS YOU GET YOUR POWERS AND WE OWN YOU. THAT'S THE DEAL.
YOU AND YOUR LITTLE PALS FLY ANYWHERE TO DO ANYTHING, YOU TELL YOUR CONTACT AND HE TELLS ME.
YOU COME HERE? TO JAPAN? KNOWING WHAT IS AT STAKE AND YOU DON'T TELL US?
I SHOULD KILL YOU RIGHT HERE, YOU FAT PIG.
I DIDN'T KNOW WHAT WAS GOING ON HERE. I DIDN'T EVEN KNOW YOU WERE HERE.
THIS $%^# HAPPENS SO FAST WITH THESE GUYS, I DON'T HAVE TIME TO GO HOME AND FEED MY--
YOU LIKE YOUR POWERS, LI'L JESSICA?
YOU WANT TO GO BACK TO WHAT YOUR LIFE WAS BEFORE?
MISERABLE. JUST ONE OF THEM. YOU WANT THAT?
WE GAVE YOU YOUR POWERS BACK, AND WE CAN TAKE THEM AWAY.
NOW HIT ME WITH A VENOM BLAST AND TAKE ME DOWN.
AND WHEN I SAY SO, YOU LET ME GO. YOU GOT IT?
HIT YOU?
WHAT ARE YOU TALKING ABOUT?
NOW.
YOUR LITTLE FRIENDS ARE RIGHT BEHIND YOU.

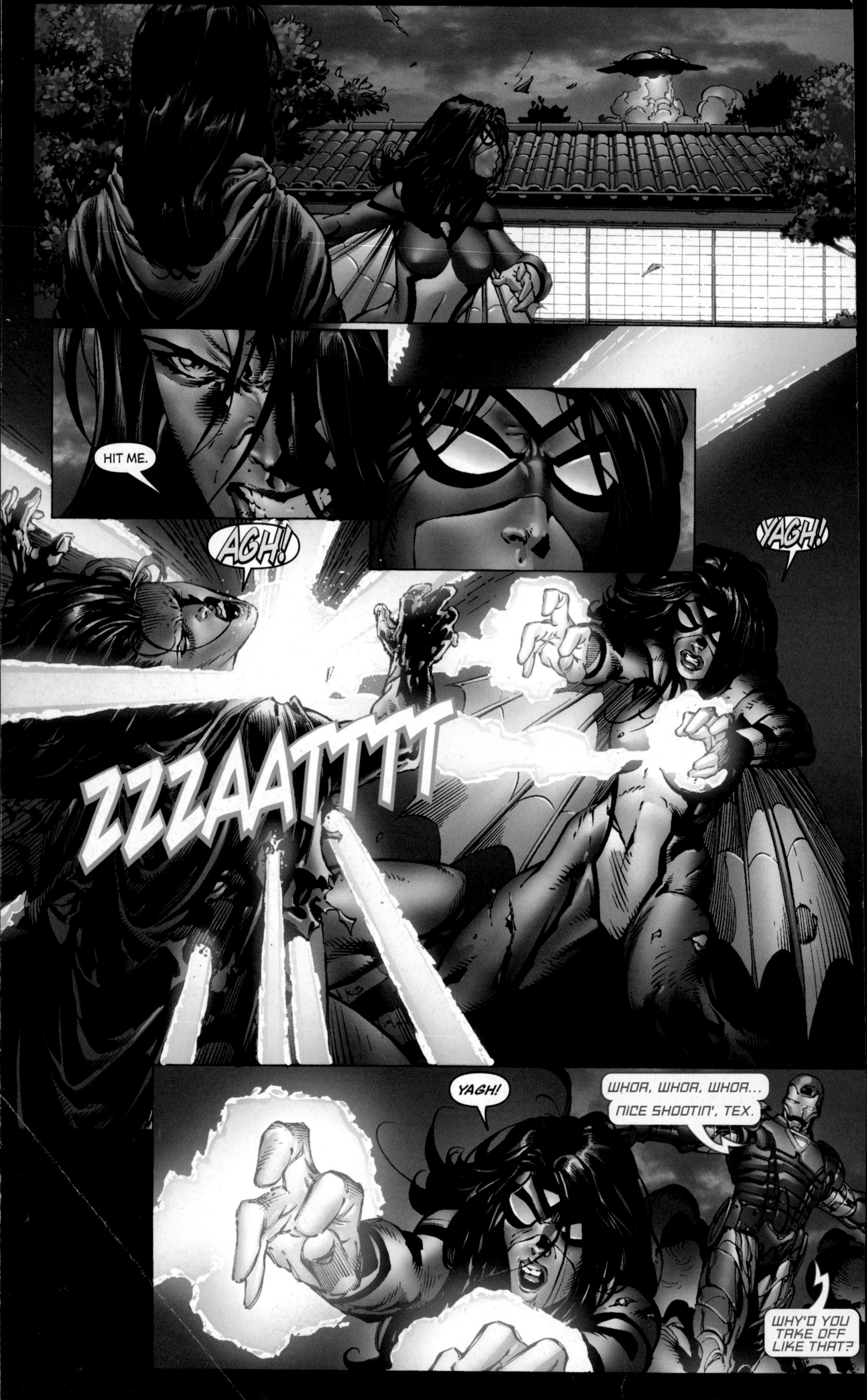
HIT ME.
AGH!
YAGH!
ZZZAATTTT
YAGH!
WHOA, WHOA, WHOA...
NICE SHOOTIN', TEX.
WHY'D YOU TAKE OFF LIKE THAT?

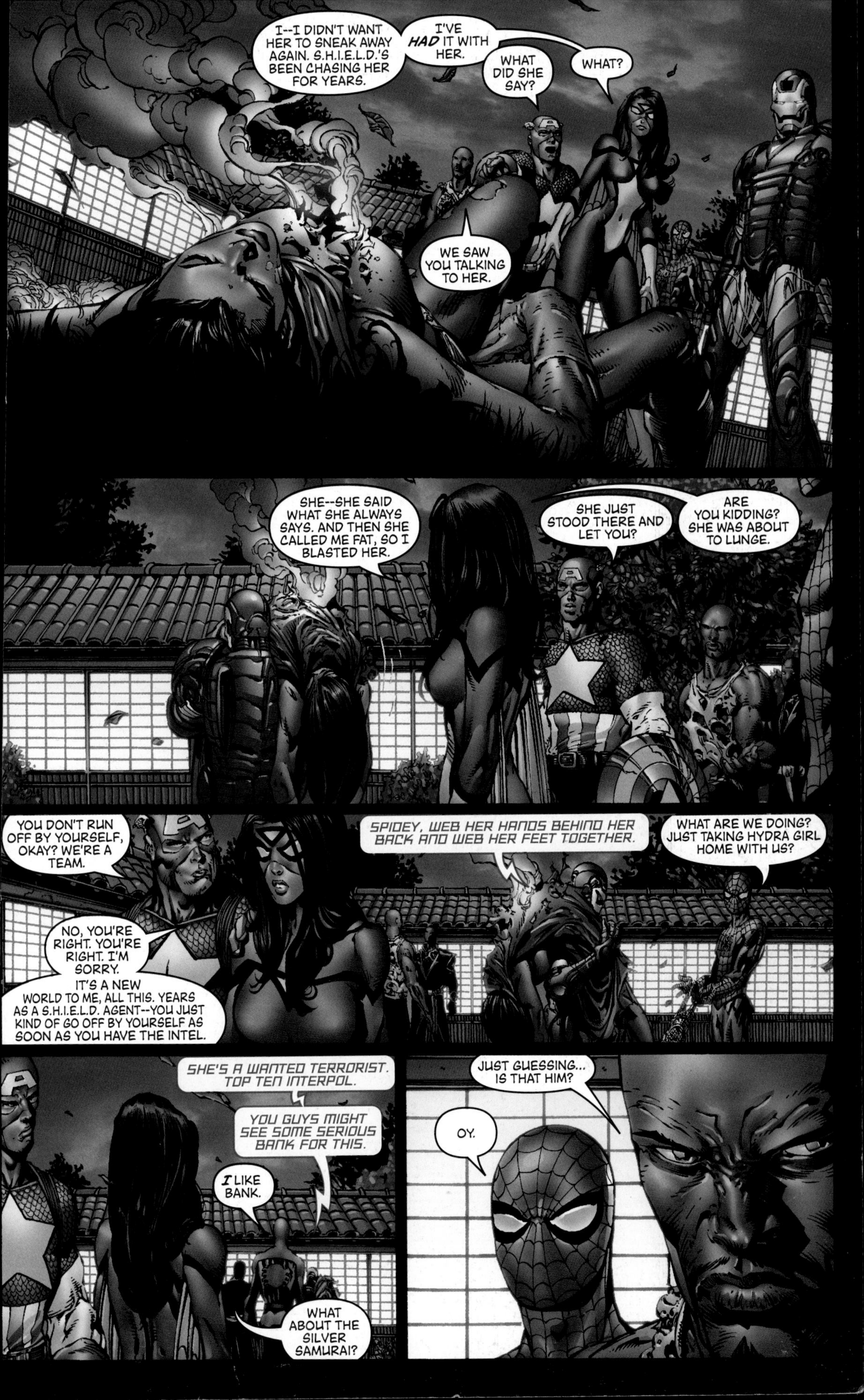
I--I DIDN'T WANT HER TO SNEAK AWAY AGAIN. S.H.I.E.L.D.'S BEEN CHASING HER FOR YEARS.
I'VE HAD IT WITH HER.
WHAT DID SHE SAY?
WHAT?
WE SAW YOU TALKING TO HER.
SHE--SHE SAID WHAT SHE ALWAYS SAYS. AND THEN SHE CALLED ME FAT, SO I BLASTED HER.
SHE JUST STOOD THERE AND LET YOU?
ARE YOU KIDDING? SHE WAS ABOUT TO LUNGE.
YOU DON'T RUN OFF BY YOURSELF, OKAY? WE'RE A TEAM.
NO, YOU'RE RIGHT. YOU'RE RIGHT. I'M SORRY.
IT'S A NEW WORLD TO ME, ALL THIS. YEARS AS A S.H.I.E.L.D. AGENT--YOU JUST KIND OF GO OFF BY YOURSELF AS SOON AS YOU HAVE THE INTEL.
SPIDEY, WEB HER HANDS BEHIND HER BACK AND WEB HER FEET TOGETHER.
WHAT ARE WE DOING? JUST TAKING HYDRA GIRL HOME WITH US?
SHE'S A WANTED TERRORIST. TOP TEN INTERPOL.
YOU GUYS MIGHT SEE SOME SERIOUS BANK FOR THIS.
I LIKE BANK.
WHAT ABOUT THE SILVER SAMURAI?
JUST GUESSING... IS THAT HIM?
OY.

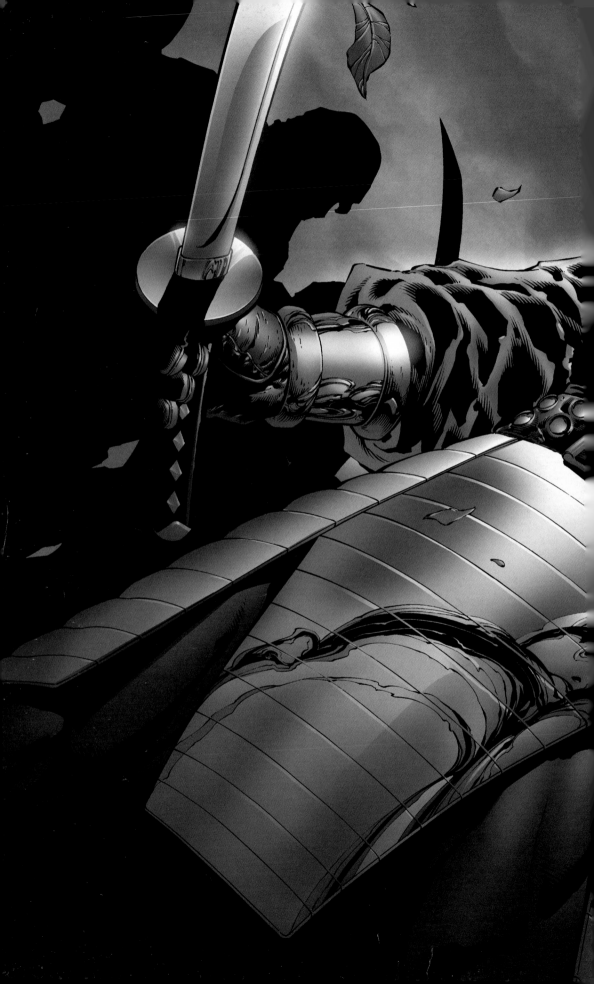

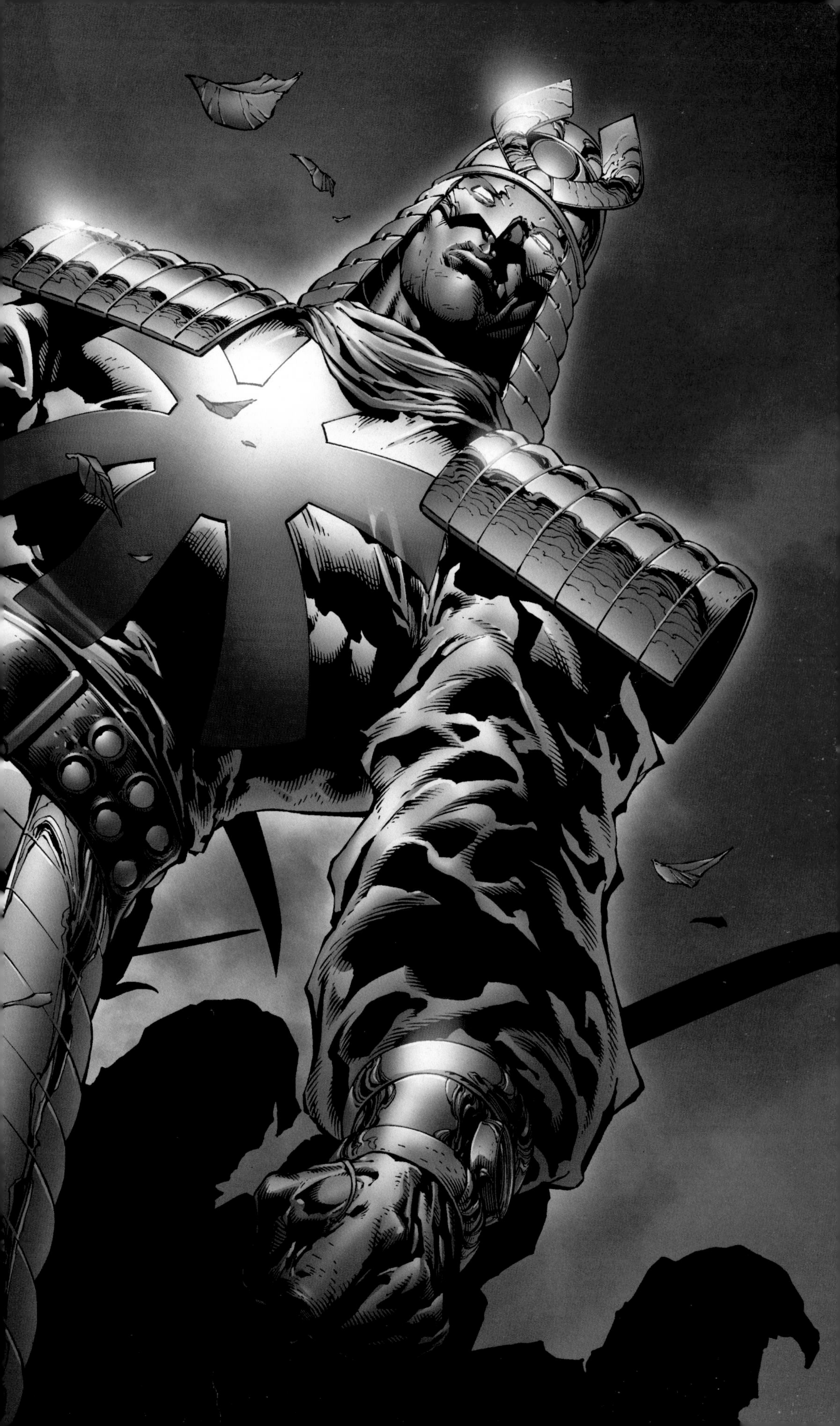

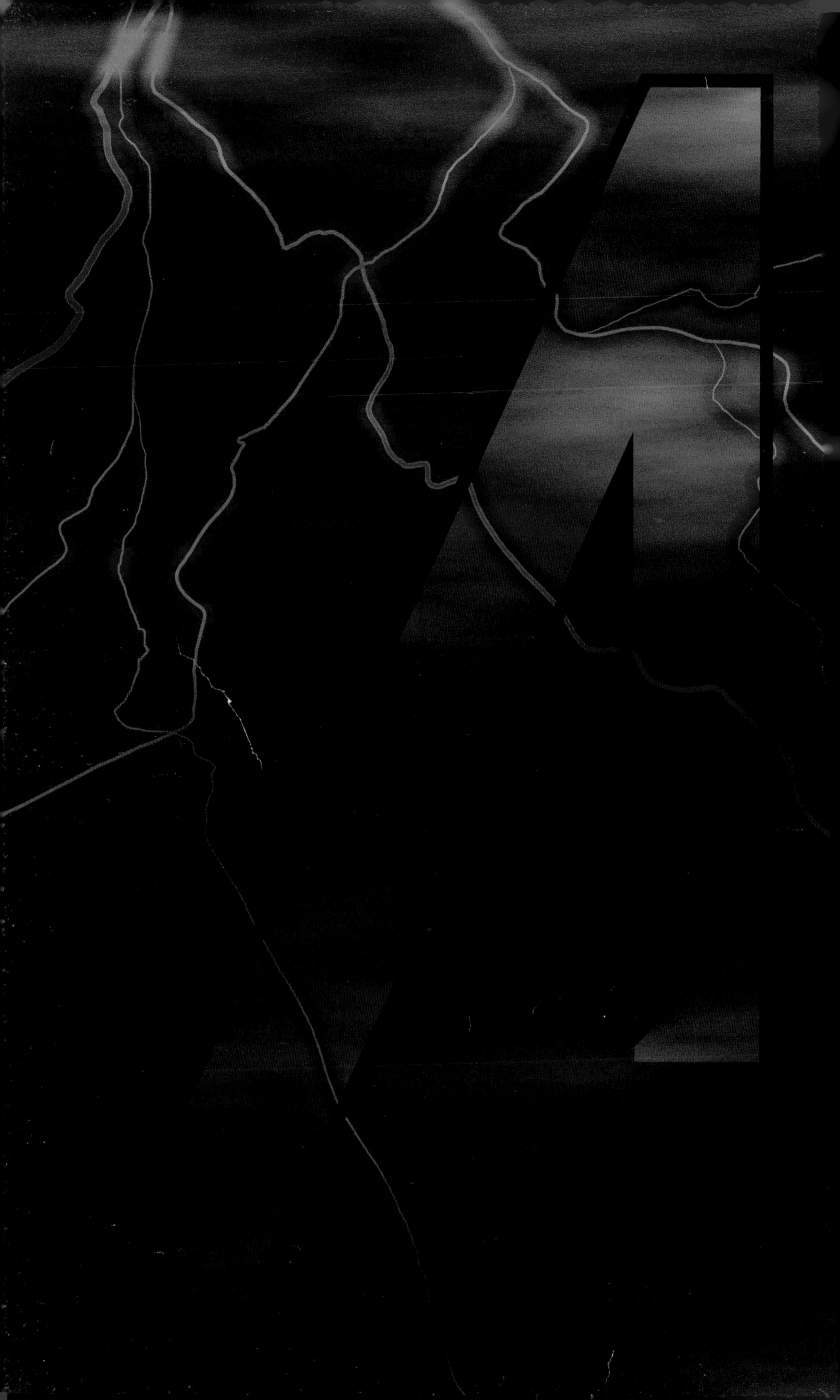

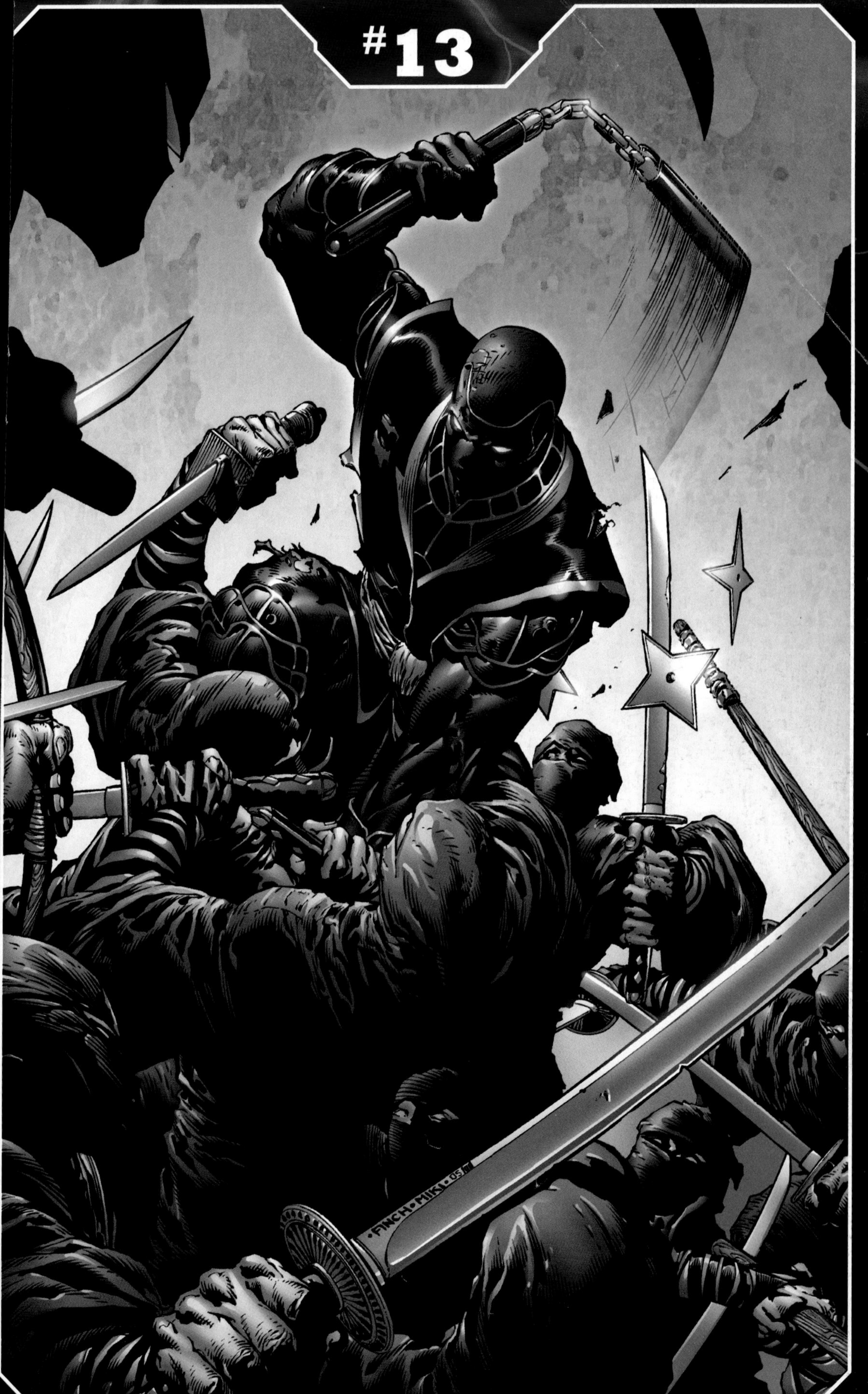
#13

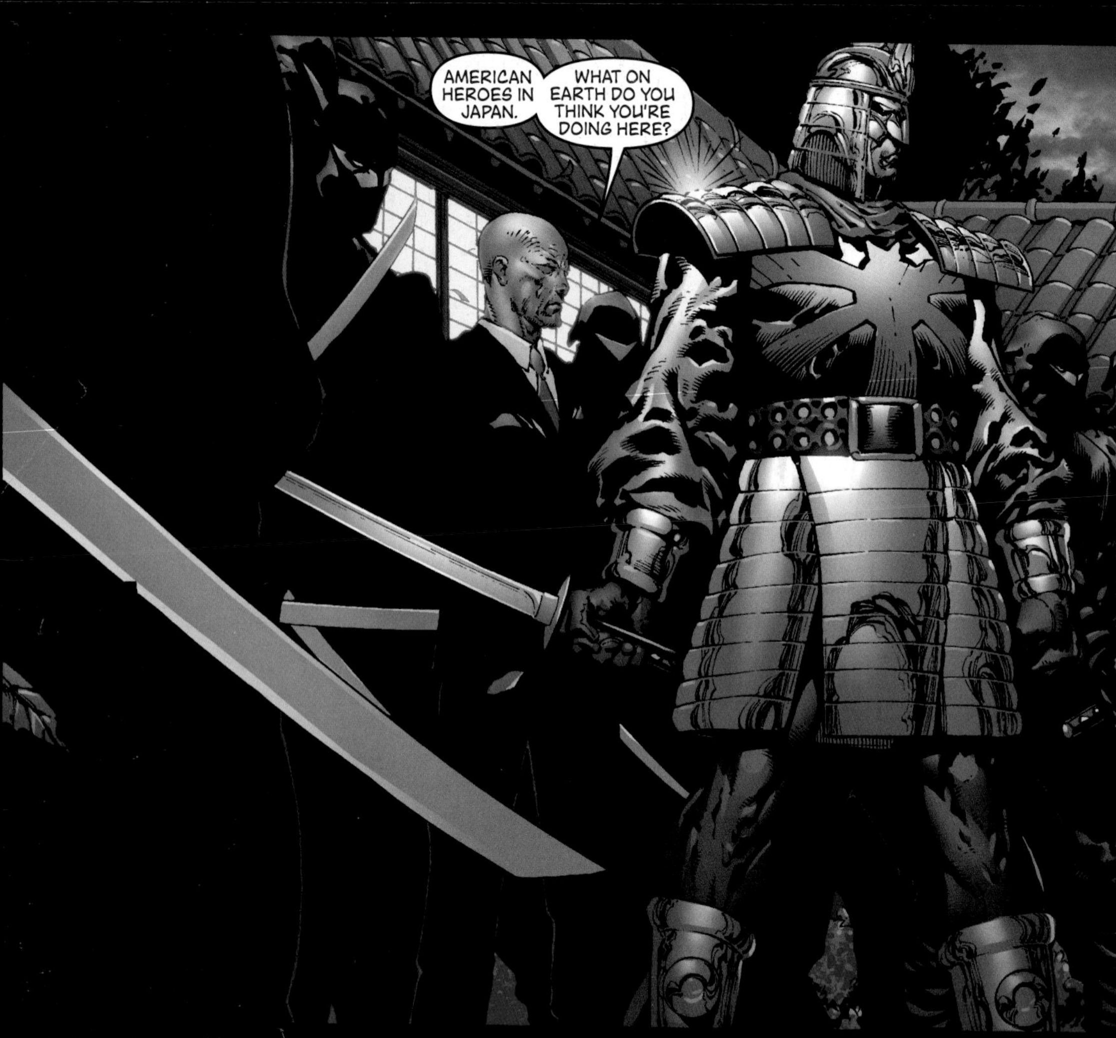
AMERICAN HEROES IN JAPAN.
WHAT ON EARTH DO YOU THINK YOU'RE DOING HERE?

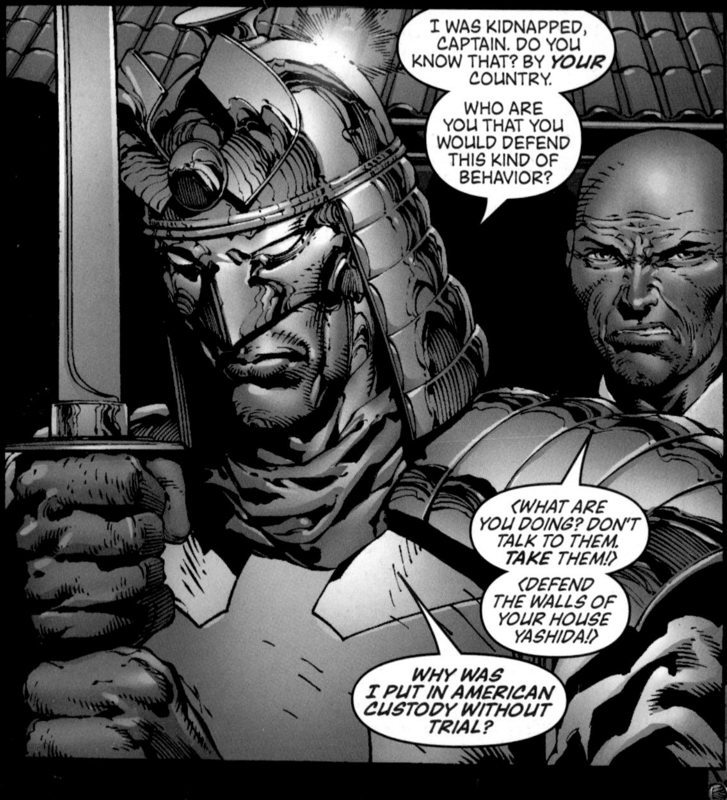
I WAS KIDNAPPED, CAPTAIN. DO YOU KNOW THAT? BY *YOUR* COUNTRY.
WHO ARE YOU THAT YOU WOULD DEFEND THIS KIND OF BEHAVIOR?

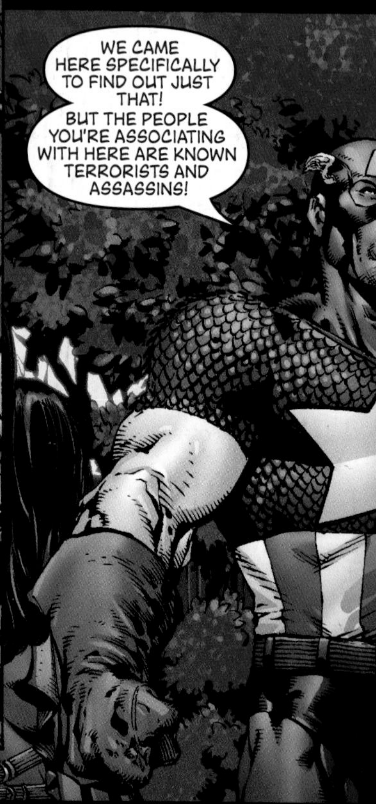
WE CAME HERE SPECIFICALLY TO FIND OUT JUST THAT!
BUT THE PEOPLE YOU'RE ASSOCIATING WITH HERE ARE KNOWN TERRORISTS AND ASSASSINS!

<WHAT ARE YOU DOING? DON'T TALK TO THEM. *TAKE* THEM!>
<DEFEND THE WALLS OF YOUR HOUSE YASHIDA!>
WHY WAS I PUT IN AMERICAN CUSTODY WITHOUT TRIAL?

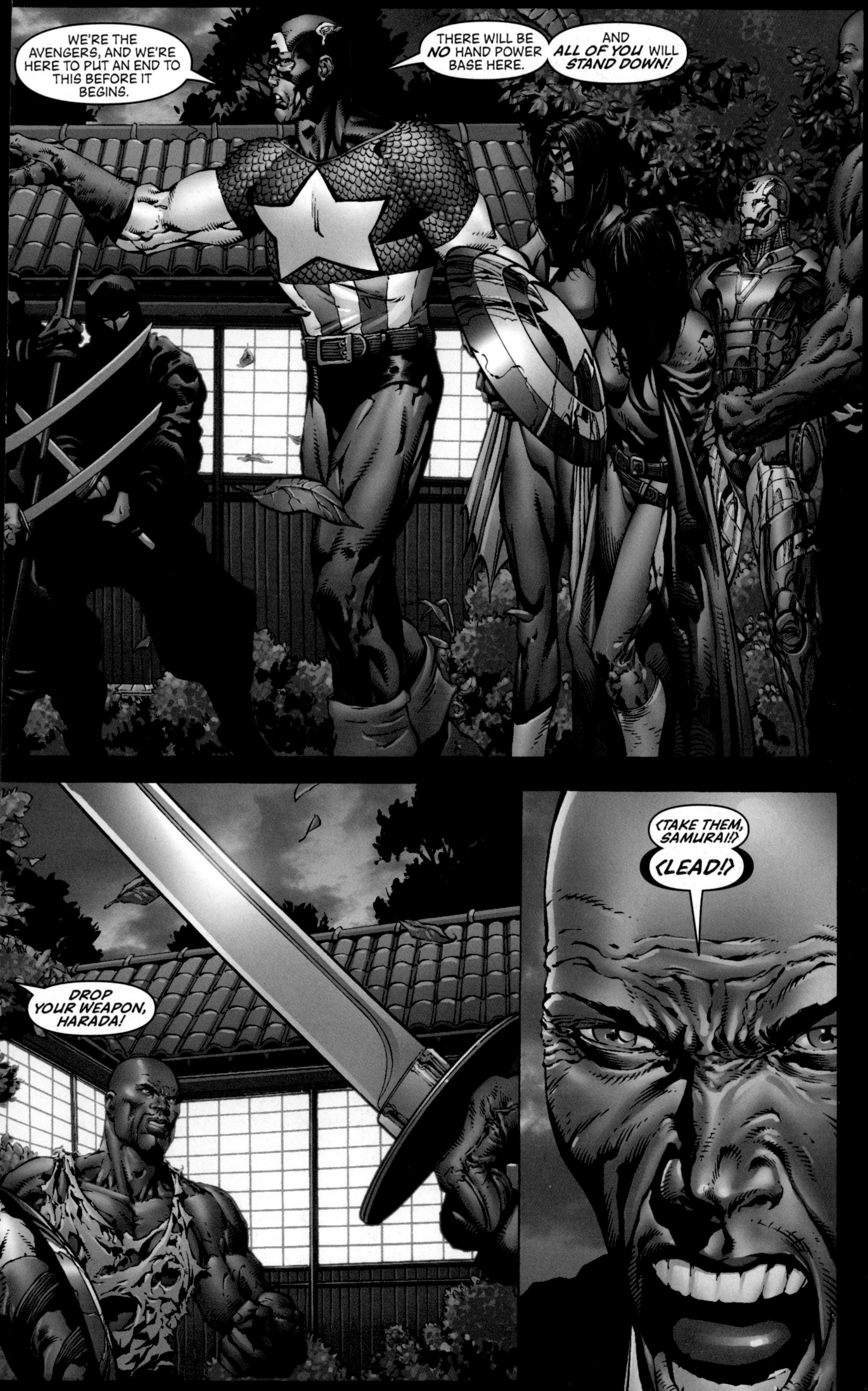
WE'RE THE AVENGERS, AND WE'RE HERE TO PUT AN END TO THIS BEFORE IT BEGINS.
THERE WILL BE NO HAND POWER BASE HERE.
AND ALL OF YOU WILL STAND DOWN!
DROP YOUR WEAPON, HARADA!
<TAKE THEM, SAMURAI!>
<LEAD!>

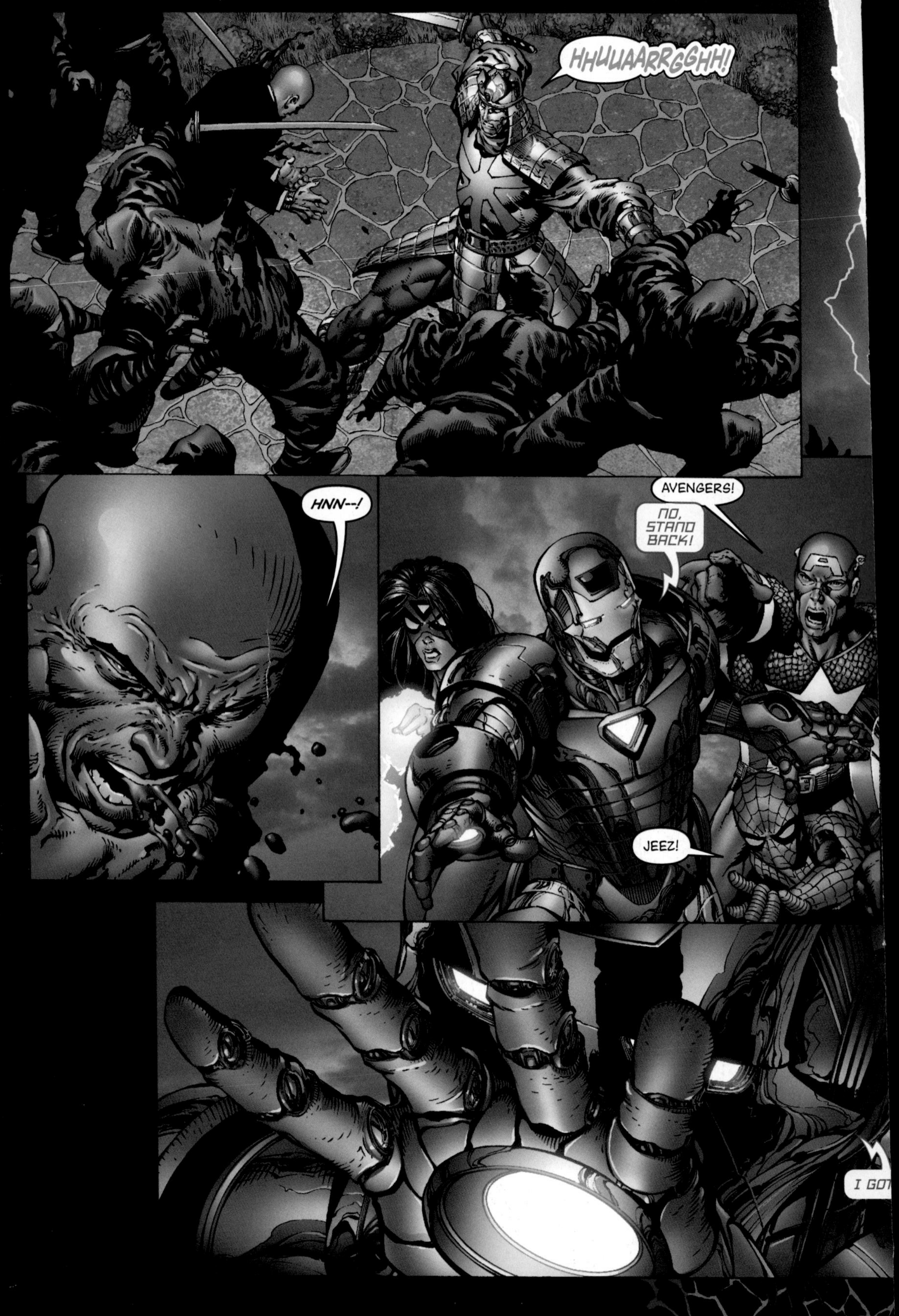
HHUUAARRGGHH!
HNN--!
AVENGERS!
NO, STAND BACK!
JEEZ!
I GOT

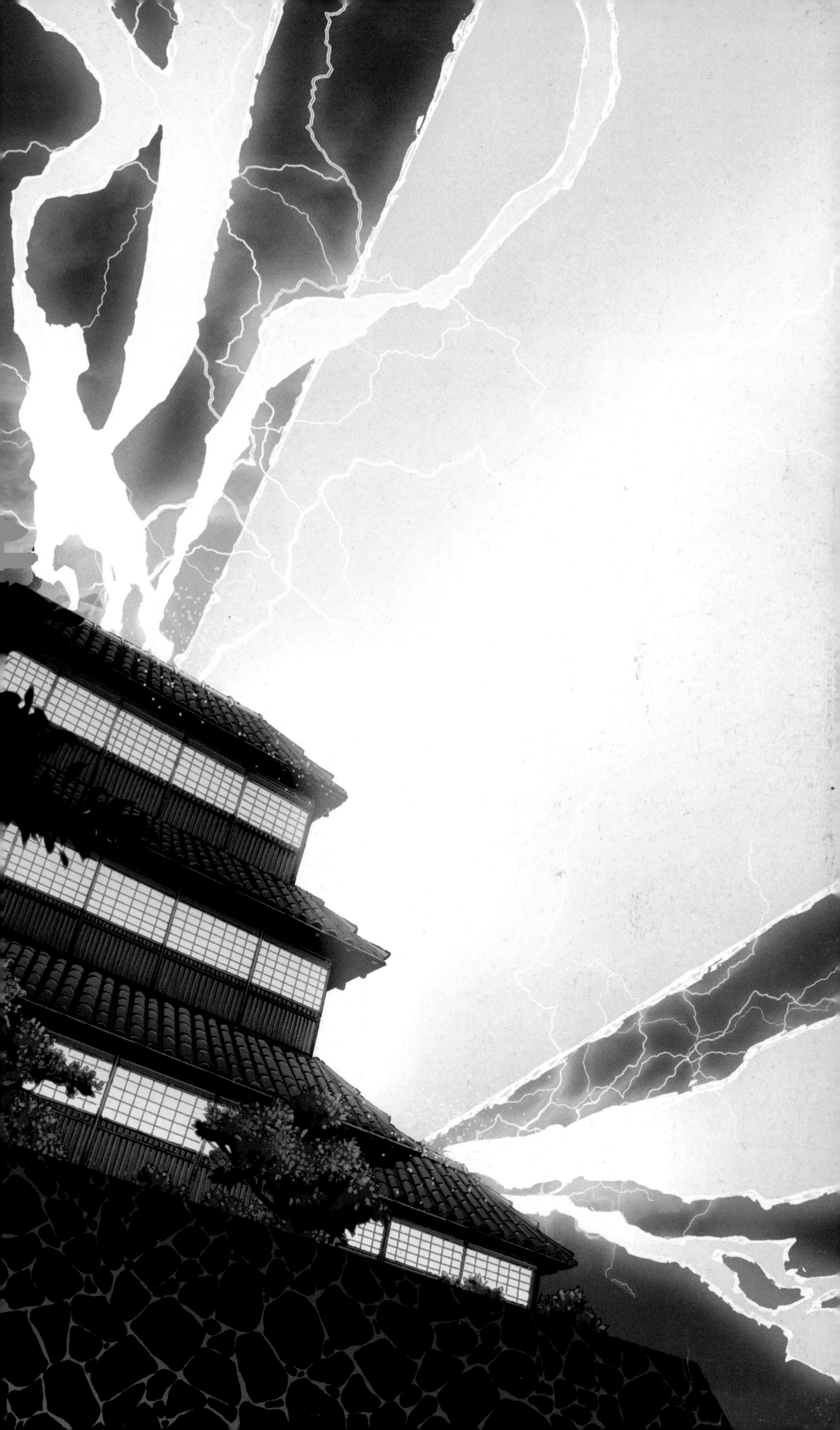

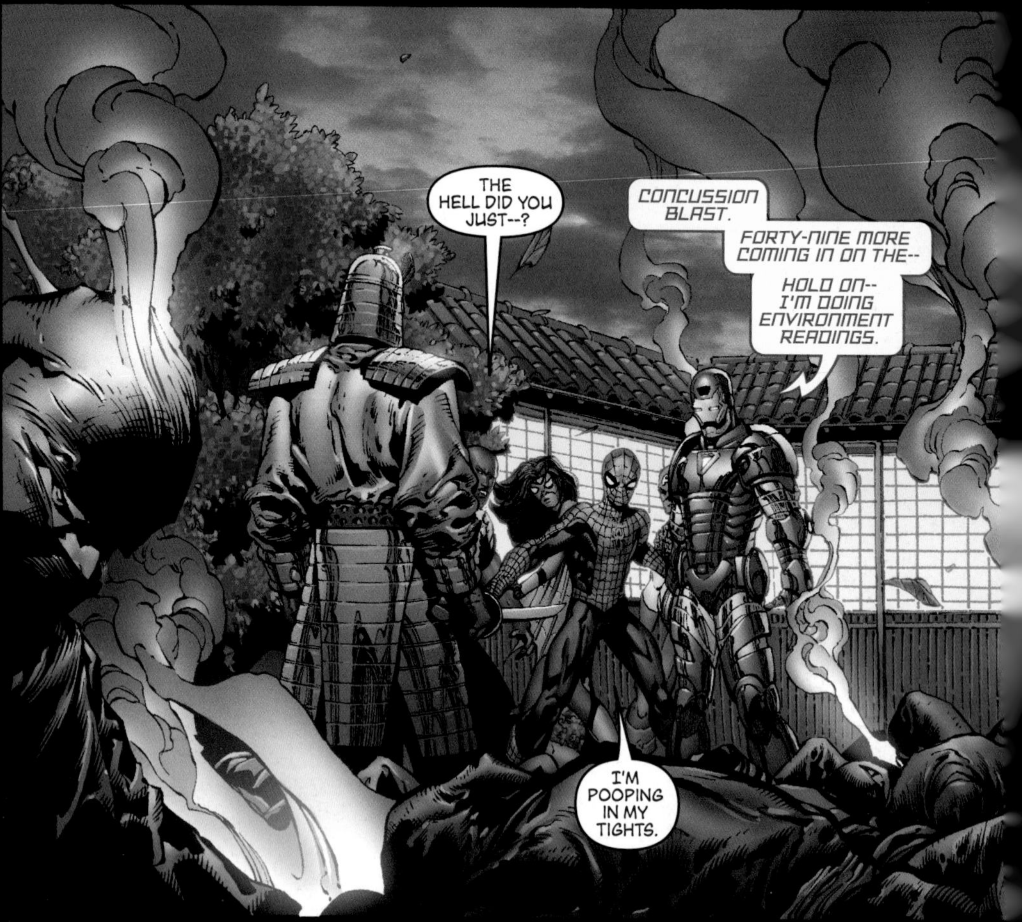
THE HELL DID YOU JUST--?
CONCUSSION BLAST.
FORTY-NINE MORE COMING IN ON THE--
HOLD ON-- I'M DOING ENVIRONMENT READINGS.
I'M POOPING IN MY TIGHTS.

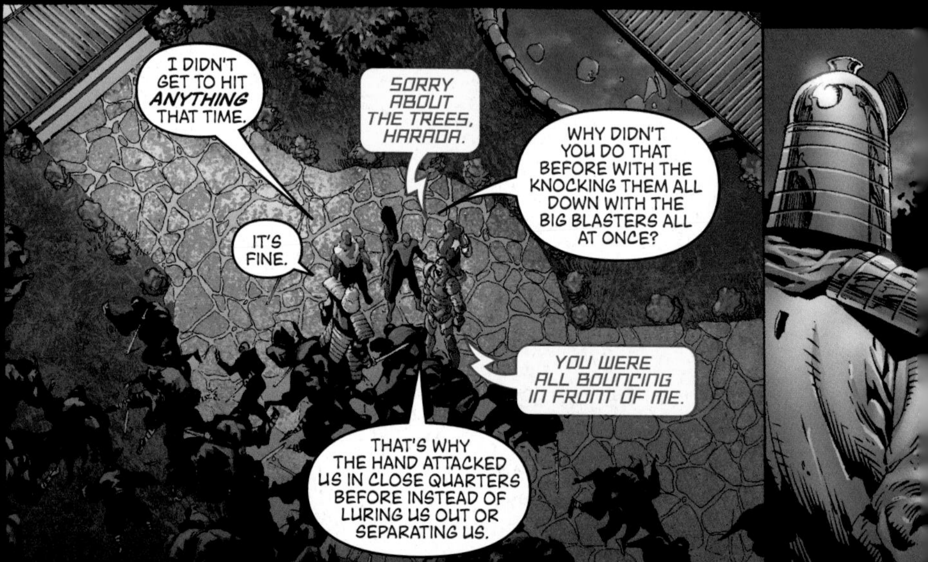
I DIDN'T GET TO HIT ANYTHING THAT TIME.
SORRY ABOUT THE TREES, HARADA.
WHY DIDN'T YOU DO THAT BEFORE WITH THE KNOCKING THEM ALL DOWN WITH THE BIG BLASTERS ALL AT ONCE?
IT'S FINE.
YOU WERE ALL BOUNCING IN FRONT OF ME.
THAT'S WHY THE HAND ATTACKED US IN CLOSE QUARTERS BEFORE INSTEAD OF LURING US OUT OR SEPARATING US.

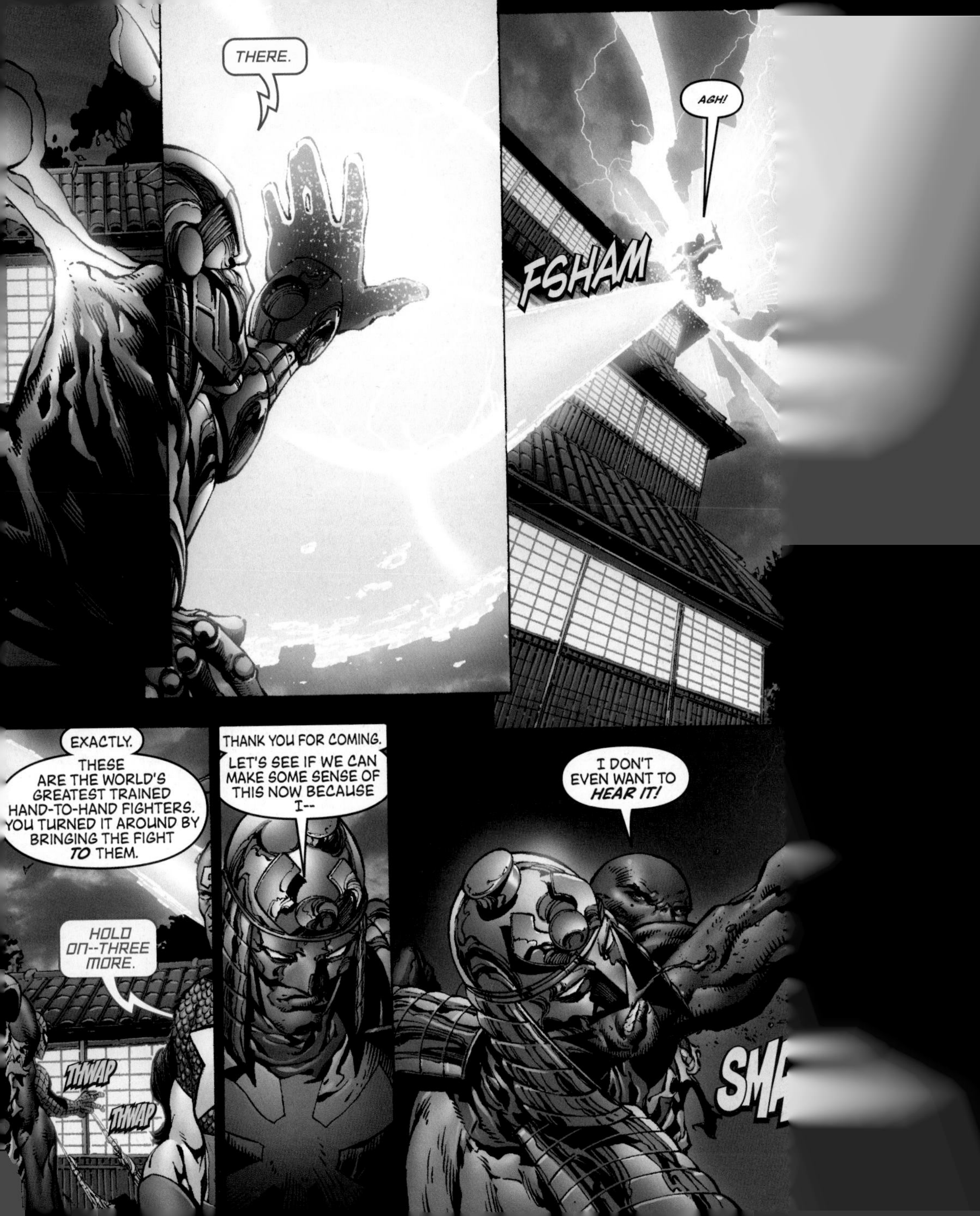
THERE.
AGH!
FSHAM
EXACTLY.
THESE ARE THE WORLD'S GREATEST TRAINED HAND-TO-HAND FIGHTERS. YOU TURNED IT AROUND BY BRINGING THE FIGHT TO THEM.
HOLD ON--THREE MORE.
THWAP
THWAP
THANK YOU FOR COMING.
LET'S SEE IF WE CAN MAKE SOME SENSE OF THIS NOW BECAUSE I--
I DON'T EVEN WANT TO HEAR IT!

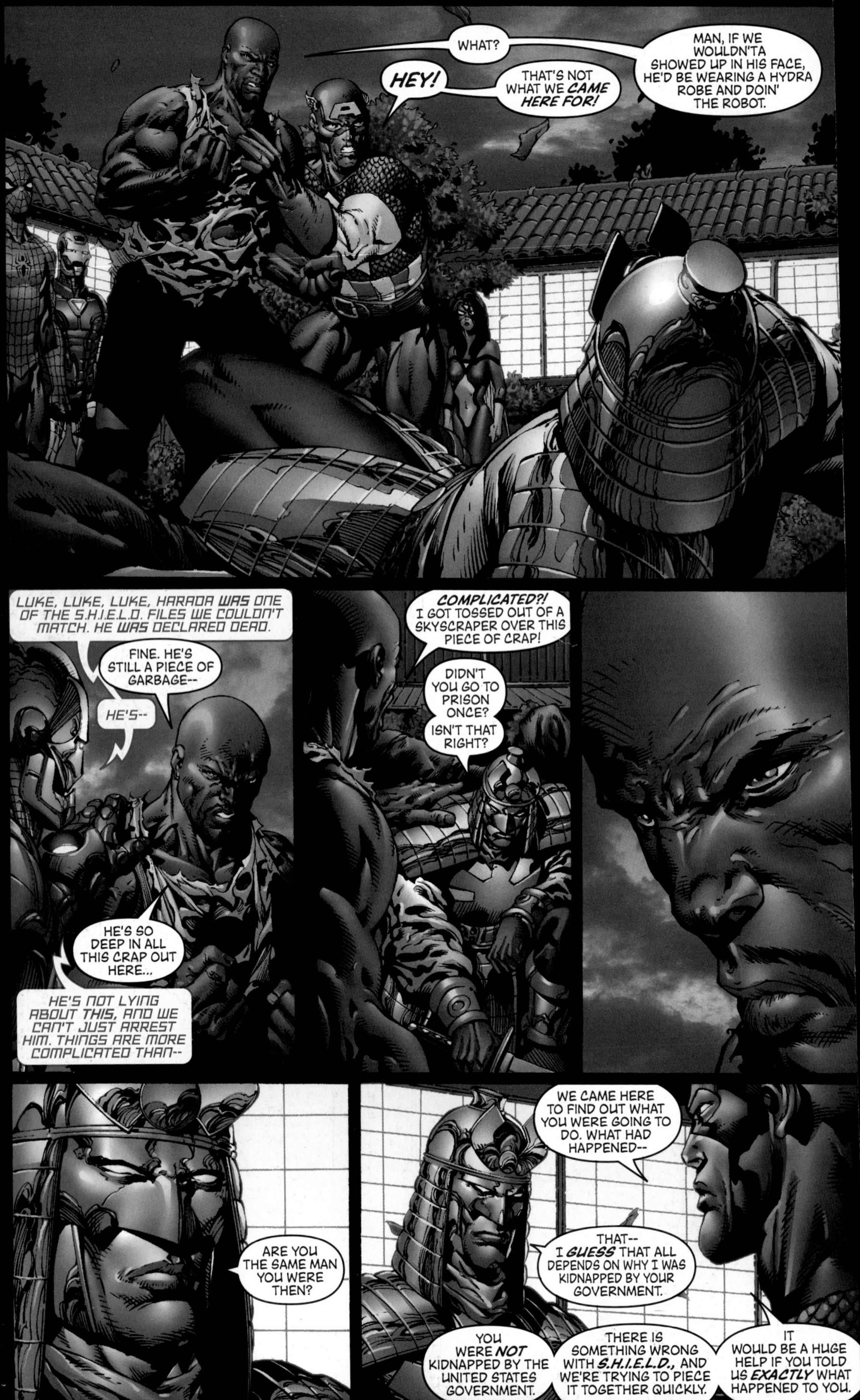
WHAT?
MAN, IF WE WOULDN'TA SHOWED UP IN HIS FACE, HE'D BE WEARING A HYDRA ROBE AND DOIN' THE ROBOT.
HEY!
THAT'S NOT WHAT WE CAME HERE FOR!
LUKE, LUKE, LUKE, HARADA WAS ONE OF THE S.H.I.E.L.D. FILES WE COULDN'T MATCH. HE WAS DECLARED DEAD.
FINE. HE'S STILL A PIECE OF GARBAGE--
HE'S--
HE'S SO DEEP IN ALL THIS CRAP OUT HERE...
HE'S NOT LYING ABOUT THIS, AND WE CAN'T JUST ARREST HIM. THINGS ARE MORE COMPLICATED THAN--
COMPLICATED?! I GOT TOSSED OUT OF A SKYSCRAPER OVER THIS PIECE OF CRAP!
DIDN'T YOU GO TO PRISON ONCE?
ISN'T THAT RIGHT?
ARE YOU THE SAME MAN YOU WERE THEN?
WE CAME HERE TO FIND OUT WHAT YOU WERE GOING TO DO. WHAT HAD HAPPENED--
THAT-- I GUESS THAT ALL DEPENDS ON WHY I WAS KIDNAPPED BY YOUR GOVERNMENT.
YOU WERE NOT KIDNAPPED BY THE UNITED STATES GOVERNMENT.
THERE IS SOMETHING WRONG WITH S.H.I.E.L.D., AND WE'RE TRYING TO PIECE IT TOGETHER QUICKLY.
IT WOULD BE A HUGE HELP IF YOU TOLD US EXACTLY WHAT HAPPENED TO YOU.

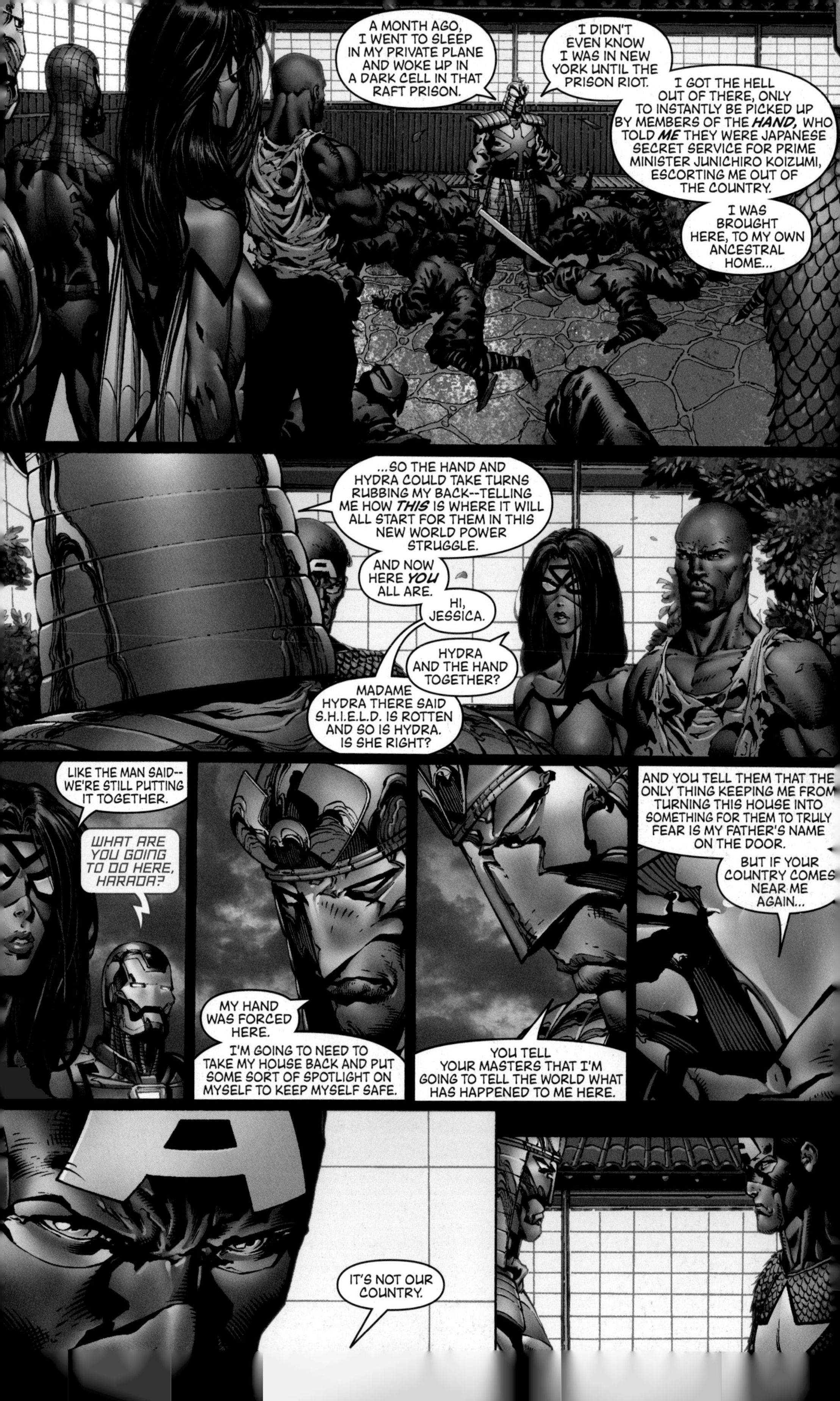
A MONTH AGO, I WENT TO SLEEP IN MY PRIVATE PLANE AND WOKE UP IN A DARK CELL IN THAT RAFT PRISON.
I DIDN'T EVEN KNOW I WAS IN NEW YORK UNTIL THE PRISON RIOT.
I GOT THE HELL OUT OF THERE, ONLY TO INSTANTLY BE PICKED UP BY MEMBERS OF THE HAND, WHO TOLD ME THEY WERE JAPANESE SECRET SERVICE FOR PRIME MINISTER JUNICHIRO KOIZUMI, ESCORTING ME OUT OF THE COUNTRY.
I WAS BROUGHT HERE, TO MY OWN ANCESTRAL HOME...
...SO THE HAND AND HYDRA COULD TAKE TURNS RUBBING MY BACK--TELLING ME HOW THIS IS WHERE IT WILL ALL START FOR THEM IN THIS NEW WORLD POWER STRUGGLE.
AND NOW HERE YOU ALL ARE.
HI, JESSICA.
HYDRA AND THE HAND TOGETHER?
MADAME HYDRA THERE SAID S.H.I.E.L.D. IS ROTTEN AND SO IS HYDRA. IS SHE RIGHT?
LIKE THE MAN SAID-- WE'RE STILL PUTTING IT TOGETHER.
WHAT ARE YOU GOING TO DO HERE, HARADA?
MY HAND WAS FORCED HERE.
I'M GOING TO NEED TO TAKE MY HOUSE BACK AND PUT SOME SORT OF SPOTLIGHT ON MYSELF TO KEEP MYSELF SAFE.
YOU TELL YOUR MASTERS THAT I'M GOING TO TELL THE WORLD WHAT HAS HAPPENED TO ME HERE.
AND YOU TELL THEM THAT THE ONLY THING KEEPING ME FROM TURNING THIS HOUSE INTO SOMETHING FOR THEM TO TRULY FEAR IS MY FATHER'S NAME ON THE DOOR.
BUT IF YOUR COUNTRY COMES NEAR ME AGAIN...
IT'S NOT OUR COUNTRY.

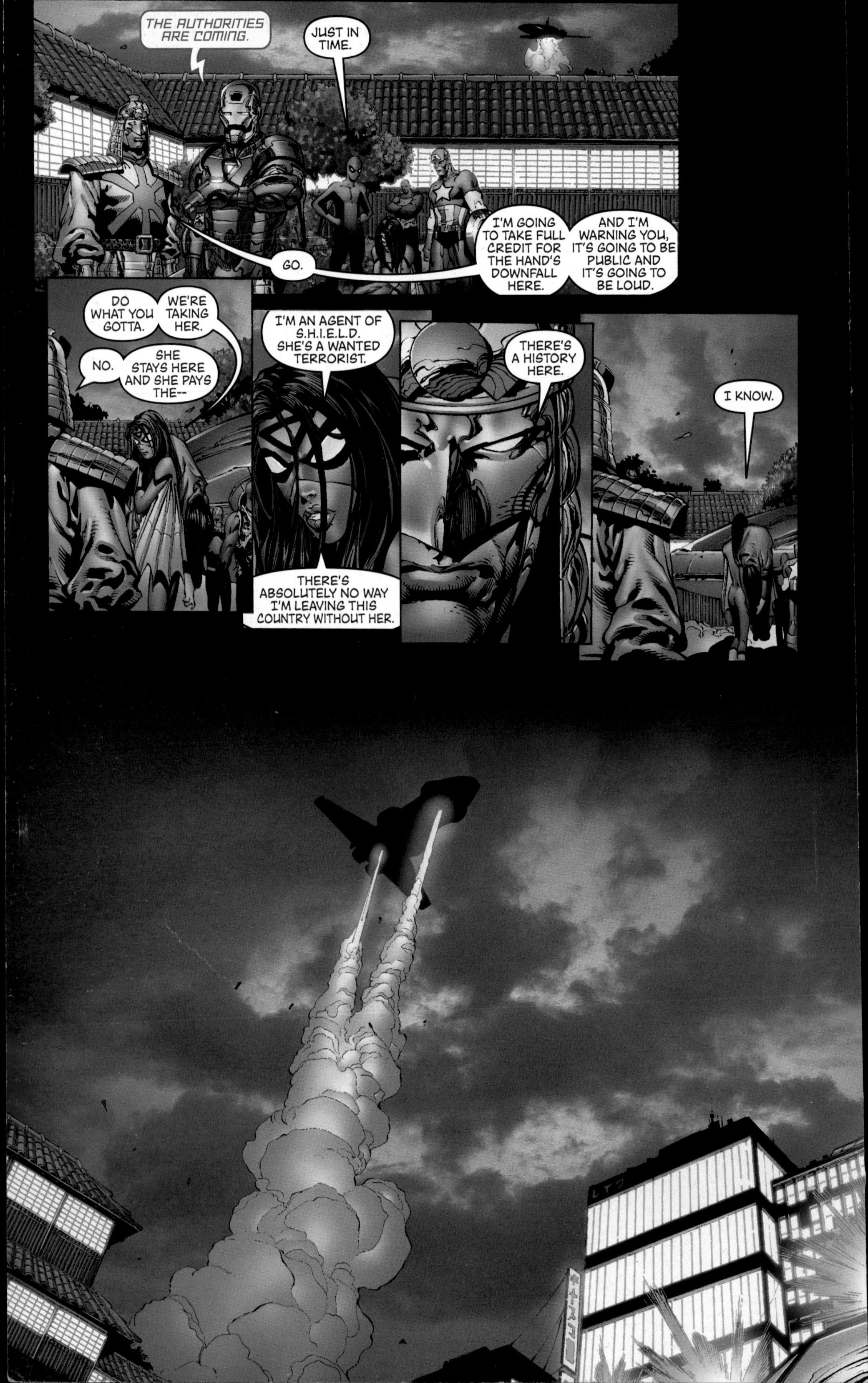
THE AUTHORITIES ARE COMING.
JUST IN TIME.
GO.
I'M GOING TO TAKE FULL CREDIT FOR THE HAND'S DOWNFALL HERE.
AND I'M WARNING YOU, IT'S GOING TO BE PUBLIC AND IT'S GOING TO BE LOUD.
DO WHAT YOU GOTTA.
WE'RE TAKING HER.
NO.
SHE STAYS HERE AND SHE PAYS THE--
I'M AN AGENT OF S.H.I.E.L.D. SHE'S A WANTED TERRORIST.
THERE'S ABSOLUTELY NO WAY I'M LEAVING THIS COUNTRY WITHOUT HER.
THERE'S A HISTORY HERE.
I KNOW.

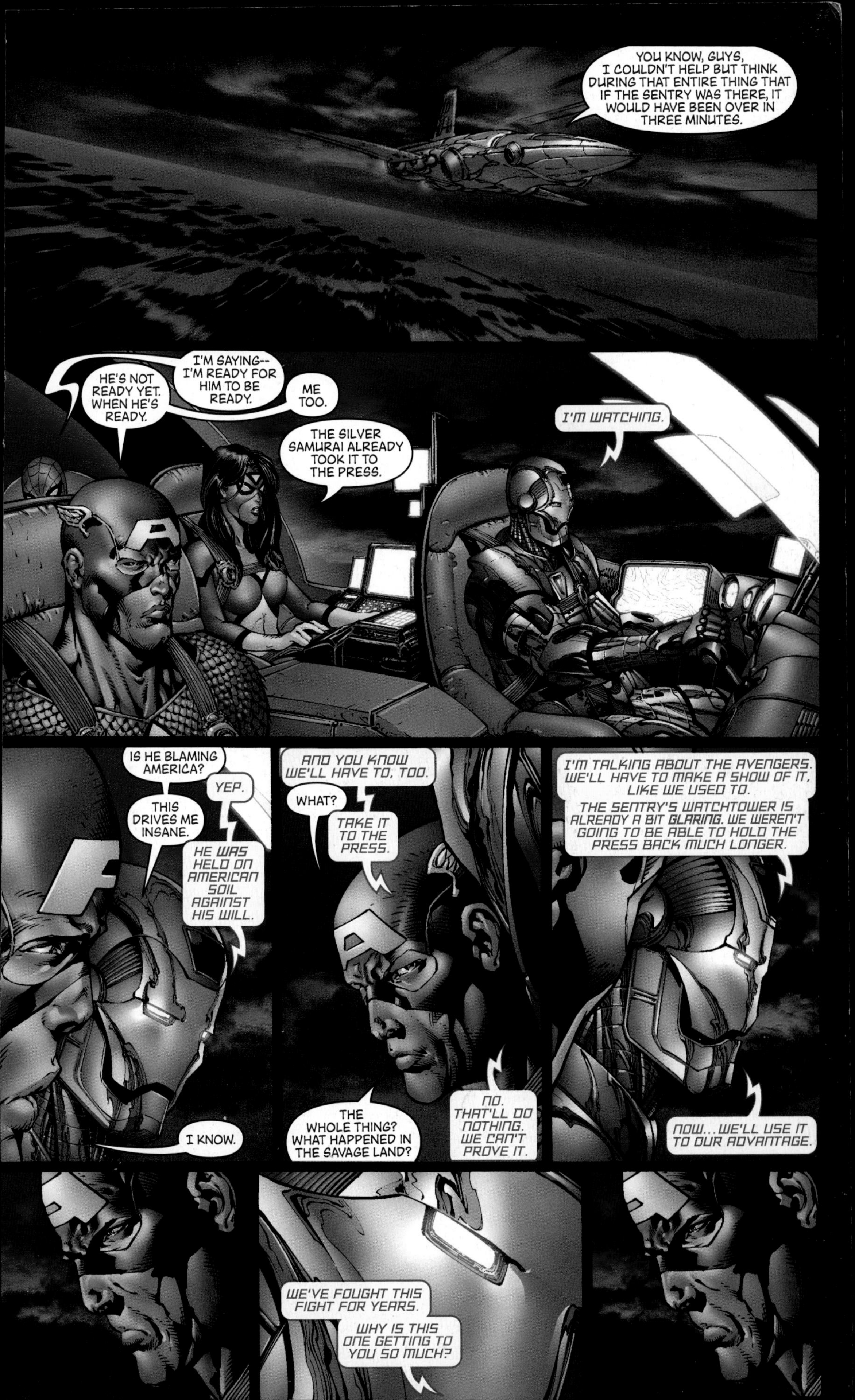
YOU KNOW, GUYS, I COULDN'T HELP BUT THINK DURING THAT ENTIRE THING THAT IF THE SENTRY WAS THERE, IT WOULD HAVE BEEN OVER IN THREE MINUTES.
HE'S NOT READY YET. WHEN HE'S READY.
I'M SAYING-- I'M READY FOR HIM TO BE READY.
ME TOO.
THE SILVER SAMURAI ALREADY TOOK IT TO THE PRESS.
I'M WATCHING.
IS HE BLAMING AMERICA?
YEP.
THIS DRIVES ME INSANE.
HE WAS HELD ON AMERICAN SOIL AGAINST HIS WILL.
I KNOW.
AND YOU KNOW WE'LL HAVE TO, TOO.
WHAT?
TAKE IT TO THE PRESS.
THE WHOLE THING? WHAT HAPPENED IN THE SAVAGE LAND?
NO. THAT'LL DO NOTHING. WE CAN'T PROVE IT.
I'M TALKING ABOUT THE AVENGERS. WE'LL HAVE TO MAKE A SHOW OF IT, LIKE WE USED TO.
THE SENTRY'S WATCHTOWER IS ALREADY A BIT GLARING. WE WEREN'T GOING TO BE ABLE TO HOLD THE PRESS BACK MUCH LONGER.
NOW... WE'LL USE IT TO OUR ADVANTAGE.
WE'VE FOUGHT THIS FIGHT FOR YEARS.
WHY IS THIS ONE GETTING TO YOU SO MUCH?

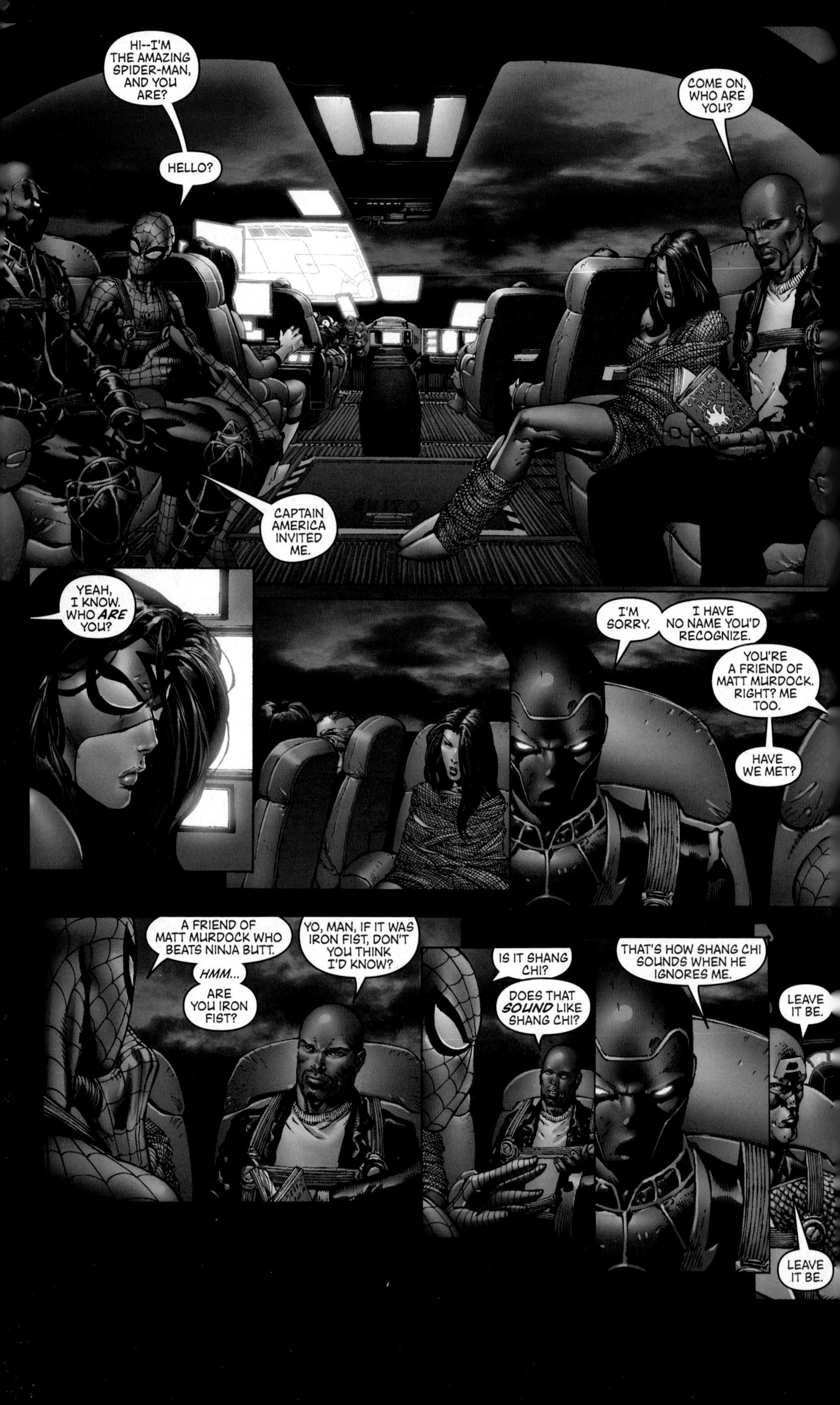
HI--I'M THE AMAZING SPIDER-MAN, AND YOU ARE?
HELLO?
COME ON, WHO ARE YOU?
CAPTAIN AMERICA INVITED ME.
YEAH, I KNOW. WHO *ARE* YOU?
I'M SORRY.
I HAVE NO NAME YOU'D RECOGNIZE.
YOU'RE A FRIEND OF MATT MURDOCK. RIGHT? ME TOO.
HAVE WE MET?
A FRIEND OF MATT MURDOCK WHO BEATS NINJA BUTT.
HMM...
ARE YOU IRON FIST?
YO, MAN, IF IT WAS IRON FIST, DON'T YOU THINK I'D KNOW?
IS IT SHANG CHI?
DOES THAT *SOUND* LIKE SHANG CHI?
THAT'S HOW SHANG CHI SOUNDS WHEN HE IGNORES ME.
LEAVE IT BE.
LEAVE IT BE.

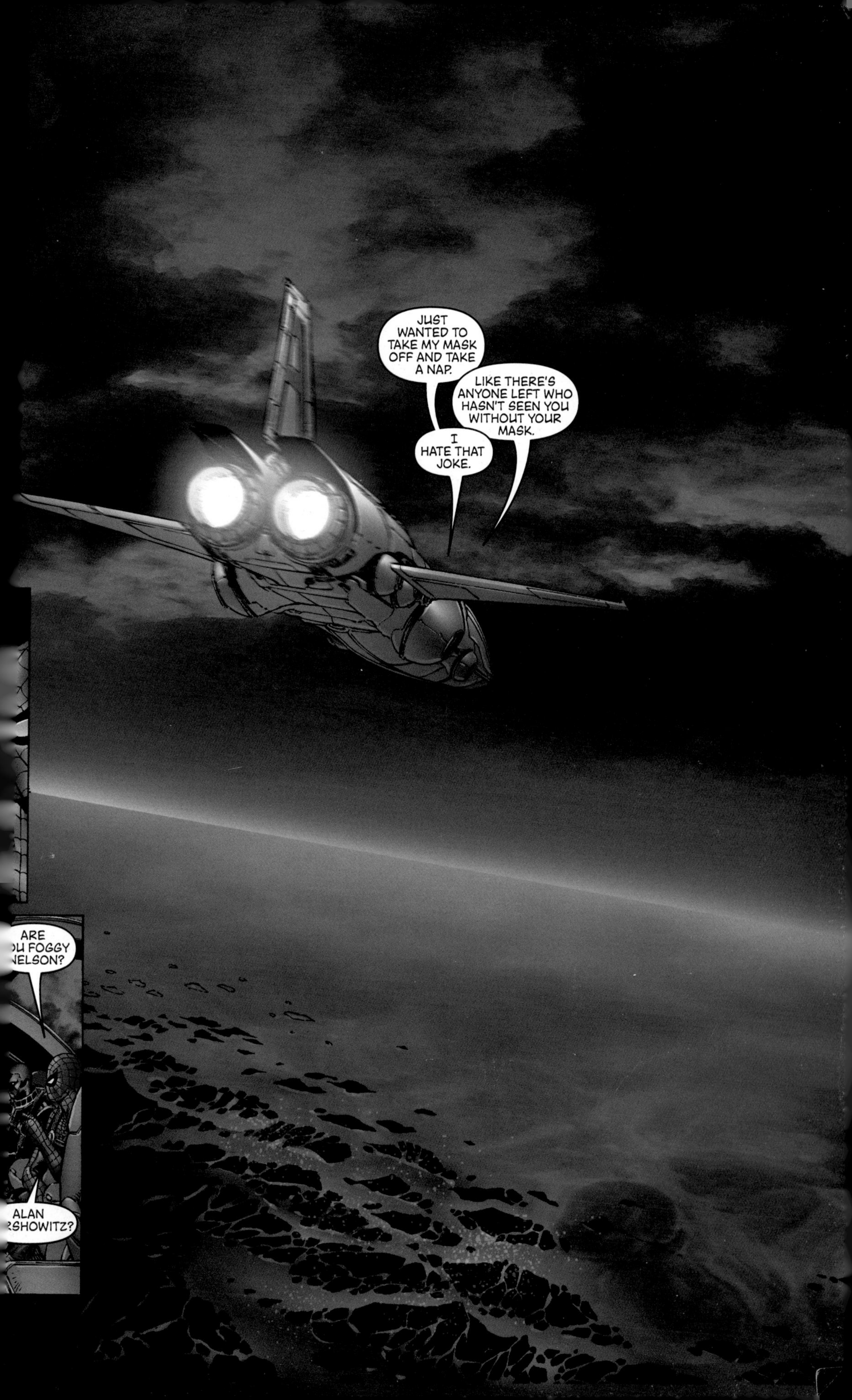
JUST WANTED TO TAKE MY MASK OFF AND TAKE A NAP.
LIKE THERE'S ANYONE LEFT WHO HASN'T SEEN YOU WITHOUT YOUR MASK.
I HATE THAT JOKE.
ARE
OU FOGGY
NELSON?
ALAN
RSHOWITZ?

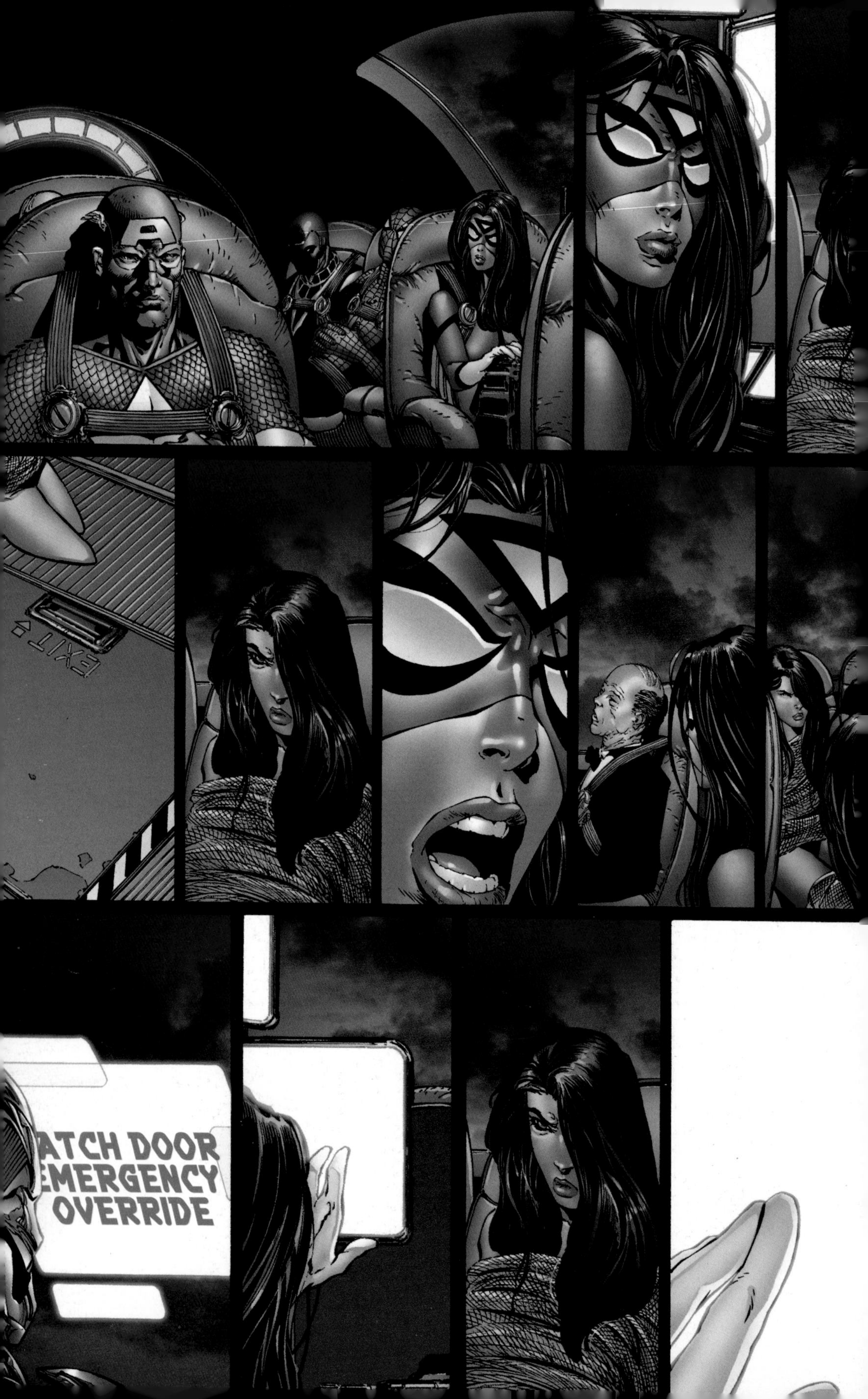
EXIT
ATCH DOOR EMERGENCY OVERRIDE

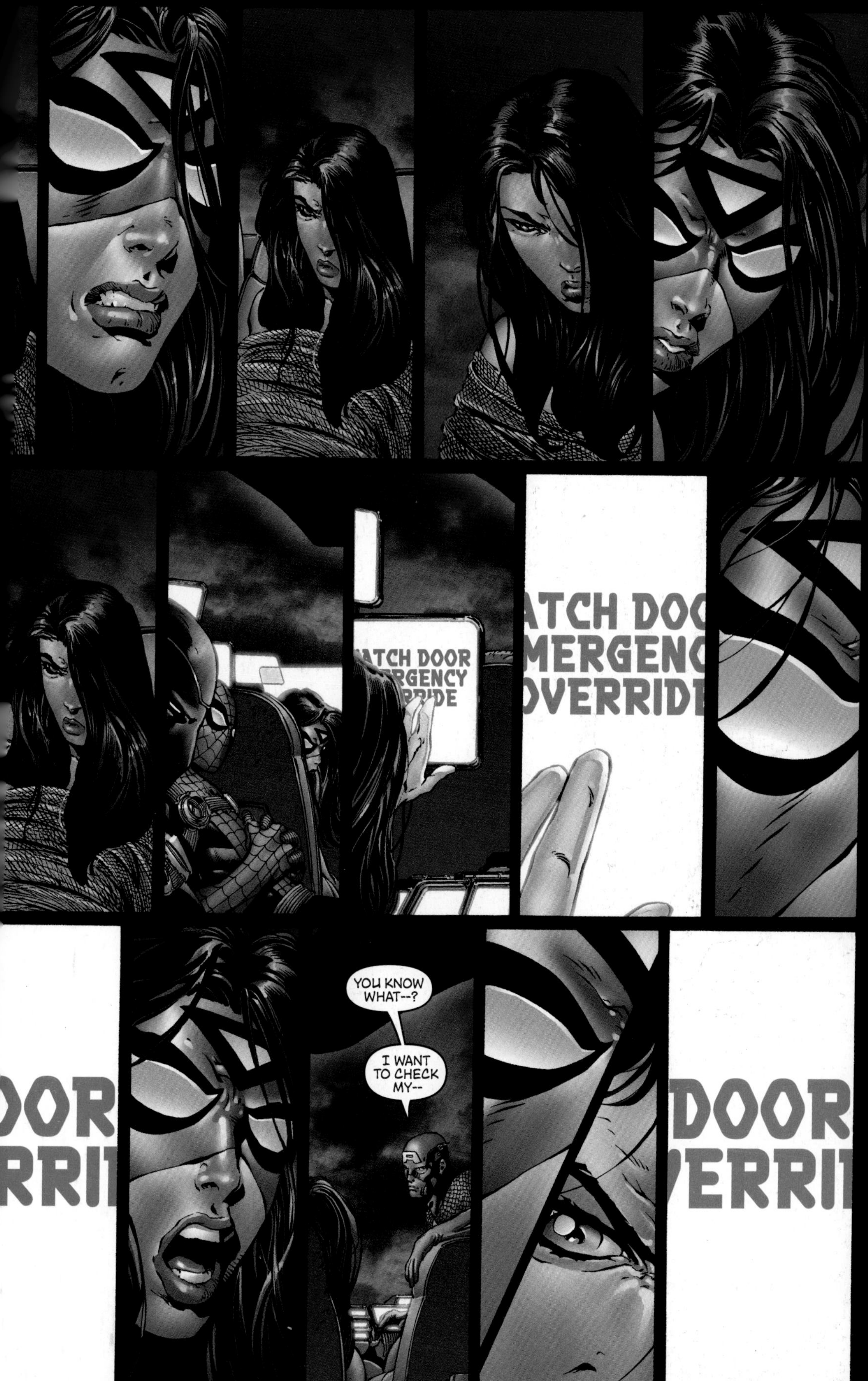
ATCH DOOR
ERGENCY
RRIDE
ATCH DOO
MERGENC
OVERRIDE
DOOR
ERRI
YOU KNOW WHAT--?
I WANT TO CHECK MY--
DOOR
VERRI

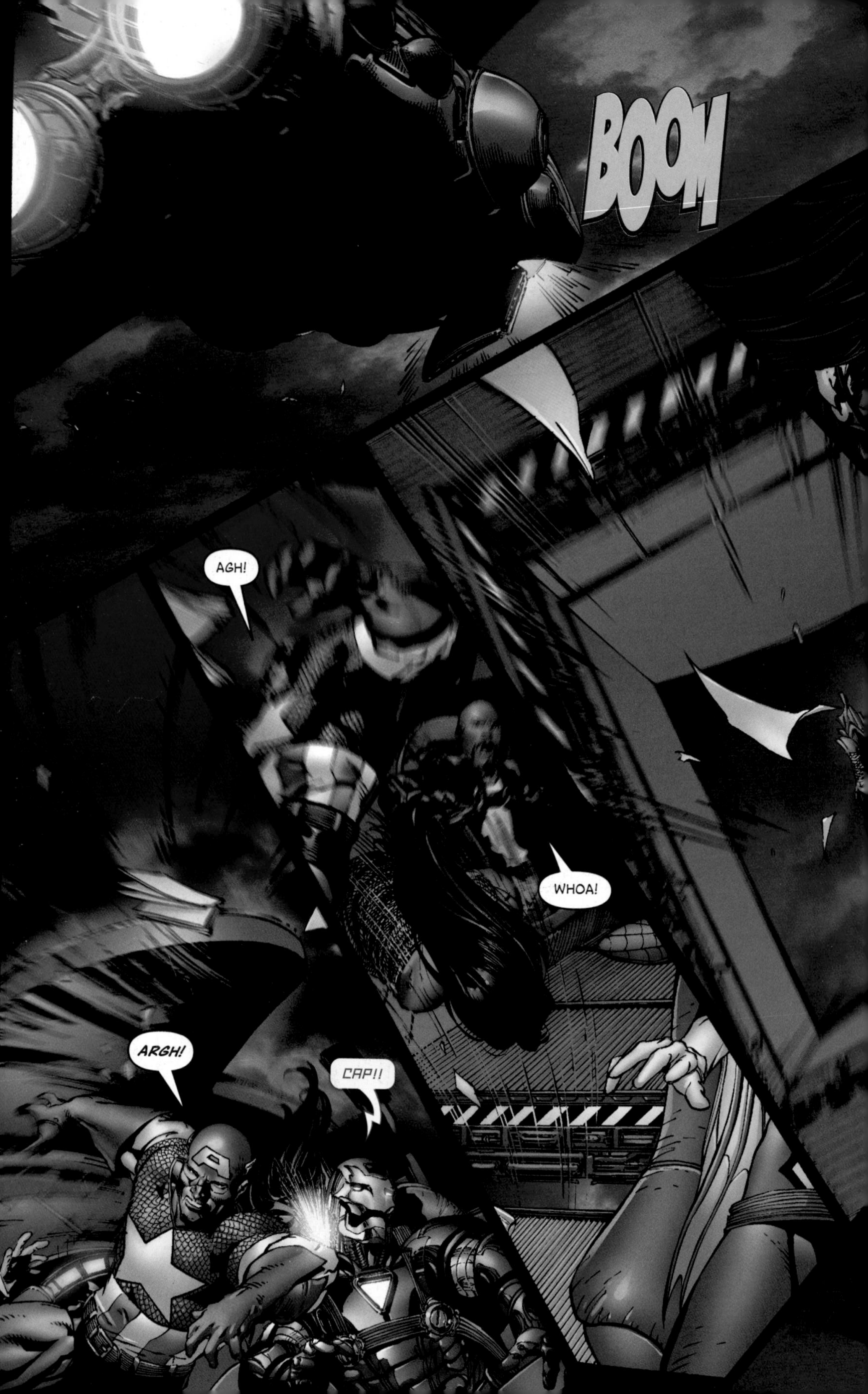
BOOM
AGH!
WHOA!
ARGH!
CAP!!

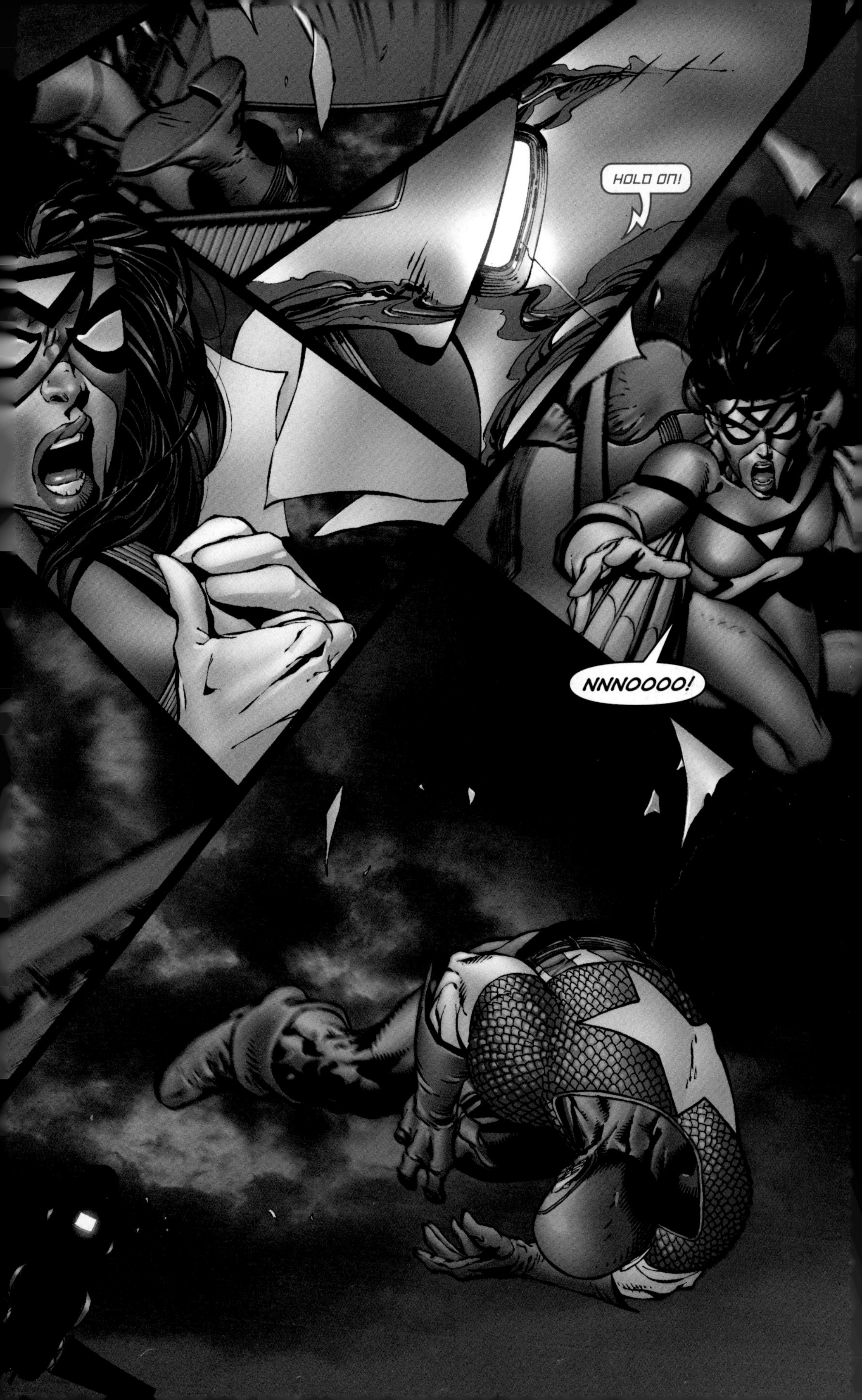
HOLD ON!
NNNOOOO!

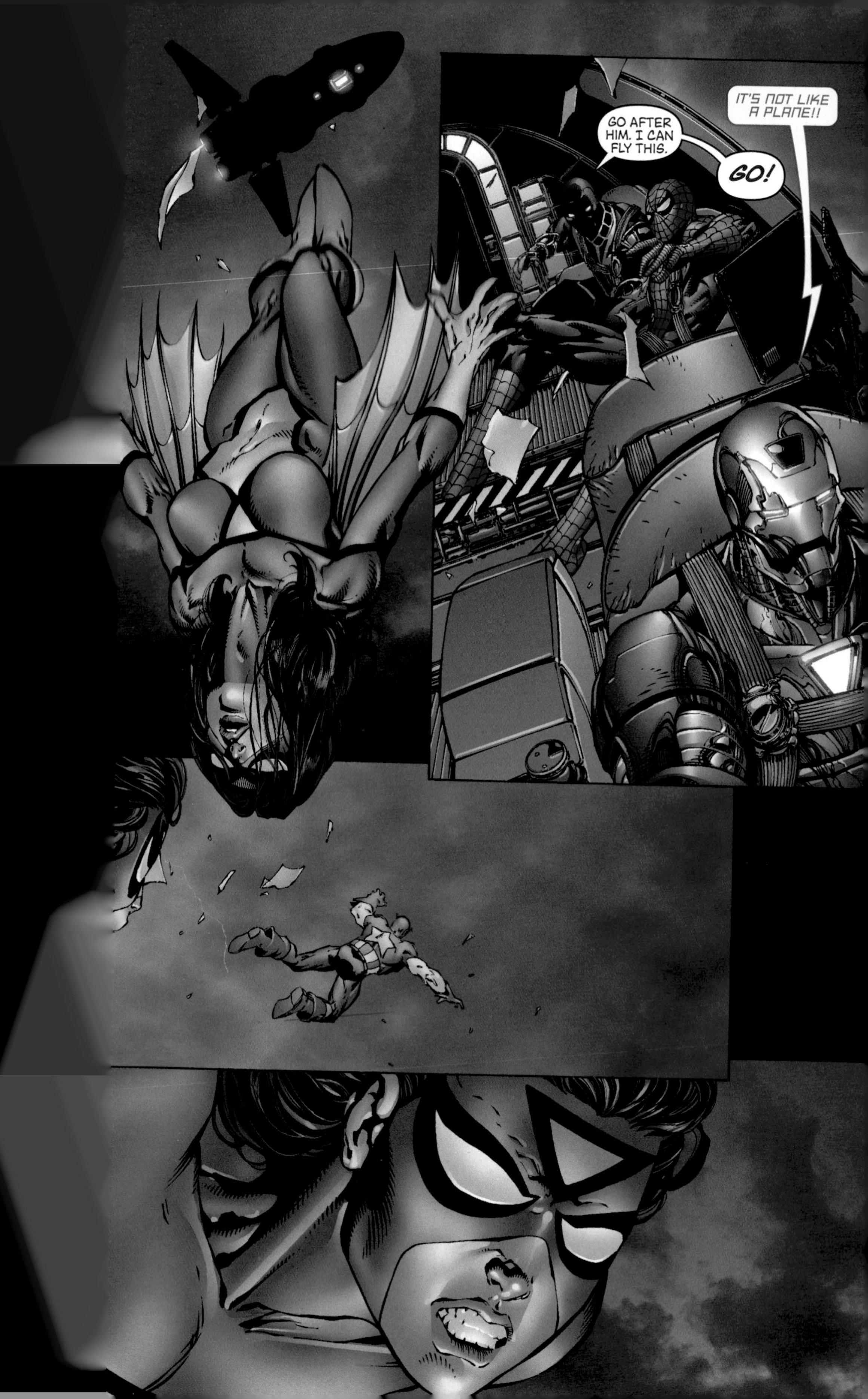
GO AFTER HIM. I CAN FLY THIS.
GO!
IT'S NOT LIKE A PLANE!!

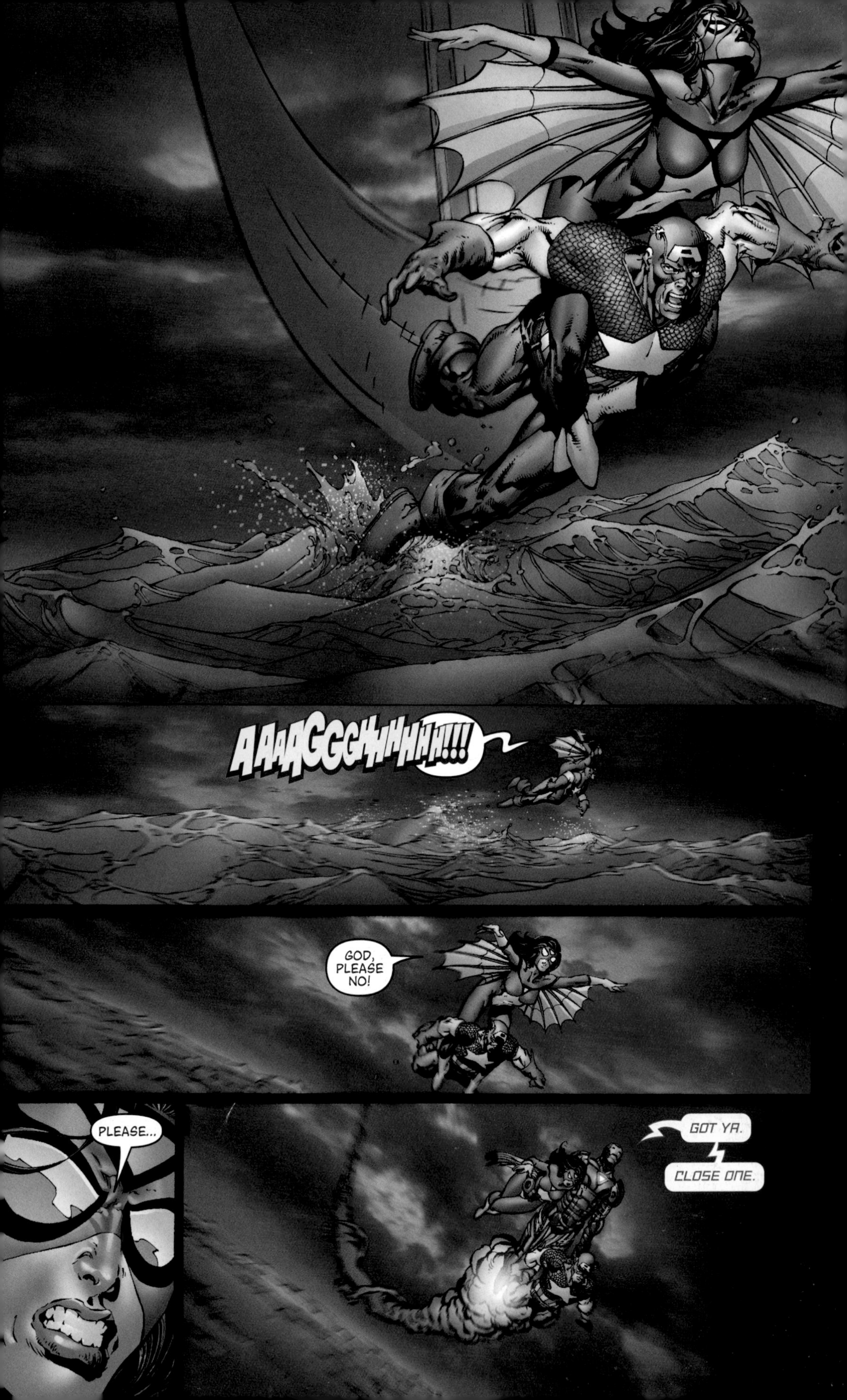
AAAAGGGHHHHHH!!!
GOD, PLEASE NO!
PLEASE...
GOT YA.
CLOSE ONE.

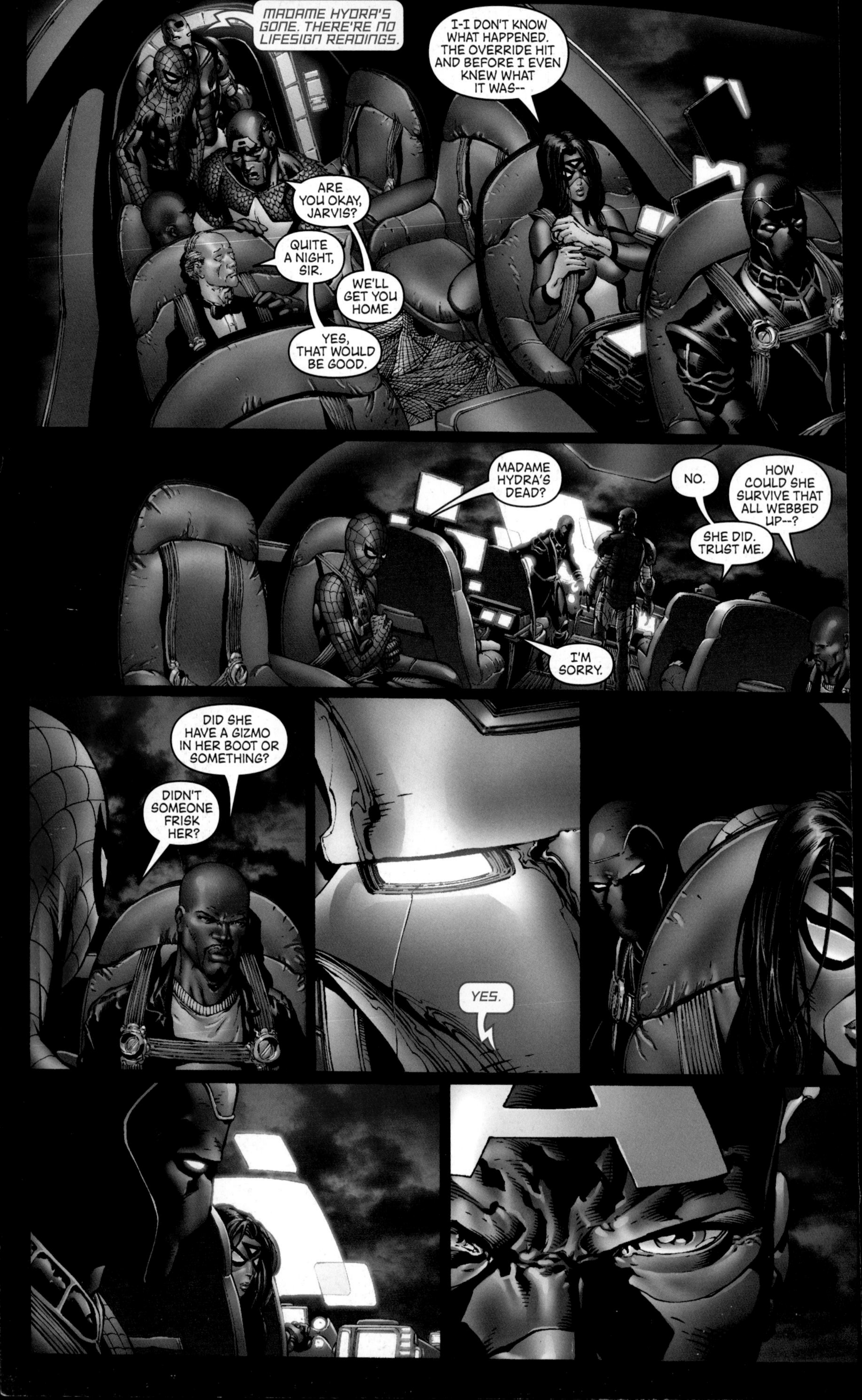
MADAME HYDRA'S GONE. THERE'RE NO LIFESIGN READINGS.
I-I DON'T KNOW WHAT HAPPENED. THE OVERRIDE HIT AND BEFORE I EVEN KNEW WHAT IT WAS--
ARE YOU OKAY, JARVIS?
QUITE A NIGHT, SIR.
WE'LL GET YOU HOME.
YES, THAT WOULD BE GOOD.
MADAME HYDRA'S DEAD?
NO.
HOW COULD SHE SURVIVE THAT ALL WEBBED UP--?
SHE DID. TRUST ME.
I'M SORRY.
DID SHE HAVE A GIZMO IN HER BOOT OR SOMETHING?
DIDN'T SOMEONE FRISK HER?
YES.

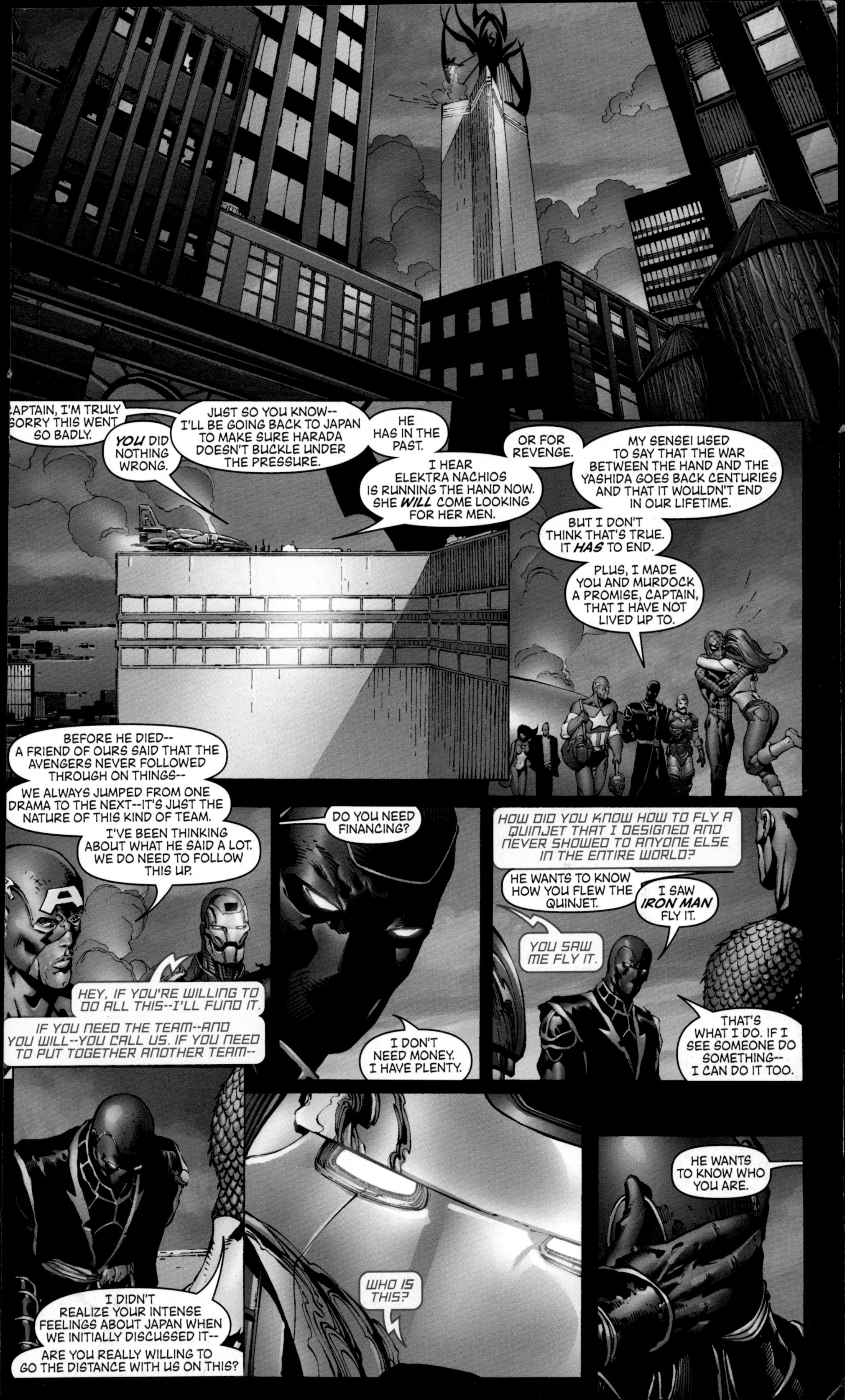
CAPTAIN, I'M TRULY SORRY THIS WENT SO BADLY.
YOU DID NOTHING WRONG.
JUST SO YOU KNOW-- I'LL BE GOING BACK TO JAPAN TO MAKE SURE HARADA DOESN'T BUCKLE UNDER THE PRESSURE.
HE HAS IN THE PAST.
I HEAR ELEKTRA NACHIOS IS RUNNING THE HAND NOW. SHE WILL COME LOOKING FOR HER MEN.
OR FOR REVENGE.
MY SENSEI USED TO SAY THAT THE WAR BETWEEN THE HAND AND THE YASHIDA GOES BACK CENTURIES AND THAT IT WOULDN'T END IN OUR LIFETIME.
BUT I DON'T THINK THAT'S TRUE. IT HAS TO END.
PLUS, I MADE YOU AND MURDOCK A PROMISE, CAPTAIN, THAT I HAVE NOT LIVED UP TO.
BEFORE HE DIED-- A FRIEND OF OURS SAID THAT THE AVENGERS NEVER FOLLOWED THROUGH ON THINGS--
WE ALWAYS JUMPED FROM ONE DRAMA TO THE NEXT--IT'S JUST THE NATURE OF THIS KIND OF TEAM.
I'VE BEEN THINKING ABOUT WHAT HE SAID A LOT. WE DO NEED TO FOLLOW THIS UP.
HEY, IF YOU'RE WILLING TO DO ALL THIS--I'LL FUND IT.
IF YOU NEED THE TEAM--AND YOU WILL--YOU CALL US. IF YOU NEED TO PUT TOGETHER ANOTHER TEAM--
DO YOU NEED FINANCING?
I DON'T NEED MONEY. I HAVE PLENTY.
HOW DID YOU KNOW HOW TO FLY A QUINJET THAT I DESIGNED AND NEVER SHOWED TO ANYONE ELSE IN THE ENTIRE WORLD?
HE WANTS TO KNOW HOW YOU FLEW THE QUINJET.
I SAW IRON MAN FLY IT.
YOU SAW ME FLY IT.
THAT'S WHAT I DO. IF I SEE SOMEONE DO SOMETHING-- I CAN DO IT TOO.
I DIDN'T REALIZE YOUR INTENSE FEELINGS ABOUT JAPAN WHEN WE INITIALLY DISCUSSED IT--
ARE YOU REALLY WILLING TO GO THE DISTANCE WITH US ON THIS?
WHO IS THIS?
HE WANTS TO KNOW WHO YOU ARE.

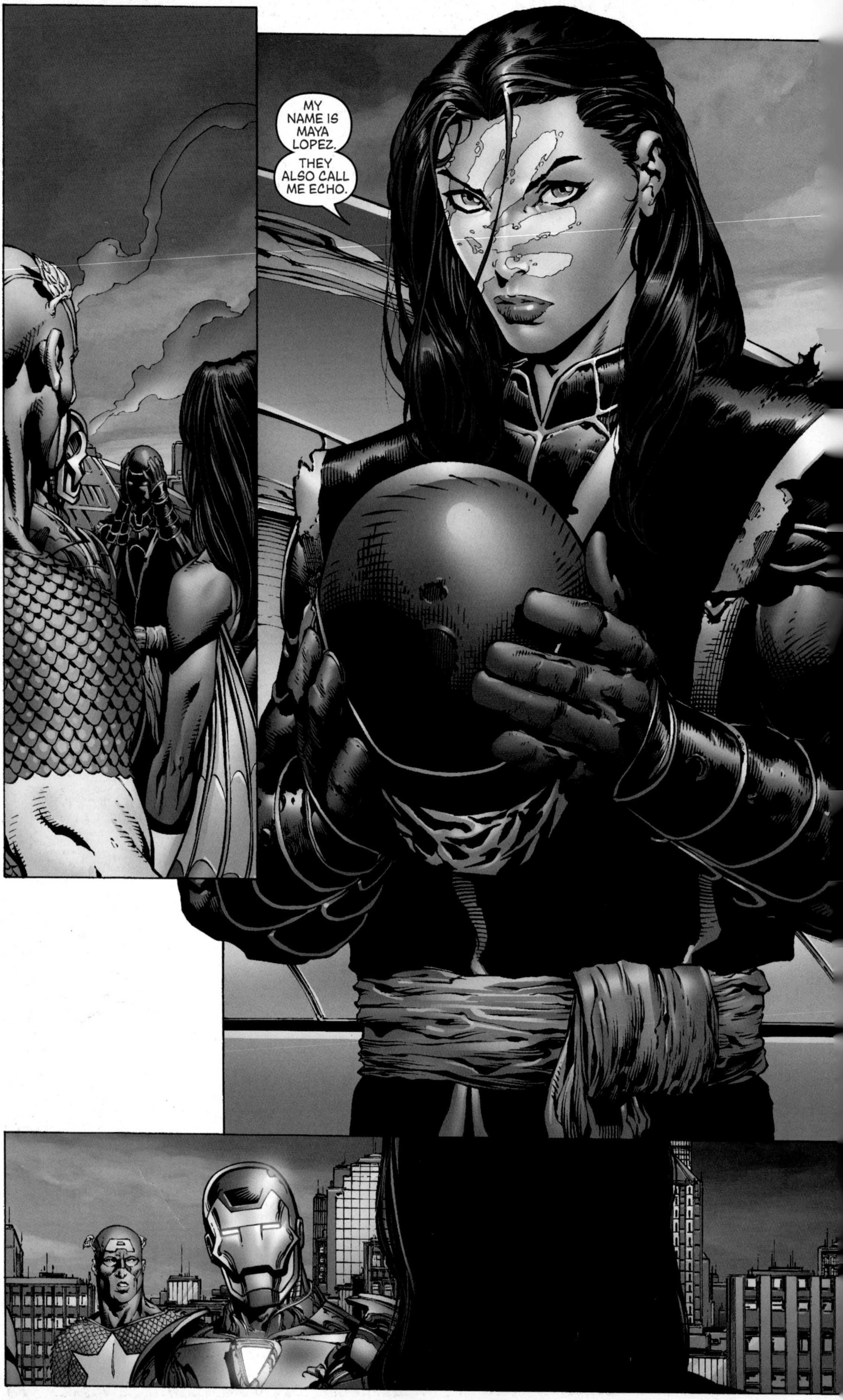
MY NAME IS MAYA LOPEZ.
THEY ALSO CALL ME ECHO.

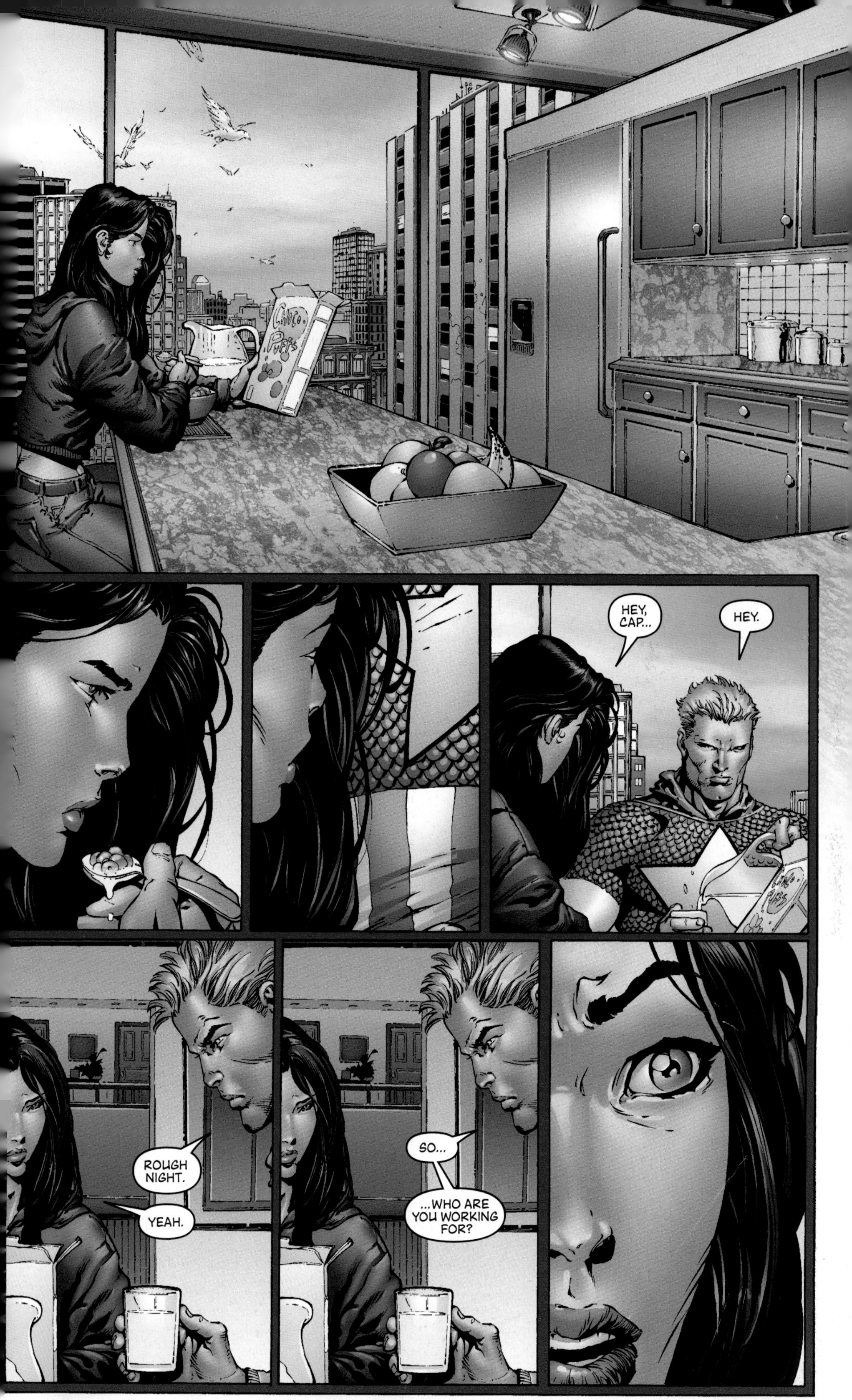

CHOCO PUFFS
HEY, CAP...
HEY.
ROUGH NIGHT.
YEAH.
SO...
...WHO ARE YOU WORKING FOR?

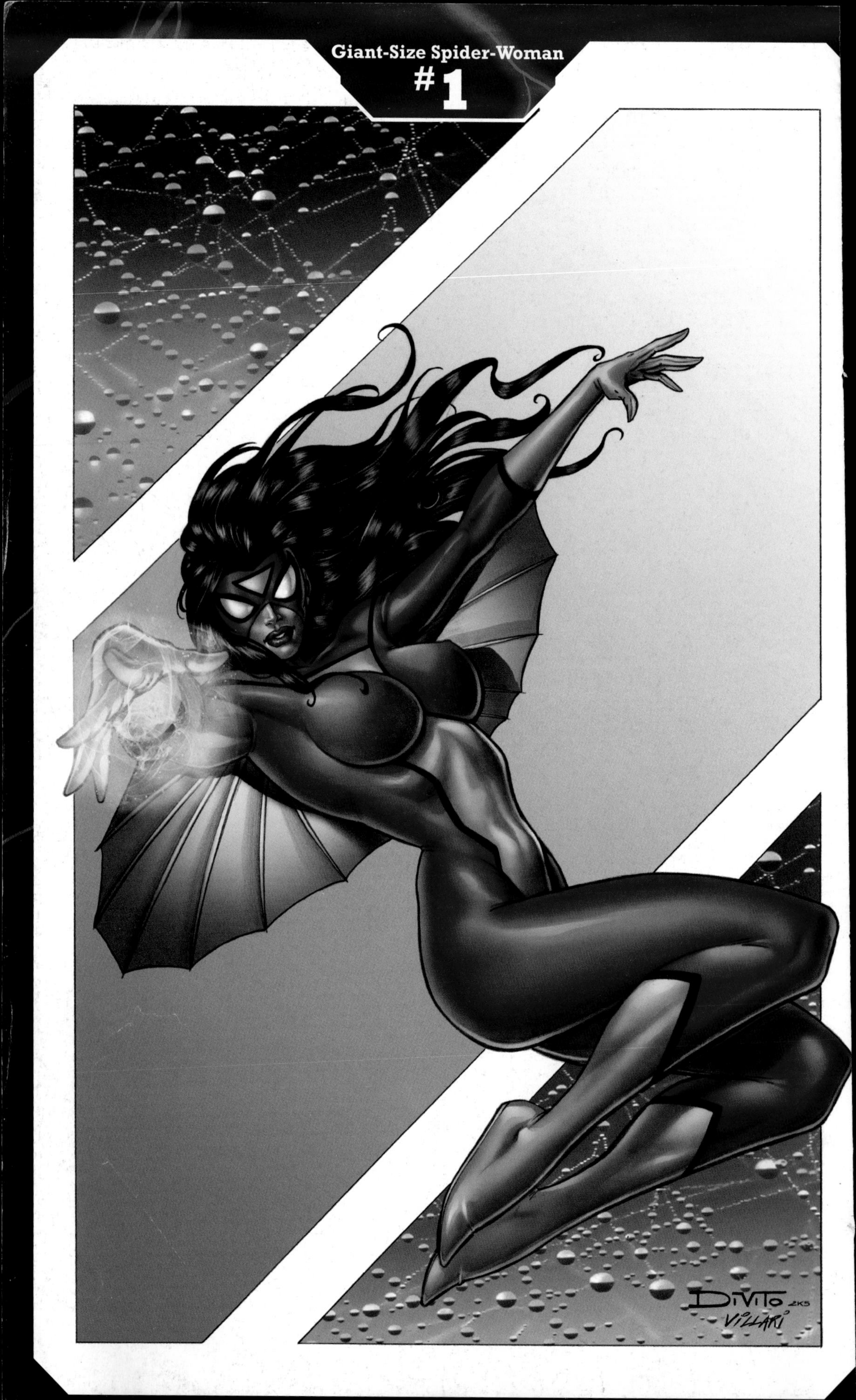
Giant-Size Spider-Woman
#1
DiVito 2K5
Villari

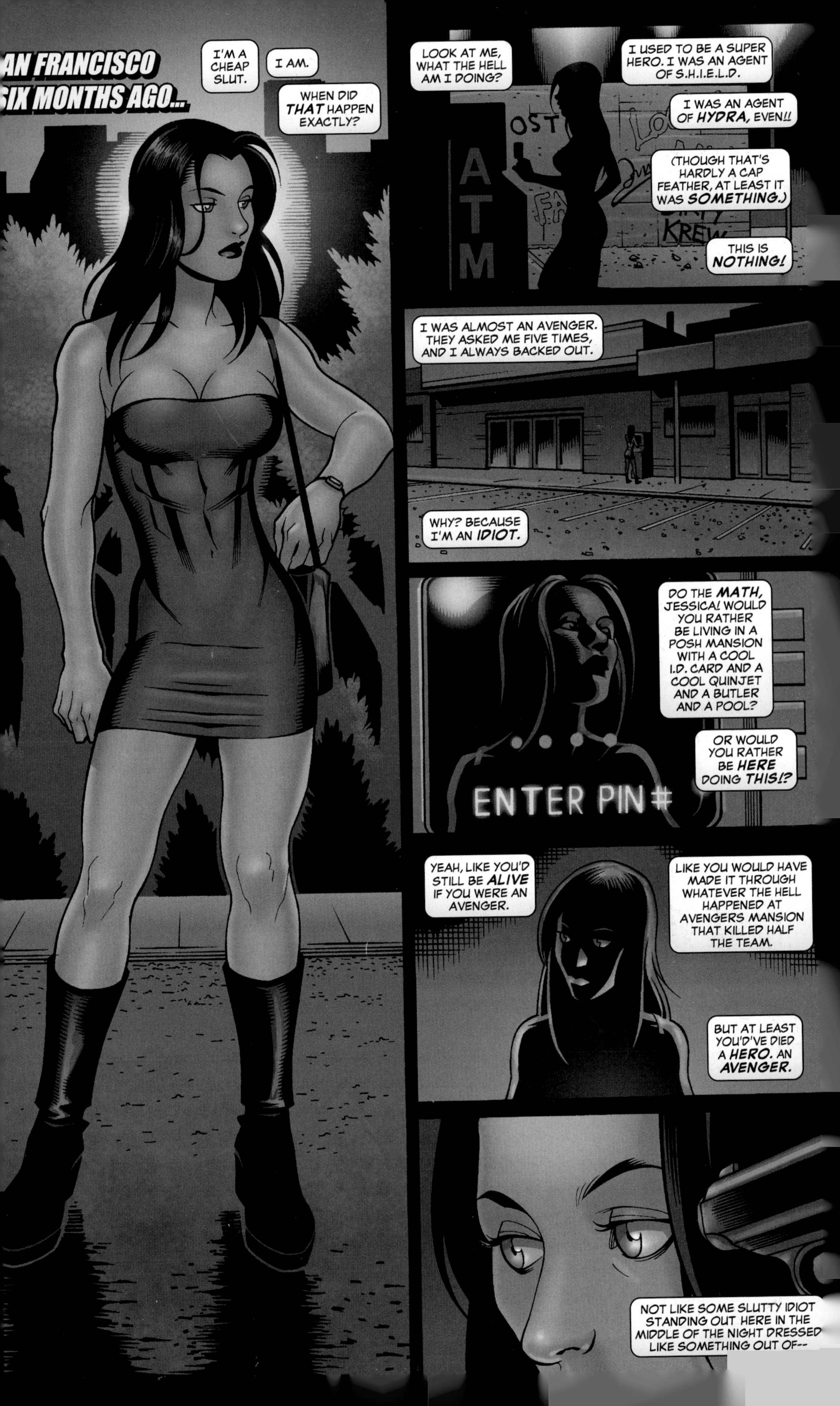
AN FRANCISCO
SIX MONTHS AGO...
I'M A CHEAP SLUT.
I AM.
WHEN DID THAT HAPPEN EXACTLY?
LOOK AT ME, WHAT THE HELL AM I DOING?
I USED TO BE A SUPER HERO. I WAS AN AGENT OF S.H.I.E.L.D.
I WAS AN AGENT OF HYDRA, EVEN!!
(THOUGH THAT'S HARDLY A CAP FEATHER, AT LEAST IT WAS SOMETHING.)
THIS IS NOTHING!
ATM
I WAS ALMOST AN AVENGER. THEY ASKED ME FIVE TIMES, AND I ALWAYS BACKED OUT.
WHY? BECAUSE I'M AN IDIOT.
DO THE MATH, JESSICA! WOULD YOU RATHER BE LIVING IN A POSH MANSION WITH A COOL I.D. CARD AND A COOL QUINJET AND A BUTLER AND A POOL?
OR WOULD YOU RATHER BE HERE DOING THIS!?
ENTER PIN#
YEAH, LIKE YOU'D STILL BE ALIVE IF YOU WERE AN AVENGER.
LIKE YOU WOULD HAVE MADE IT THROUGH WHATEVER THE HELL HAPPENED AT AVENGERS MANSION THAT KILLED HALF THE TEAM.
BUT AT LEAST YOU'D'VE DIED A HERO. AN AVENGER.
NOT LIKE SOME SLUTTY IDIOT STANDING OUT HERE IN THE MIDDLE OF THE NIGHT DRESSED LIKE SOMETHING OUT OF--

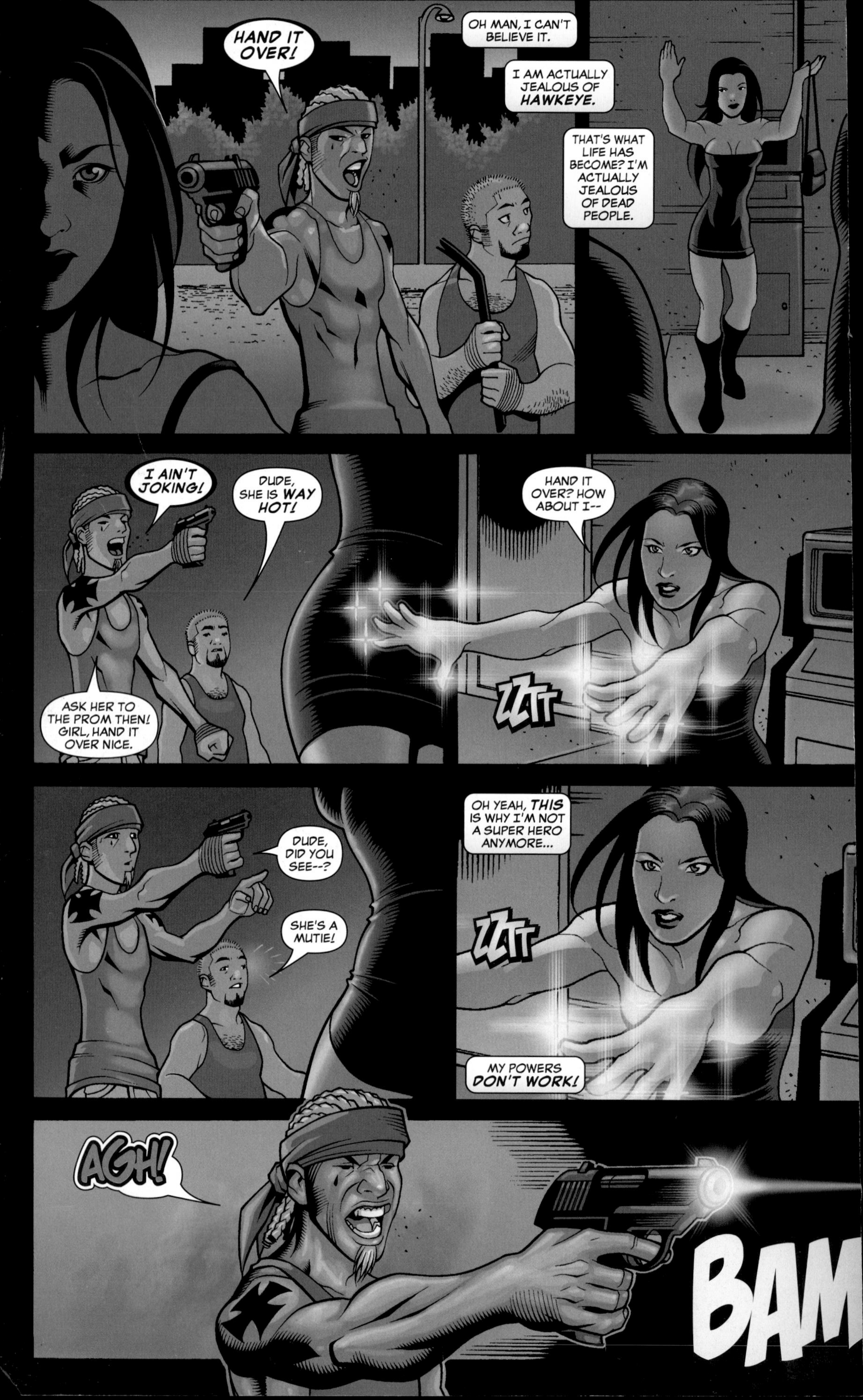
HAND IT OVER!
OH MAN, I CAN'T BELIEVE IT.
I AM ACTUALLY JEALOUS OF HAWKEYE.
THAT'S WHAT LIFE HAS BECOME? I'M ACTUALLY JEALOUS OF DEAD PEOPLE.
I AIN'T JOKING!
DUDE, SHE IS WAY HOT!
ASK HER TO THE PROM THEN! GIRL, HAND IT OVER NICE.
HAND IT OVER? HOW ABOUT I--
ZZTT
DUDE, DID YOU SEE--?
SHE'S A MUTIE!
OH YEAH, THIS IS WHY I'M NOT A SUPER HERO ANYMORE...
ZZTT
MY POWERS DON'T WORK!
AGH!
BAM

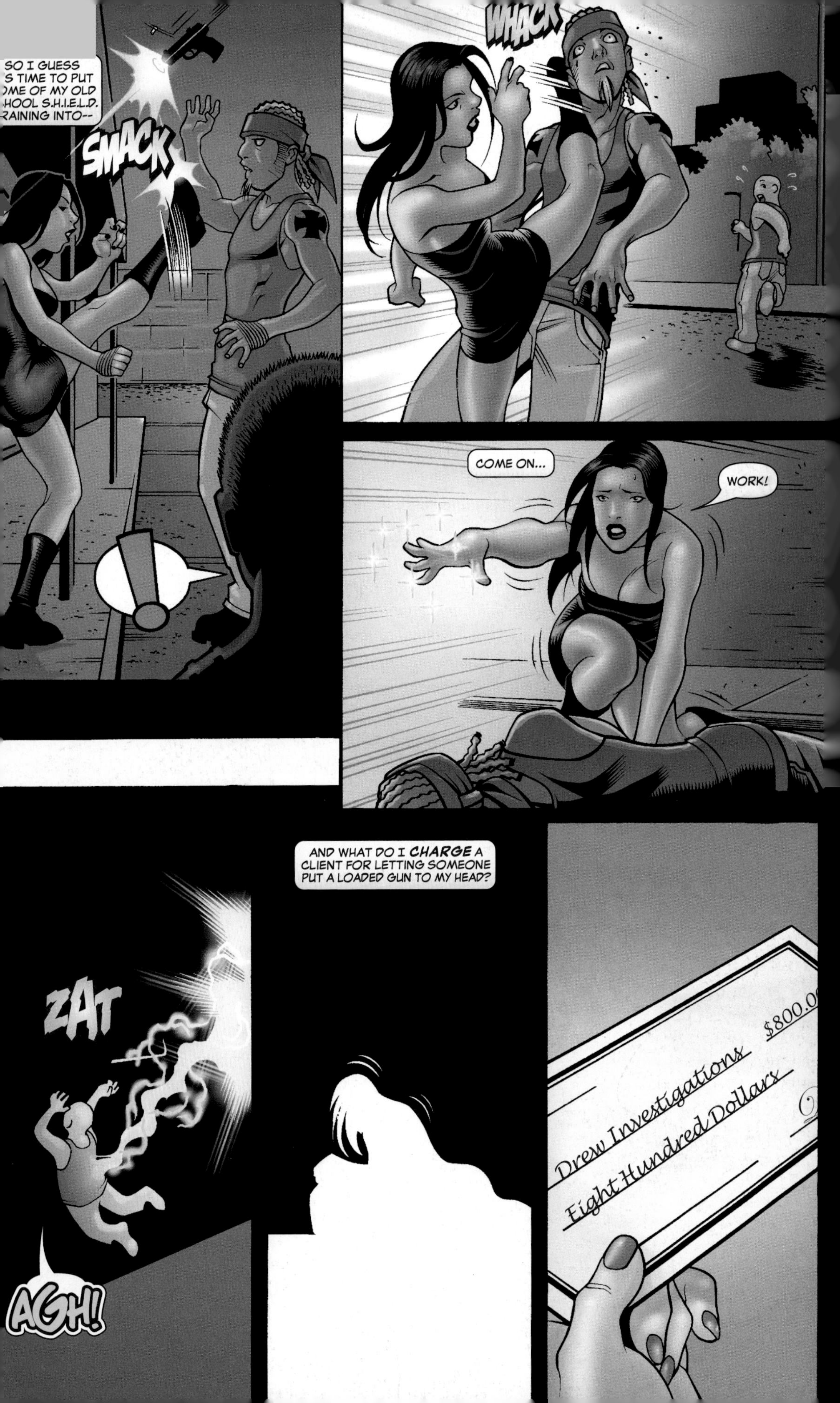
SO I GUESS 'S TIME TO PUT OME OF MY OLD HOOL S.H.I.E.L.D. RAINING INTO--
SMACK
!
WHACK
COME ON...
WORK!
ZAT
AGH!
AND WHAT DO I CHARGE A CLIENT FOR LETTING SOMEONE PUT A LOADED GUN TO MY HEAD?
$800.0
Drew Investigations
Eight Hundred Dollars

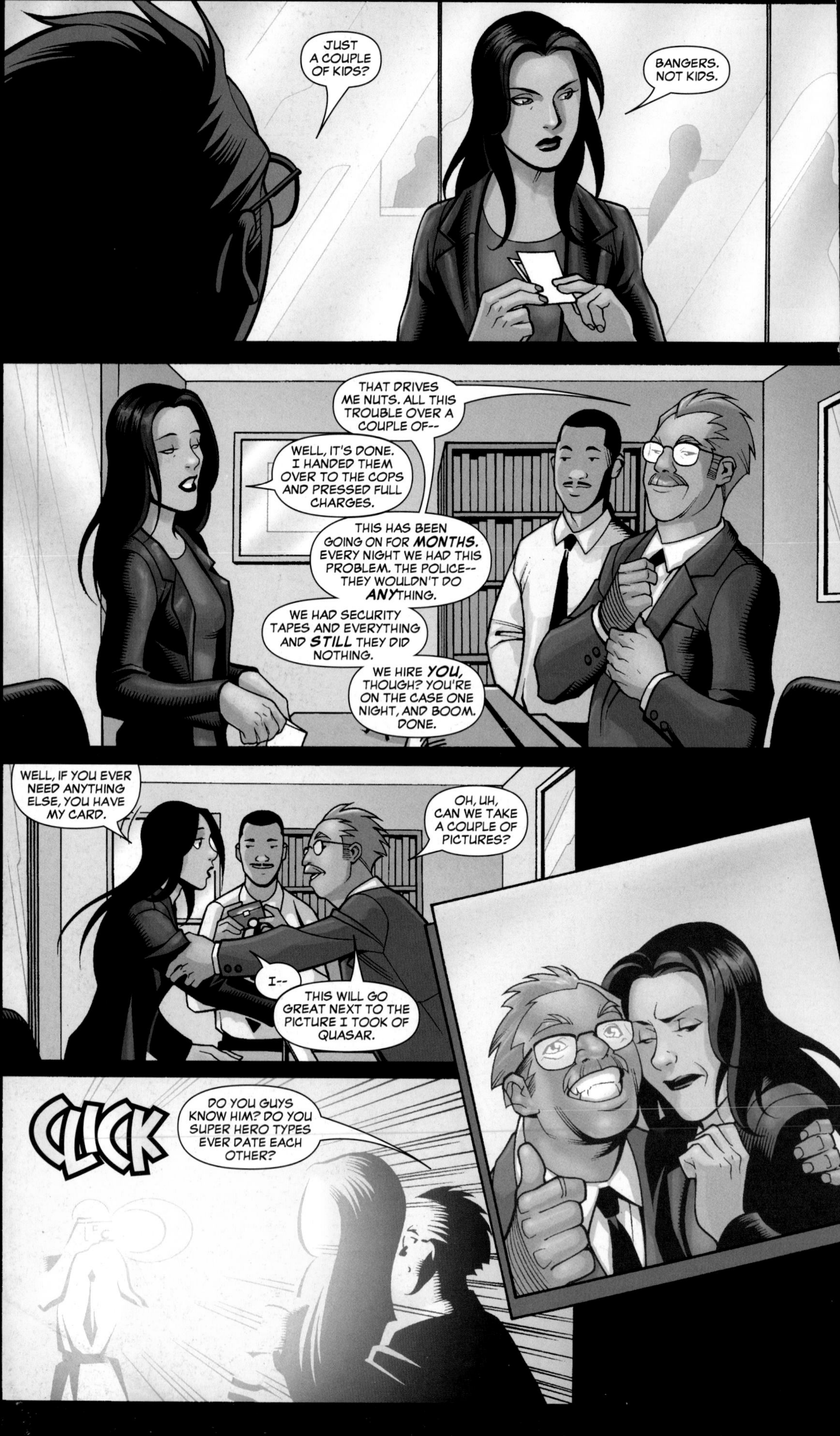
JUST A COUPLE OF KIDS?
BANGERS. NOT KIDS.
THAT DRIVES ME NUTS. ALL THIS TROUBLE OVER A COUPLE OF--
WELL, IT'S DONE. I HANDED THEM OVER TO THE COPS AND PRESSED FULL CHARGES.
THIS HAS BEEN GOING ON FOR MONTHS. EVERY NIGHT WE HAD THIS PROBLEM. THE POLICE-- THEY WOULDN'T DO ANYTHING.
WE HAD SECURITY TAPES AND EVERYTHING AND STILL THEY DID NOTHING.
WE HIRE YOU, THOUGH? YOU'RE ON THE CASE ONE NIGHT, AND BOOM. DONE.
WELL, IF YOU EVER NEED ANYTHING ELSE, YOU HAVE MY CARD.
OH, UH, CAN WE TAKE A COUPLE OF PICTURES?
I--
THIS WILL GO GREAT NEXT TO THE PICTURE I TOOK OF QUASAR.
CLICK
DO YOU GUYS KNOW HIM? DO YOU SUPER HERO TYPES EVER DATE EACH OTHER?

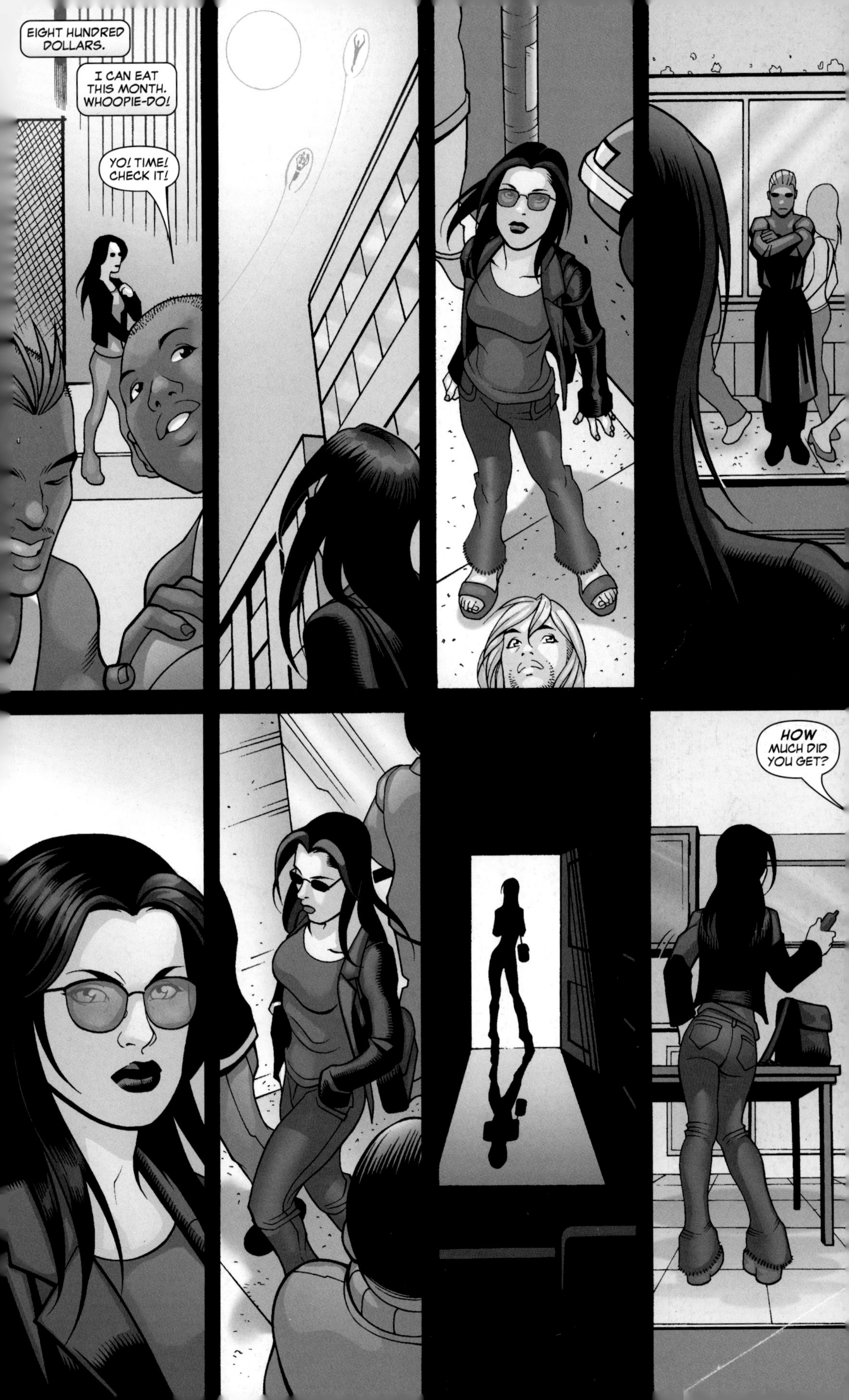
EIGHT HUNDRED DOLLARS.
I CAN EAT THIS MONTH. WHOOPIE-DO!
YO! TIME! CHECK IT!
HOW MUCH DID YOU GET?

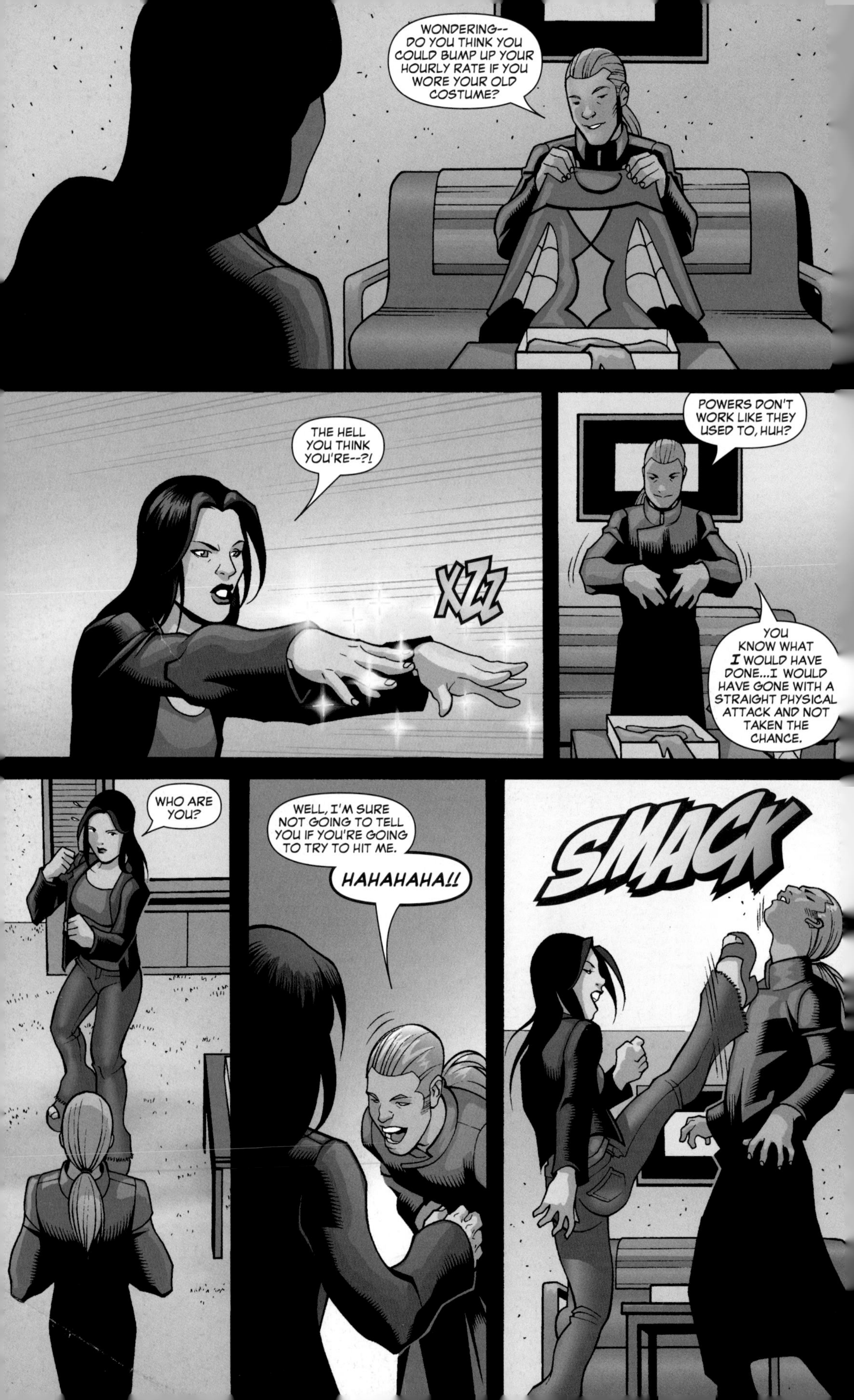
WONDERING-- DO YOU THINK YOU COULD BUMP UP YOUR HOURLY RATE IF YOU WORE YOUR OLD COSTUME?
THE HELL YOU THINK YOU'RE--?!
XZZ
POWERS DON'T WORK LIKE THEY USED TO, HUH?
YOU KNOW WHAT *I* WOULD HAVE DONE...I WOULD HAVE GONE WITH A STRAIGHT PHYSICAL ATTACK AND NOT TAKEN THE CHANCE.
WHO ARE YOU?
WELL, I'M SURE NOT GOING TO TELL YOU IF YOU'RE GOING TO TRY TO HIT ME.
HAHAHAHA!!
SMACK

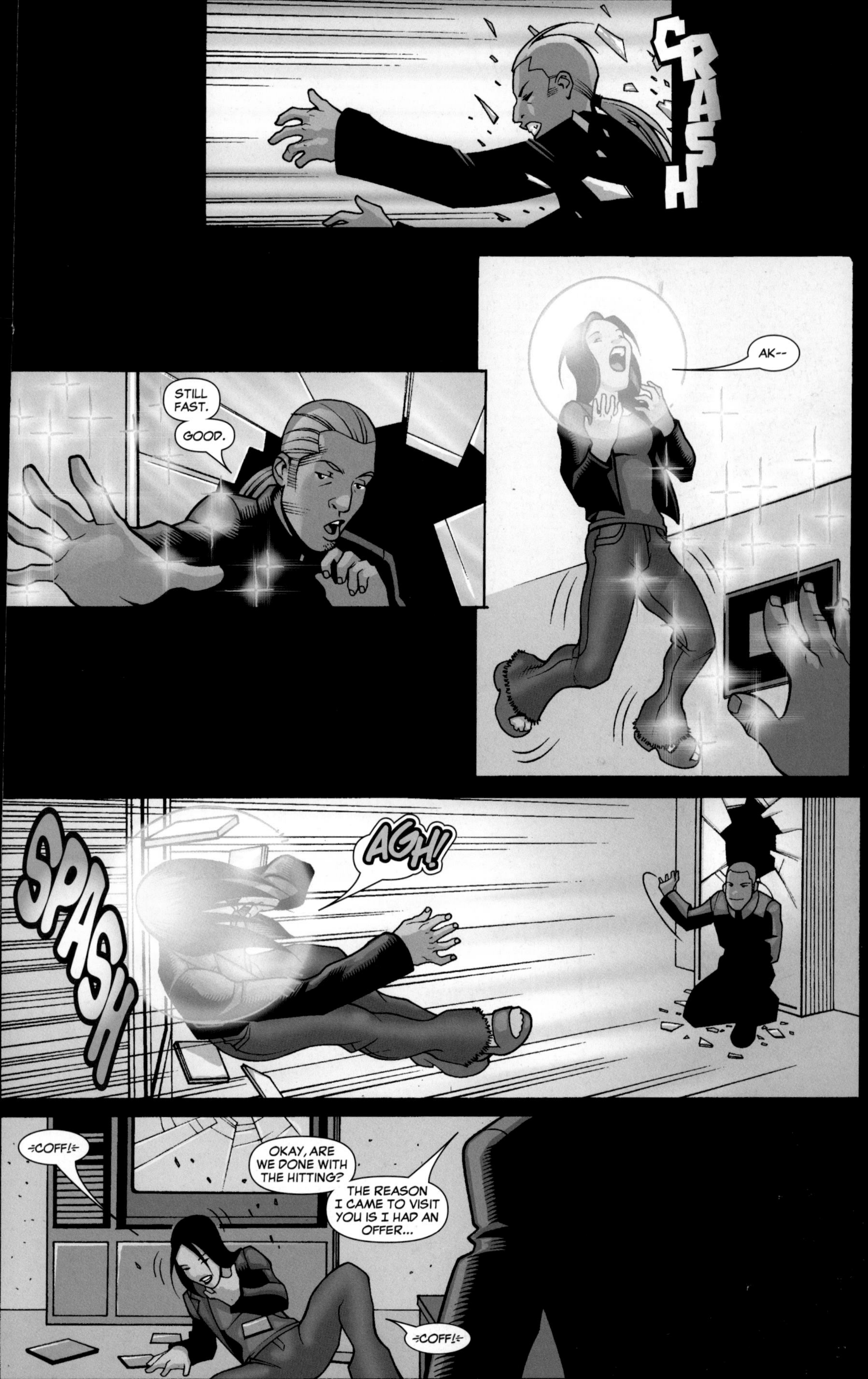
CRASH
STILL FAST.
GOOD.
AK--
SPASH
AGH!
=COFF!=
OKAY, ARE WE DONE WITH THE HITTING?
THE REASON I CAME TO VISIT YOU IS I HAD AN OFFER...
=COFF!=

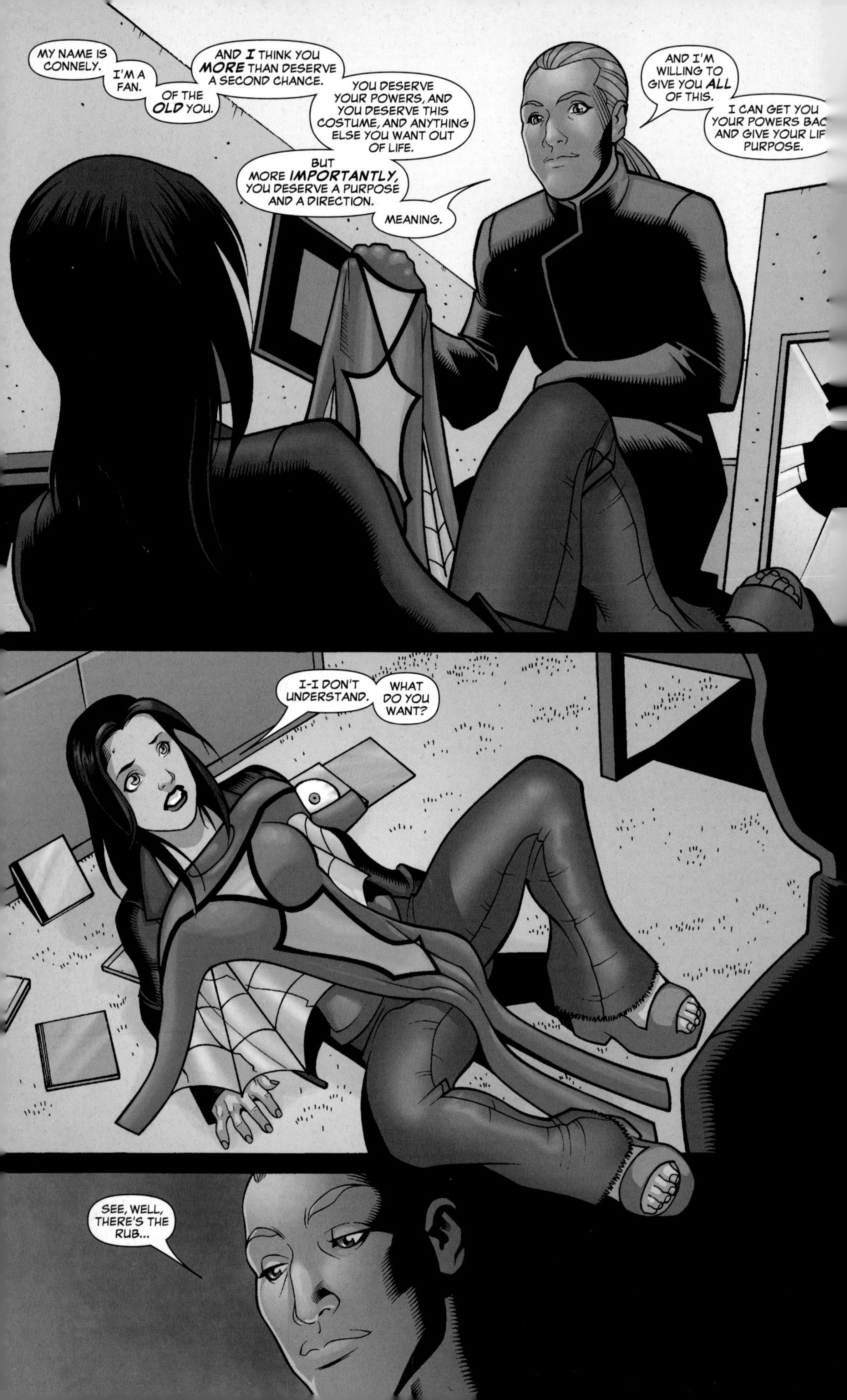
MY NAME IS CONNELY.
I'M A FAN.
OF THE OLD YOU.
AND I THINK YOU MORE THAN DESERVE A SECOND CHANCE.
YOU DESERVE YOUR POWERS, AND YOU DESERVE THIS COSTUME, AND ANYTHING ELSE YOU WANT OUT OF LIFE.
BUT MORE IMPORTANTLY, YOU DESERVE A PURPOSE AND A DIRECTION.
MEANING.
AND I'M WILLING TO GIVE YOU ALL OF THIS.
I CAN GET YOU YOUR POWERS BAC
AND GIVE YOUR LIF
PURPOSE.
I-I DON'T UNDERSTAND.
WHAT DO YOU WANT?
SEE, WELL, THERE'S THE RUB...

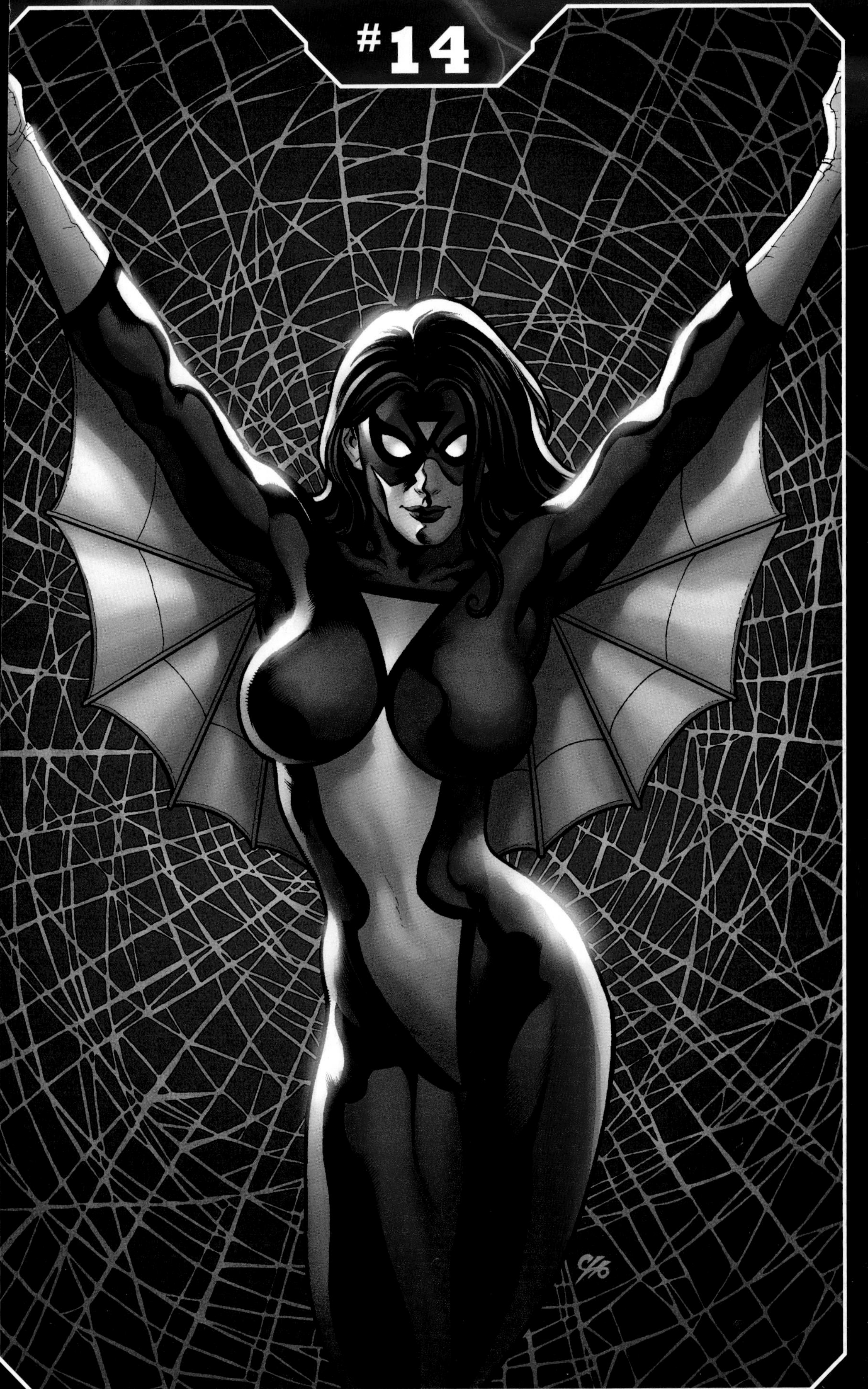
#14

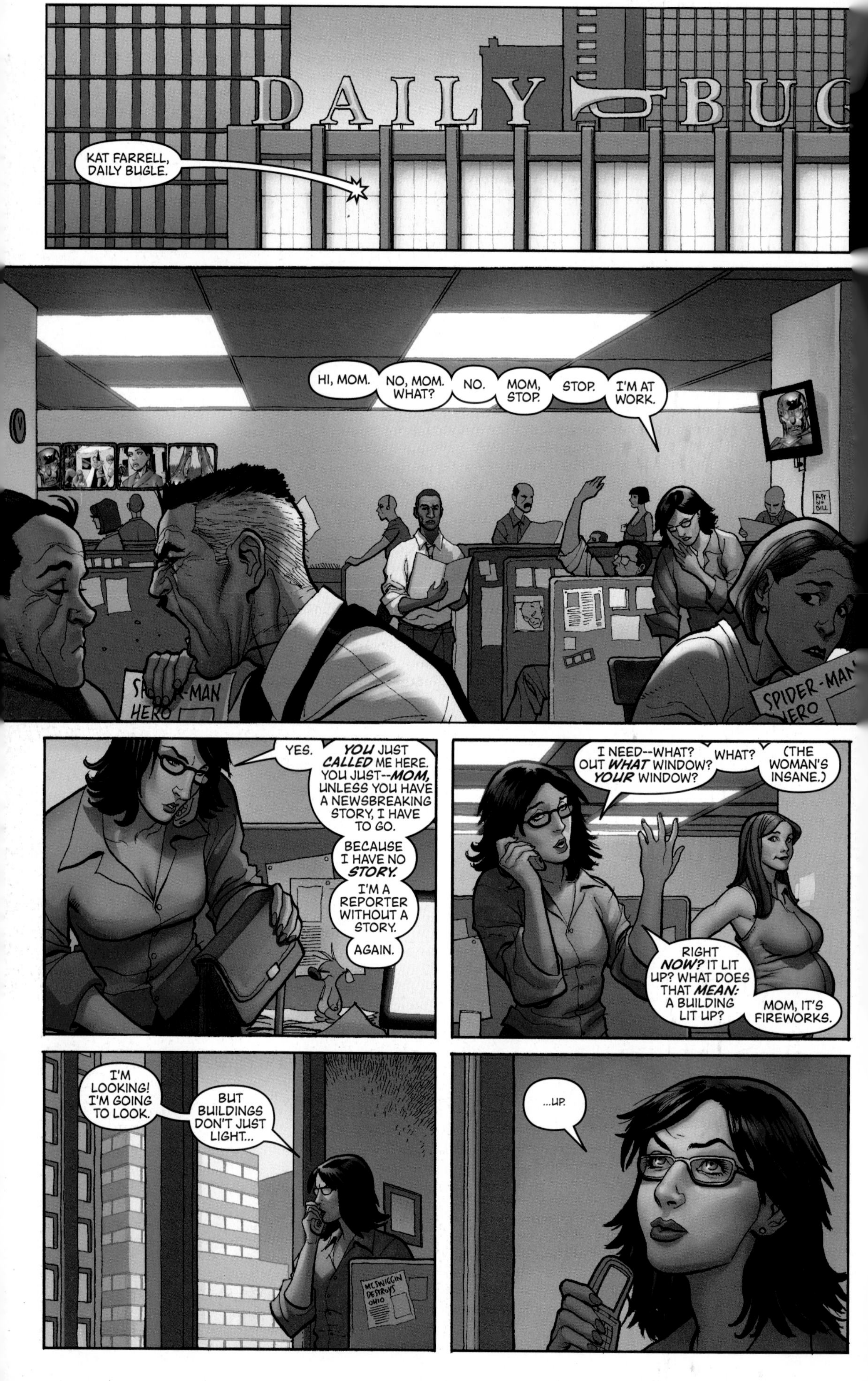
DAILY BUG
KAT FARRELL, DAILY BUGLE.
HI, MOM.
NO, MOM. WHAT?
NO.
MOM, STOP.
STOP.
I'M AT WORK.
SPIDER-MAN HERO
YES.
YOU JUST CALLED ME HERE. YOU JUST--MOM, UNLESS YOU HAVE A NEWSBREAKING STORY, I HAVE TO GO.
BECAUSE I HAVE NO STORY.
I'M A REPORTER WITHOUT A STORY.
AGAIN.
I NEED--WHAT? OUT WHAT WINDOW? YOUR WINDOW?
WHAT?
(THE WOMAN'S INSANE.)
RIGHT NOW? IT LIT UP? WHAT DOES THAT MEAN: A BUILDING LIT UP?
MOM, IT'S FIREWORKS.
I'M LOOKING! I'M GOING TO LOOK.
BUT BUILDINGS DON'T JUST LIGHT...
MCSWIGGIN DESTROYS OHIO
...UP.

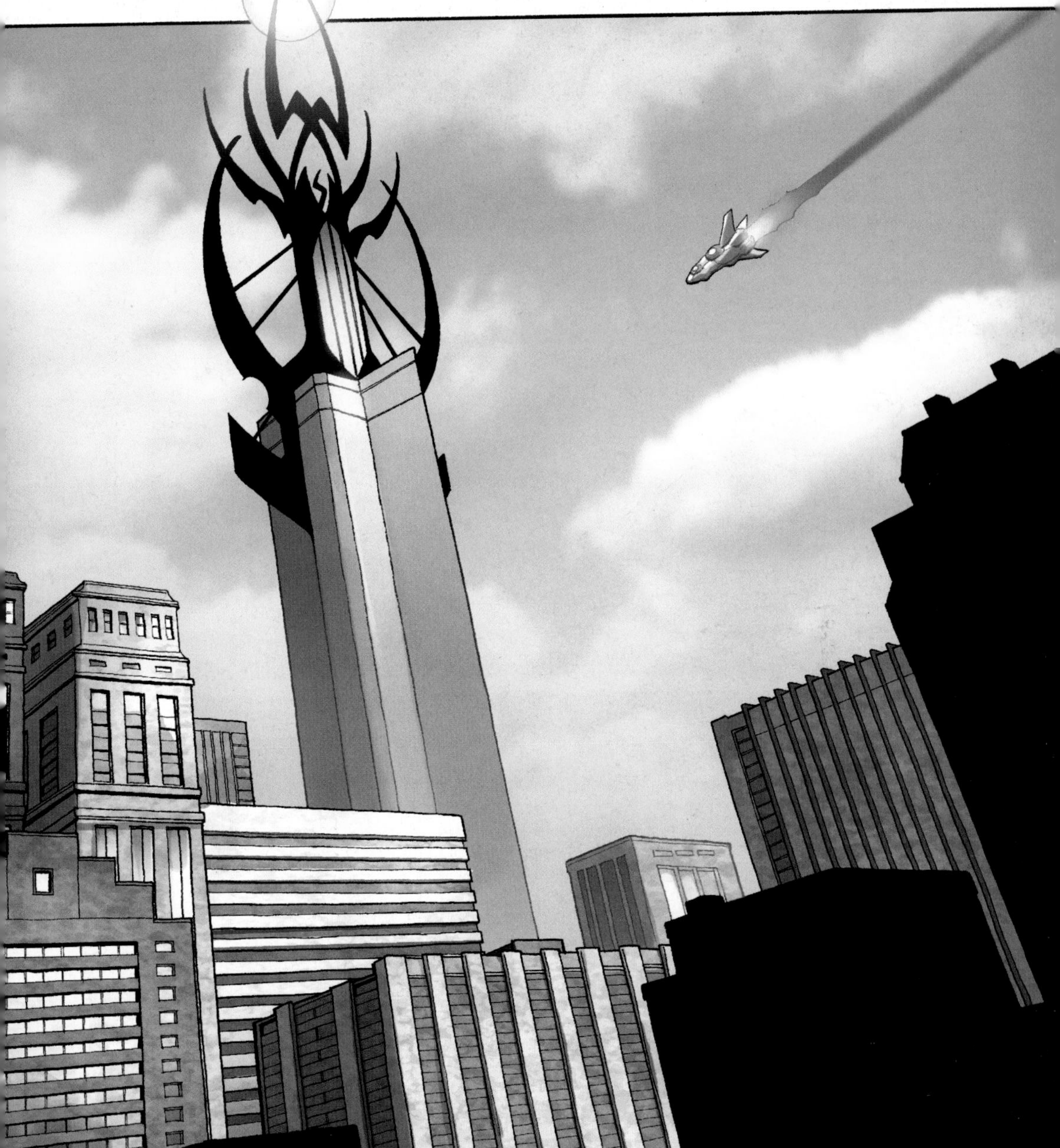

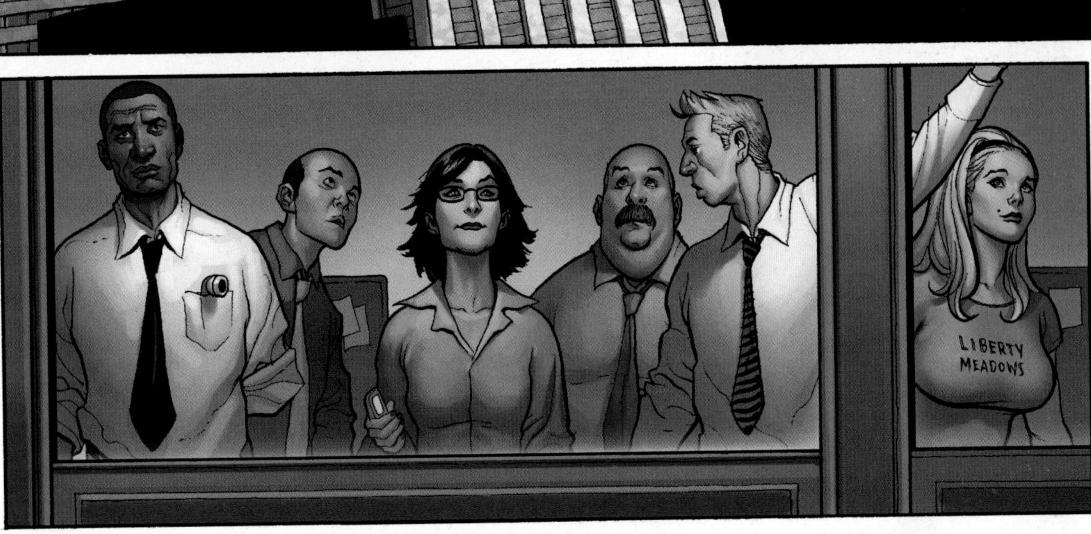
LIBERTY MEADOWS

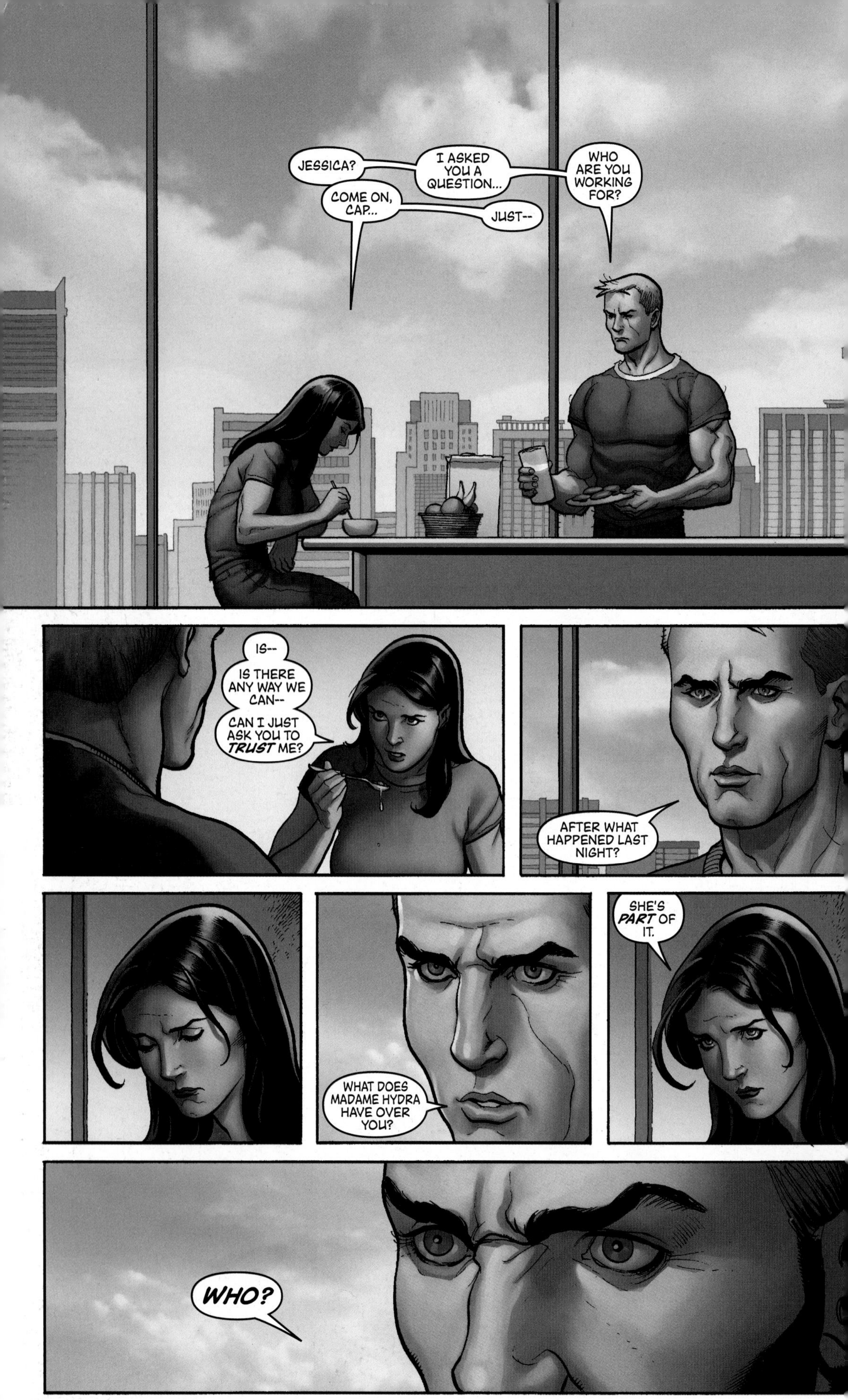
JESSICA?
I ASKED YOU A QUESTION...
WHO ARE YOU WORKING FOR?
COME ON, CAP...
JUST--
IS--
IS THERE ANY WAY WE CAN--
CAN I JUST ASK YOU TO TRUST ME?
AFTER WHAT HAPPENED LAST NIGHT?
WHAT DOES MADAME HYDRA HAVE OVER YOU?
SHE'S PART OF IT.
WHO?

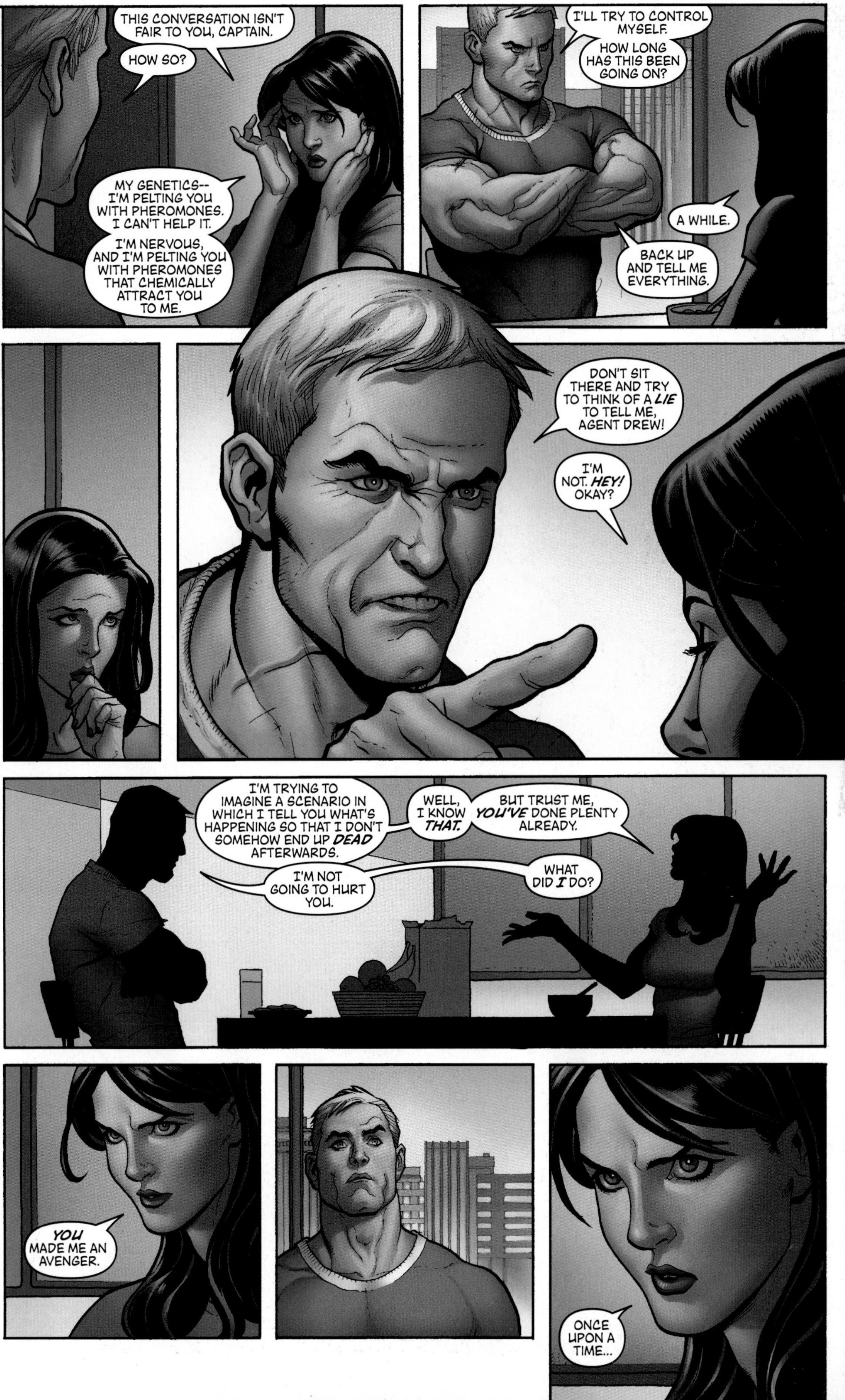
THIS CONVERSATION ISN'T FAIR TO YOU, CAPTAIN.
HOW SO?
MY GENETICS-- I'M PELTING YOU WITH PHEROMONES. I CAN'T HELP IT.
I'M NERVOUS, AND I'M PELTING YOU WITH PHEROMONES THAT CHEMICALLY ATTRACT YOU TO ME.
I'LL TRY TO CONTROL MYSELF.
HOW LONG HAS THIS BEEN GOING ON?
A WHILE.
BACK UP AND TELL ME EVERYTHING.
DON'T SIT THERE AND TRY TO THINK OF A LIE TO TELL ME, AGENT DREW!
I'M NOT. HEY! OKAY?
I'M TRYING TO IMAGINE A SCENARIO IN WHICH I TELL YOU WHAT'S HAPPENING SO THAT I DON'T SOMEHOW END UP DEAD AFTERWARDS.
WELL, I KNOW THAT.
BUT TRUST ME, YOU'VE DONE PLENTY ALREADY.
I'M NOT GOING TO HURT YOU.
WHAT DID I DO?
YOU MADE ME AN AVENGER.
ONCE UPON A TIME...

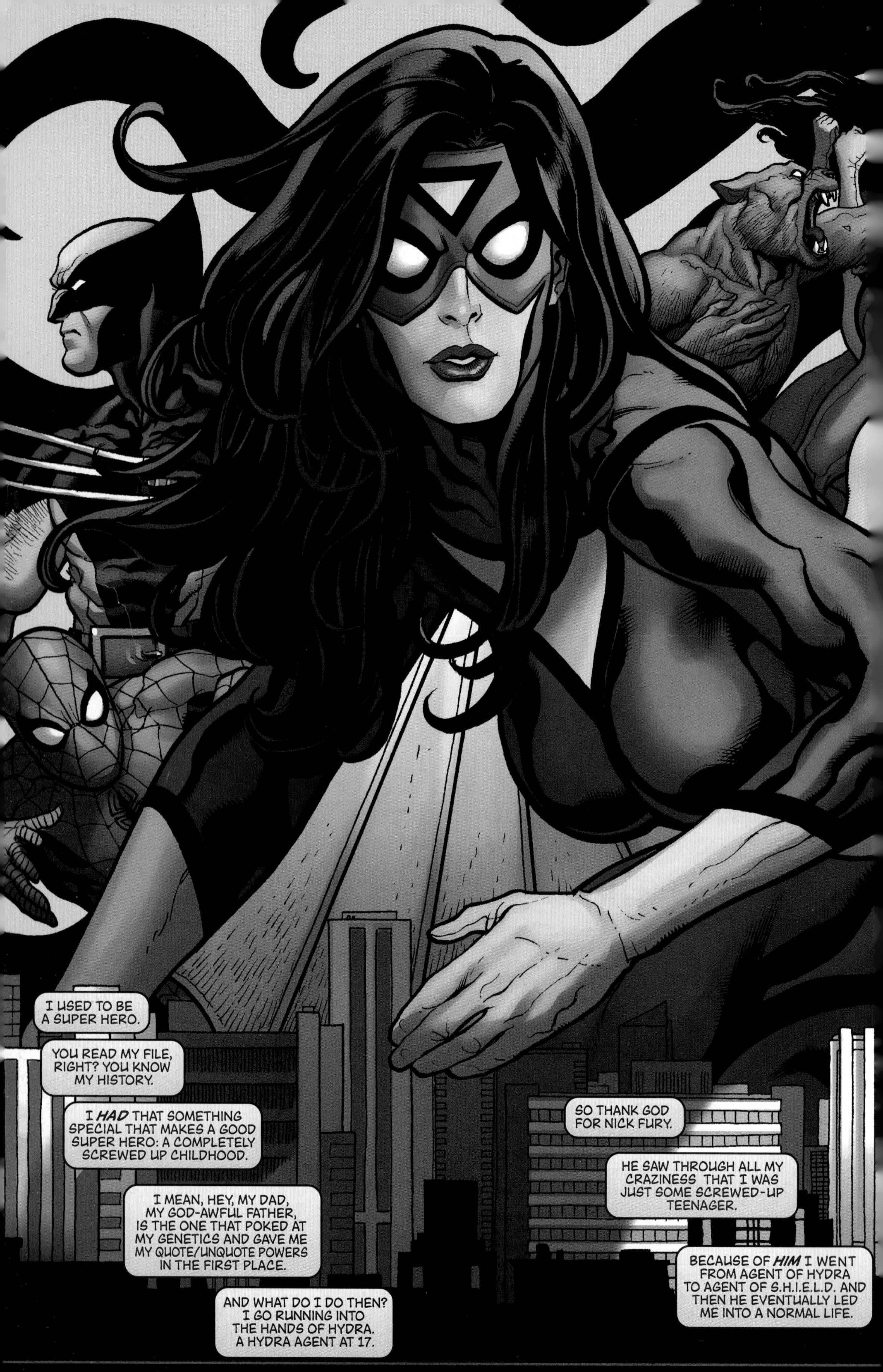
I USED TO BE A SUPER HERO.
YOU READ MY FILE, RIGHT? YOU KNOW MY HISTORY.
I HAD THAT SOMETHING SPECIAL THAT MAKES A GOOD SUPER HERO: A COMPLETELY SCREWED UP CHILDHOOD.
I MEAN, HEY, MY DAD, MY GOD-AWFUL FATHER, IS THE ONE THAT POKED AT MY GENETICS AND GAVE ME MY QUOTE/UNQUOTE POWERS IN THE FIRST PLACE.
AND WHAT DO I DO THEN? I GO RUNNING INTO THE HANDS OF HYDRA. A HYDRA AGENT AT 17.
SO THANK GOD FOR NICK FURY.
HE SAW THROUGH ALL MY CRAZINESS THAT I WAS JUST SOME SCREWED-UP TEENAGER.
BECAUSE OF HIM I WENT FROM AGENT OF HYDRA TO AGENT OF S.H.I.E.L.D. AND THEN HE EVENTUALLY LED ME INTO A NORMAL LIFE.

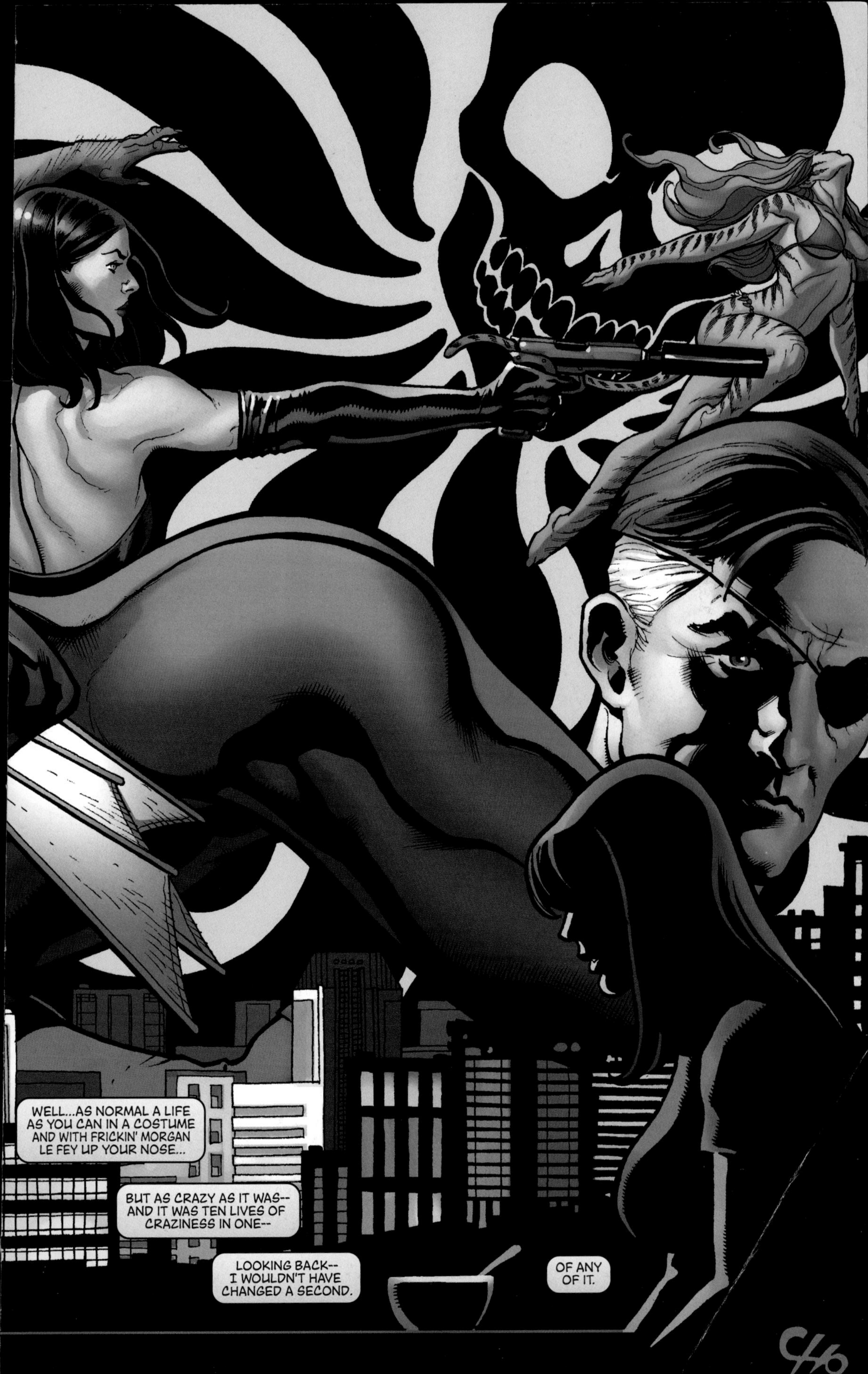
WELL...AS NORMAL A LIFE AS YOU CAN IN A COSTUME AND WITH FRICKIN' MORGAN LE FEY UP YOUR NOSE...
BUT AS CRAZY AS IT WAS-- AND IT WAS TEN LIVES OF CRAZINESS IN ONE--
LOOKING BACK-- I WOULDN'T HAVE CHANGED A SECOND.
OF ANY OF IT.

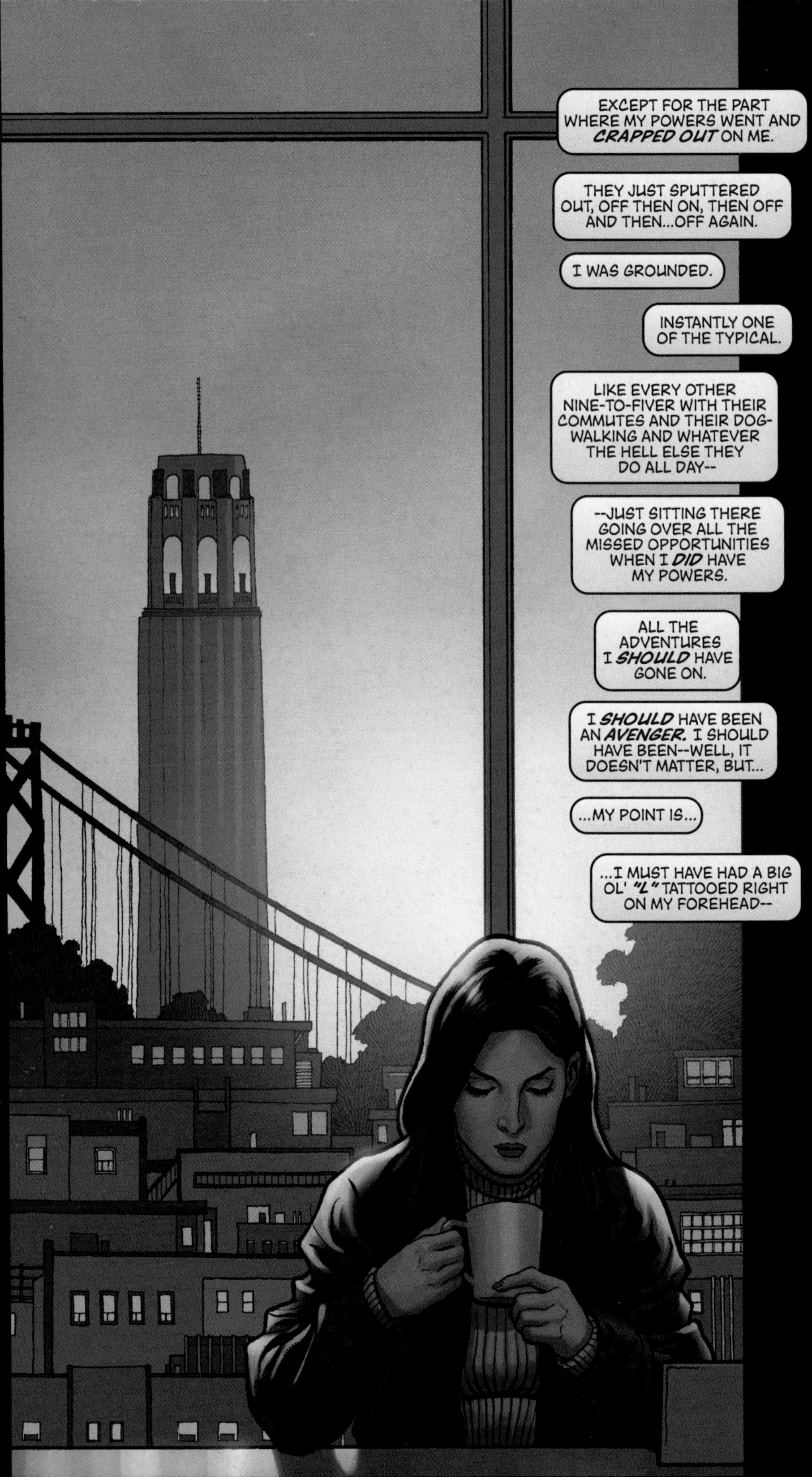
EXCEPT FOR THE PART WHERE MY POWERS WENT AND *CRAPPED OUT* ON ME.
THEY JUST SPUTTERED OUT, OFF THEN ON, THEN OFF AND THEN...OFF AGAIN.
I WAS GROUNDED.
INSTANTLY ONE OF THE TYPICAL.
LIKE EVERY OTHER NINE-TO-FIVER WITH THEIR COMMUTES AND THEIR DOG-WALKING AND WHATEVER THE HELL ELSE THEY DO ALL DAY--
--JUST SITTING THERE GOING OVER ALL THE MISSED OPPORTUNITIES WHEN I *DID* HAVE MY POWERS.
ALL THE ADVENTURES I *SHOULD* HAVE GONE ON.
I *SHOULD* HAVE BEEN AN *AVENGER.* I SHOULD HAVE BEEN--WELL, IT DOESN'T MATTER, BUT...
...MY POINT IS...
...I MUST HAVE HAD A BIG OL' *"L"* TATTOOED RIGHT ON MY FOREHEAD--

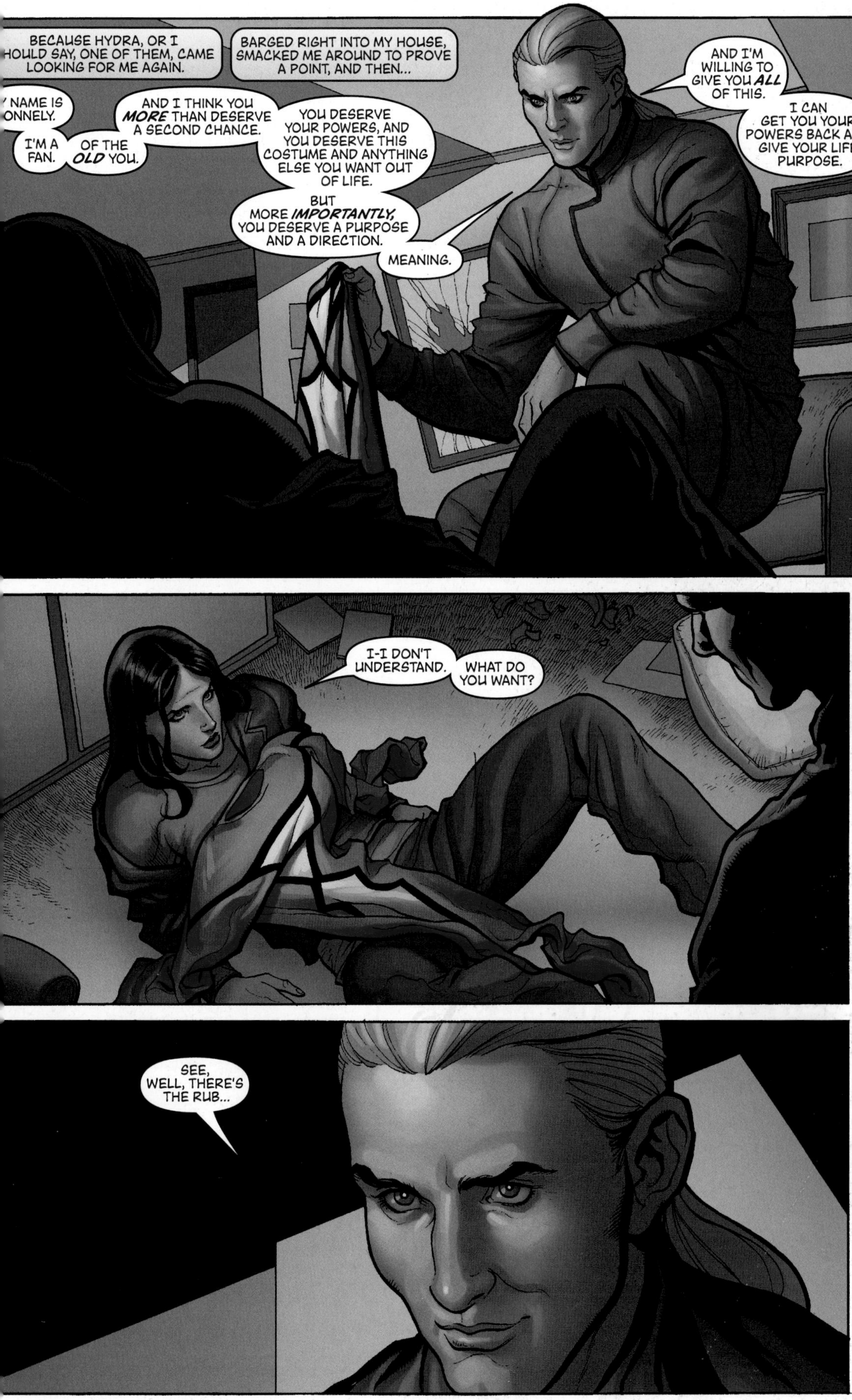
BECAUSE HYDRA, OR I HOULD SAY, ONE OF THEM, CAME LOOKING FOR ME AGAIN.
BARGED RIGHT INTO MY HOUSE, SMACKED ME AROUND TO PROVE A POINT, AND THEN...
Y NAME IS ONNELY.
I'M A FAN.
OF THE OLD YOU.
AND I THINK YOU MORE THAN DESERVE A SECOND CHANCE.
YOU DESERVE YOUR POWERS, AND YOU DESERVE THIS COSTUME AND ANYTHING ELSE YOU WANT OUT OF LIFE.
BUT MORE IMPORTANTLY, YOU DESERVE A PURPOSE AND A DIRECTION.
MEANING.
AND I'M WILLING TO GIVE YOU ALL OF THIS.
I CAN GET YOU YOUR POWERS BACK AND GIVE YOUR LIFE PURPOSE.
I-I DON'T UNDERSTAND.
WHAT DO YOU WANT?
SEE, WELL, THERE'S THE RUB...

THEY OFFERED ME MY POWERS BACK *IF* I GOT MY S.H.I.E.L.D. STATUS REINSTATED.

DOUBLE AGENT.

YEAH.

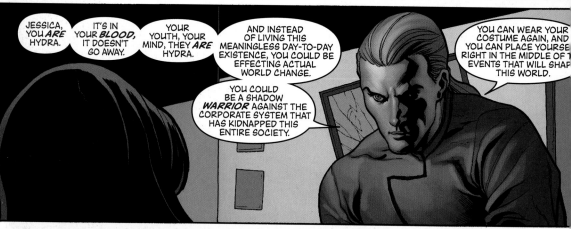

JESSICA, YOU *ARE* HYDRA.

IT'S IN YOUR *BLOOD*, IT DOESN'T GO AWAY.

YOUR YOUTH, YOUR MIND, THEY *ARE* HYDRA.

AND INSTEAD OF LIVING THIS MEANINGLESS DAY-TO-DAY EXISTENCE, YOU COULD BE EFFECTING ACTUAL WORLD CHANGE.

YOU COULD BE A SHADOW *WARRIOR* AGAINST THE CORPORATE SYSTEM THAT HAS KIDNAPPED THIS ENTIRE SOCIETY.

YOU CAN WEAR YOUR COSTUME AGAIN, AND YOU CAN PLACE YOURSELF RIGHT IN THE MIDDLE OF THE EVENTS THAT WILL SHAPE THIS WORLD.

YEAH.

AND HERE'S THE THING--AND YOU KNOW THIS IS TRUE...

...AN OFFER LIKE *THIS* IS MADE?

BY *HYDRA?*

YOU DON'T SAY: "EH, I'LL TAKE A PASS."

YOU SAY "YES" OR THEY *KILL* YOU.

THAT'S WHAT HE WAS OFFERING.

JOIN US OR *DIE.*

I WAS A WEAK LITTLE WORM PERSON. THEY *SAW* THIS, AND THEY *POUNCED* ON ME.

THEY WANTED ME TO CALL FURY AND GET REINSTATED.

I HAD NO CHOICE.

I HAD TO CALL HIM.

JACKPOT RECORDS.

I NEED TO SPEAK TO THE MANAGER.

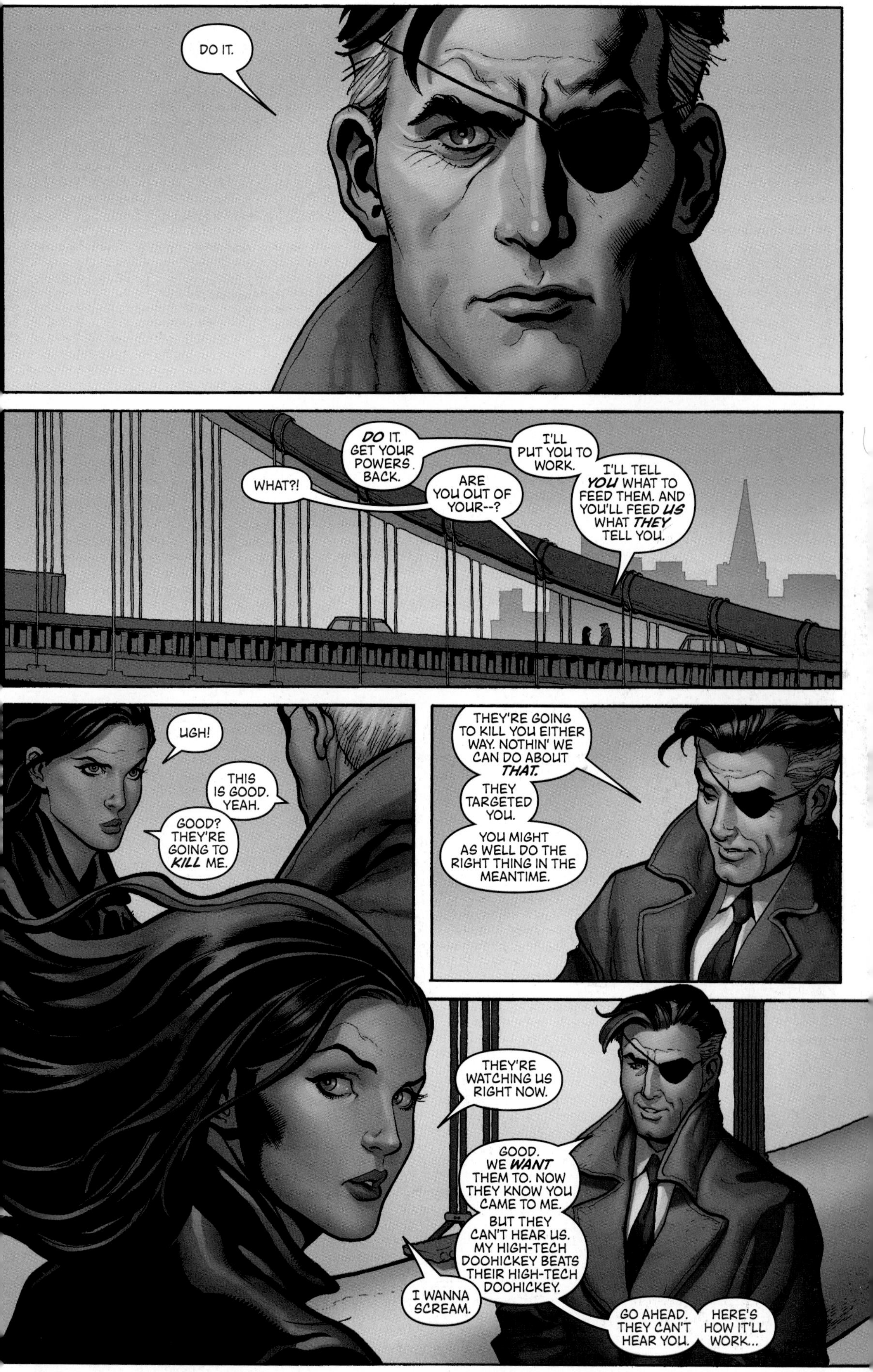
DO IT.
WHAT?!
DO IT. GET YOUR POWERS BACK.
ARE YOU OUT OF YOUR--?
I'LL PUT YOU TO WORK.
I'LL TELL YOU WHAT TO FEED THEM. AND YOU'LL FEED US WHAT THEY TELL YOU.
UGH!
THIS IS GOOD. YEAH.
GOOD? THEY'RE GOING TO KILL ME.
THEY'RE GOING TO KILL YOU EITHER WAY. NOTHIN' WE CAN DO ABOUT THAT.
THEY TARGETED YOU.
YOU MIGHT AS WELL DO THE RIGHT THING IN THE MEANTIME.
THEY'RE WATCHING US RIGHT NOW.
GOOD. WE WANT THEM TO. NOW THEY KNOW YOU CAME TO ME.
BUT THEY CAN'T HEAR US. MY HIGH-TECH DOOHICKEY BEATS THEIR HIGH-TECH DOOHICKEY.
I WANNA SCREAM.
GO AHEAD. THEY CAN'T HEAR YOU.
HERE'S HOW IT'LL WORK...

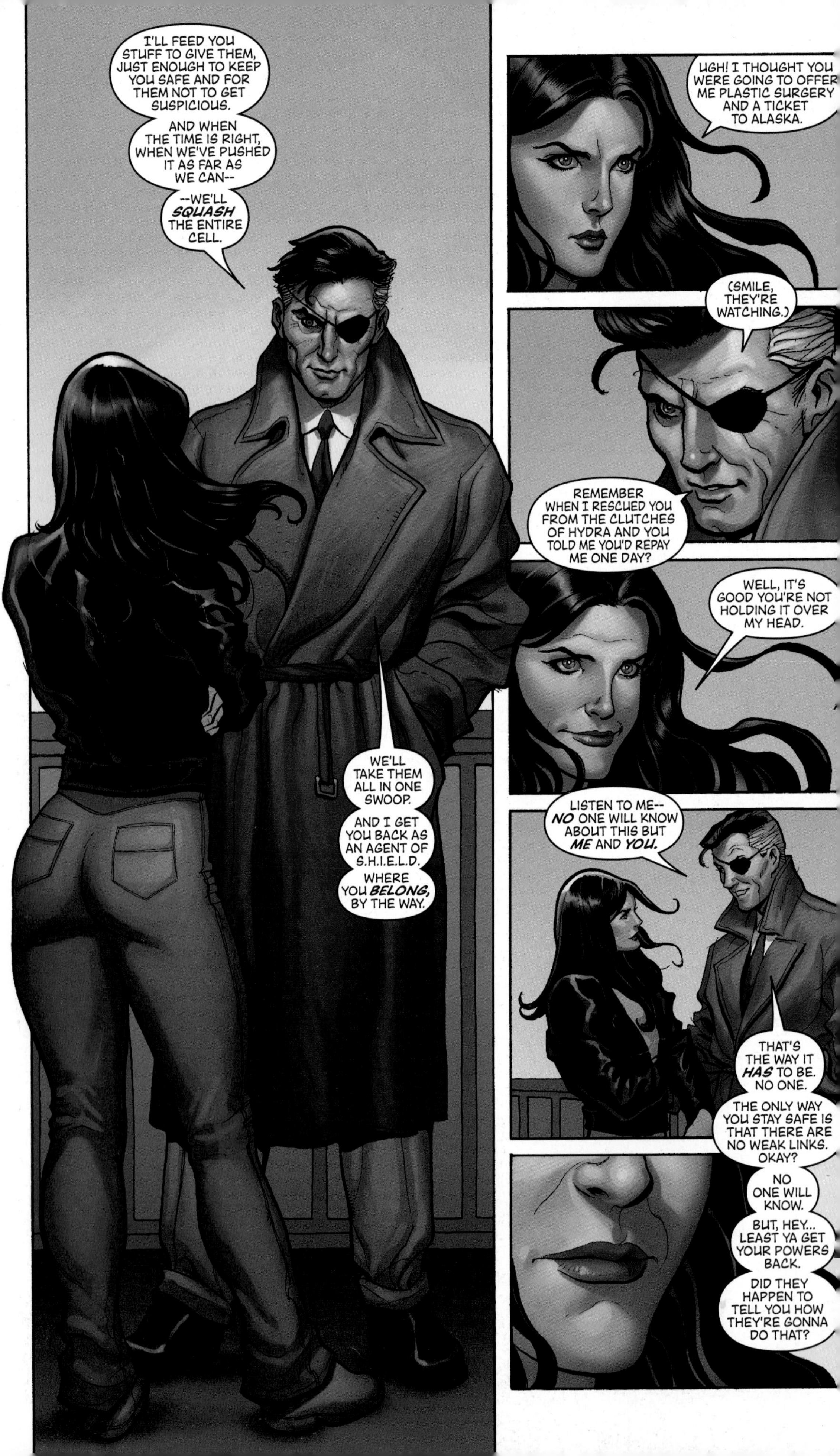

I'LL FEED YOU STUFF TO GIVE THEM, JUST ENOUGH TO KEEP YOU SAFE AND FOR THEM NOT TO GET SUSPICIOUS.
AND WHEN THE TIME IS RIGHT, WHEN WE'VE PUSHED IT AS FAR AS WE CAN--
--WE'LL *SQUASH* THE ENTIRE CELL.
WE'LL TAKE THEM ALL IN ONE SWOOP.
AND I GET YOU BACK AS AN AGENT OF S.H.I.E.L.D.
WHERE YOU *BELONG,* BY THE WAY.
UGH! I THOUGHT YOU WERE GOING TO OFFER ME PLASTIC SURGERY AND A TICKET TO ALASKA.
(SMILE, THEY'RE WATCHING.)
REMEMBER WHEN I RESCUED YOU FROM THE CLUTCHES OF HYDRA AND YOU TOLD ME YOU'D REPAY ME ONE DAY?
WELL, IT'S GOOD YOU'RE NOT HOLDING IT OVER MY HEAD.
LISTEN TO ME-- *NO* ONE WILL KNOW ABOUT THIS BUT *ME* AND *YOU.*
THAT'S THE WAY IT *HAS* TO BE. NO ONE.
THE ONLY WAY YOU STAY SAFE IS THAT THERE ARE NO WEAK LINKS. OKAY?
NO ONE WILL KNOW.
BUT, HEY... LEAST YA GET YOUR POWERS BACK.
DID THEY HAPPEN TO TELL YOU HOW THEY'RE GONNA DO THAT?

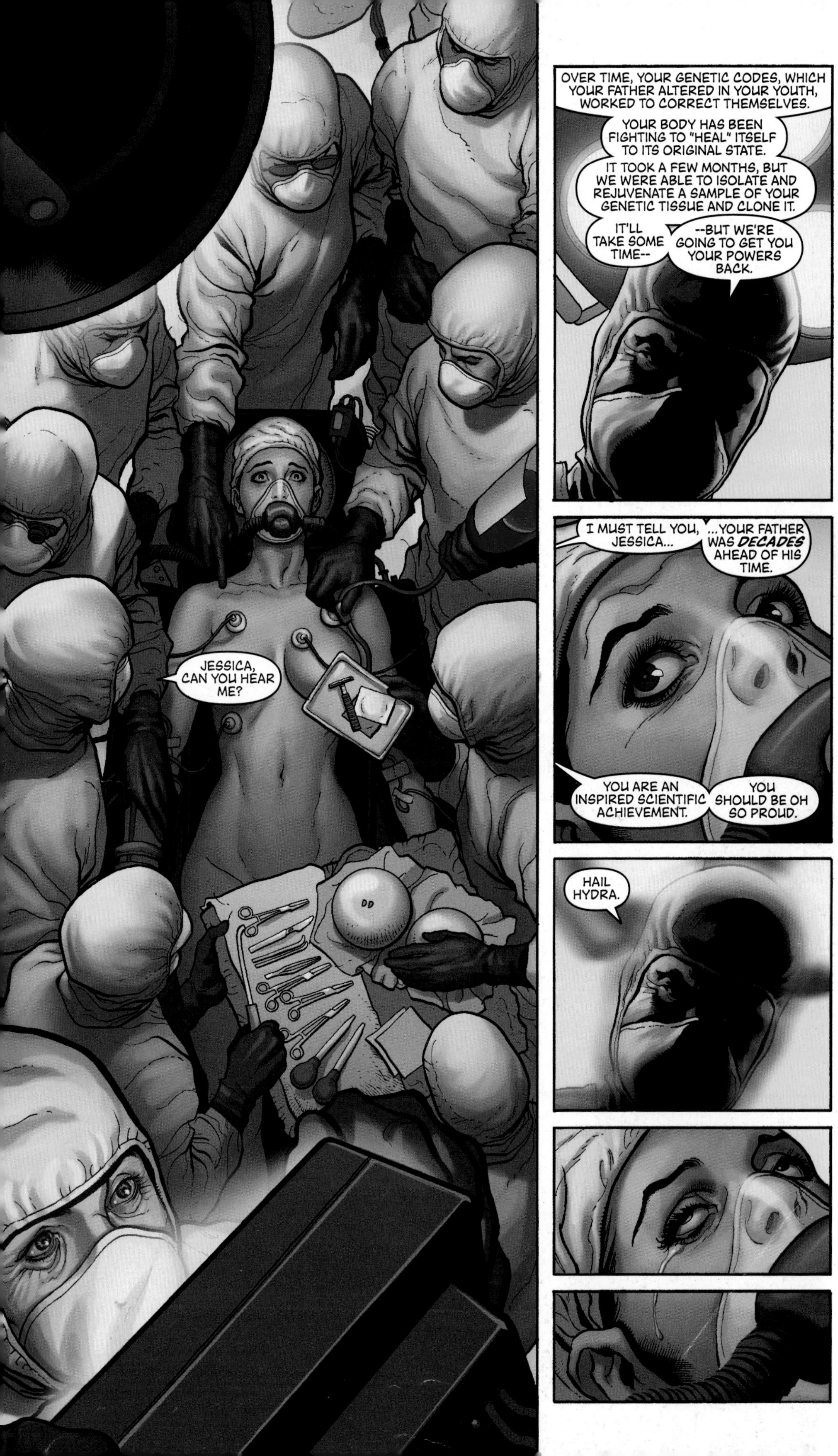

JESSICA, CAN YOU HEAR ME?
OVER TIME, YOUR GENETIC CODES, WHICH YOUR FATHER ALTERED IN YOUR YOUTH, WORKED TO CORRECT THEMSELVES.
YOUR BODY HAS BEEN FIGHTING TO "HEAL" ITSELF TO ITS ORIGINAL STATE.
IT TOOK A FEW MONTHS, BUT WE WERE ABLE TO ISOLATE AND REJUVENATE A SAMPLE OF YOUR GENETIC TISSUE AND CLONE IT.
IT'LL TAKE SOME TIME--
--BUT WE'RE GOING TO GET YOU YOUR POWERS BACK.
I MUST TELL YOU, JESSICA...
...YOUR FATHER WAS ***DECADES*** AHEAD OF HIS TIME.
YOU ARE AN INSPIRED SCIENTIFIC ACHIEVEMENT.
YOU SHOULD BE OH SO PROUD.
HAIL HYDRA.

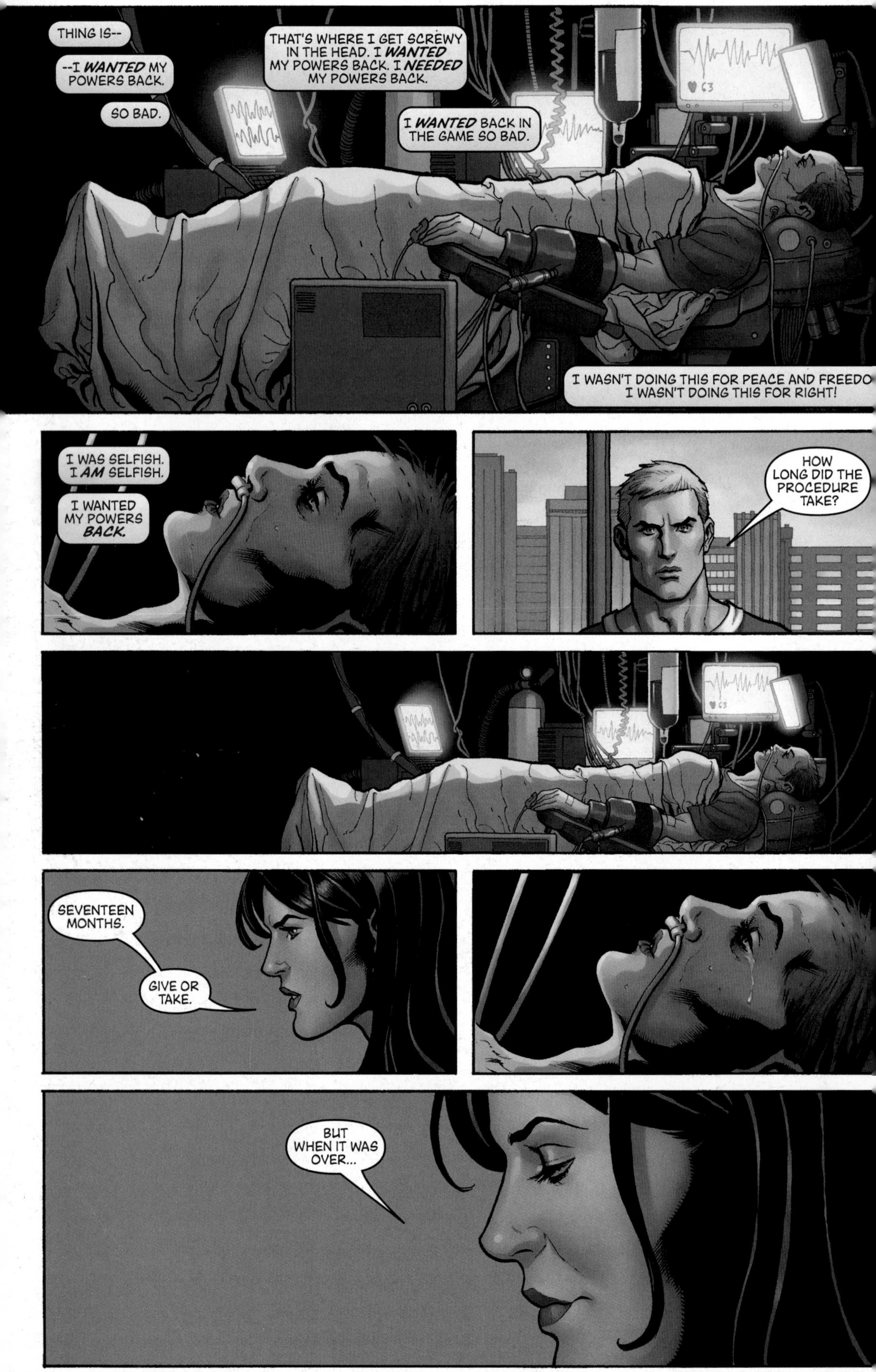
THING IS--
--I WANTED MY POWERS BACK.
SO BAD.
THAT'S WHERE I GET SCREWY IN THE HEAD. I WANTED MY POWERS BACK. I NEEDED MY POWERS BACK.
I WANTED BACK IN THE GAME SO BAD.
I WASN'T DOING THIS FOR PEACE AND FREEDO
I WASN'T DOING THIS FOR RIGHT!
I WAS SELFISH. I AM SELFISH.
I WANTED MY POWERS BACK.
HOW LONG DID THE PROCEDURE TAKE?
SEVENTEEN MONTHS.
GIVE OR TAKE.
BUT WHEN IT WAS OVER...

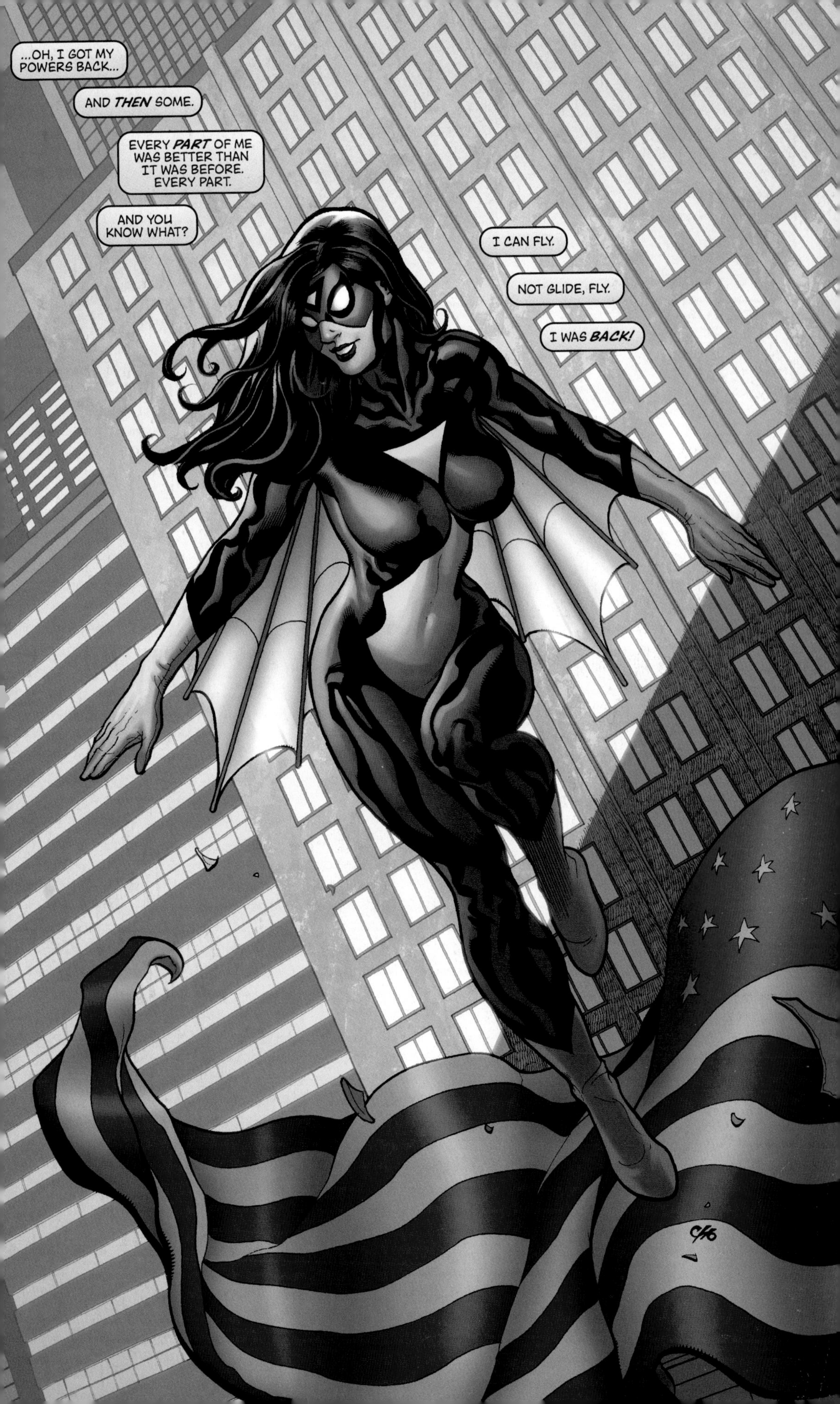

...OH, I GOT MY POWERS BACK...
AND THEN SOME.
EVERY PART OF ME WAS BETTER THAN IT WAS BEFORE. EVERY PART.
AND YOU KNOW WHAT?
I CAN FLY.
NOT GLIDE, FLY.
I WAS BACK!
CHO

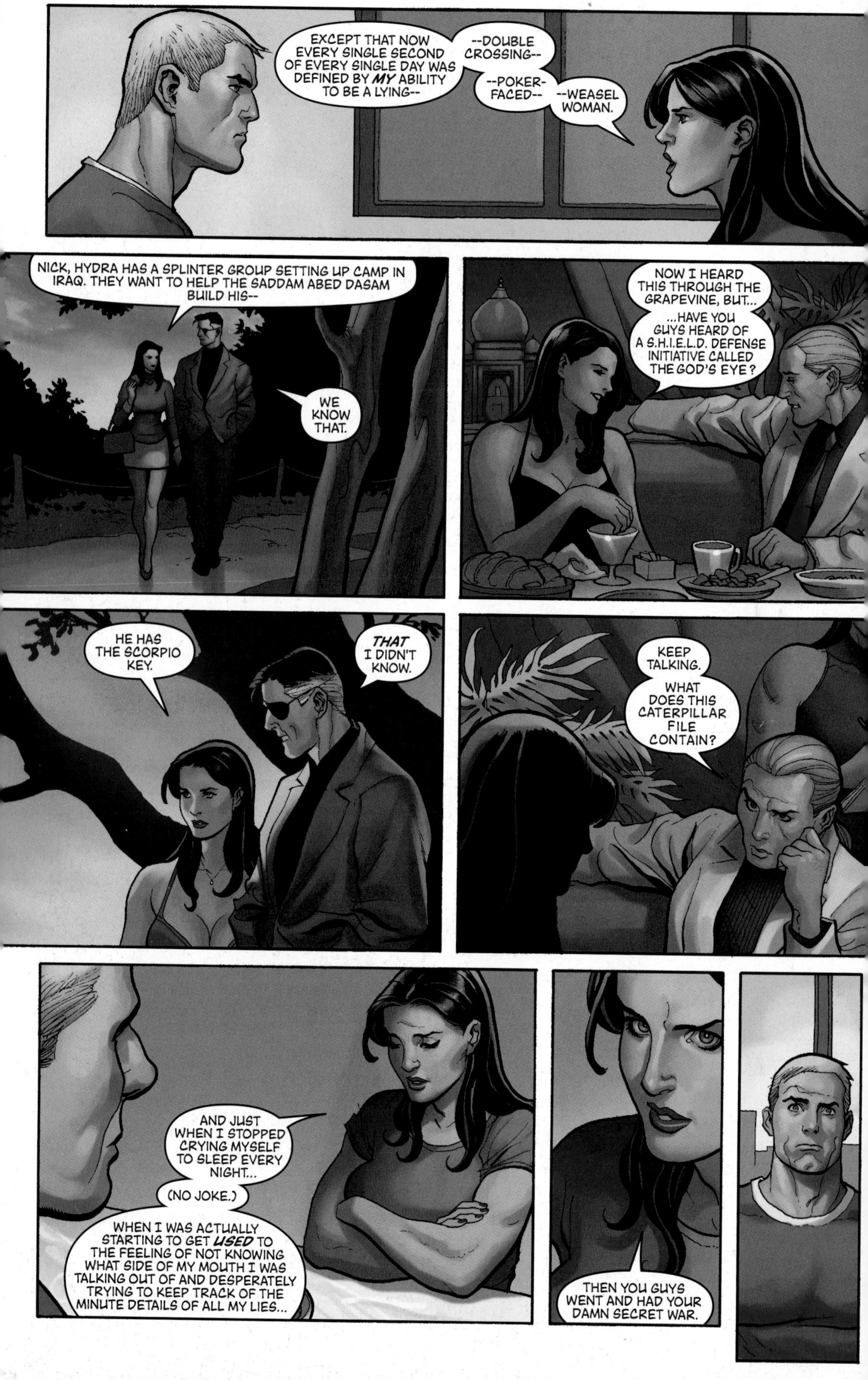

EXCEPT THAT NOW EVERY SINGLE SECOND OF EVERY SINGLE DAY WAS DEFINED BY *MY* ABILITY TO BE A LYING--
--DOUBLE CROSSING--
--POKER-FACED--
--WEASEL WOMAN.
NICK, HYDRA HAS A SPLINTER GROUP SETTING UP CAMP IN IRAQ. THEY WANT TO HELP THE SADDAM ABED DASAM BUILD HIS--
WE KNOW THAT.
NOW I HEARD THIS THROUGH THE GRAPEVINE, BUT...
...HAVE YOU GUYS HEARD OF A S.H.I.E.L.D. DEFENSE INITIATIVE CALLED THE GOD'S EYE?
HE HAS THE SCORPIO KEY.
THAT I DIDN'T KNOW.
KEEP TALKING.
WHAT DOES THIS CATERPILLAR FILE CONTAIN?
AND JUST WHEN I STOPPED CRYING MYSELF TO SLEEP EVERY NIGHT...
(NO JOKE.)
WHEN I WAS ACTUALLY STARTING TO GET *USED* TO THE FEELING OF NOT KNOWING WHAT SIDE OF MY MOUTH I WAS TALKING OUT OF AND DESPERATELY TRYING TO KEEP TRACK OF THE MINUTE DETAILS OF ALL MY LIES...
THEN YOU GUYS WENT AND HAD YOUR DAMN SECRET WAR.

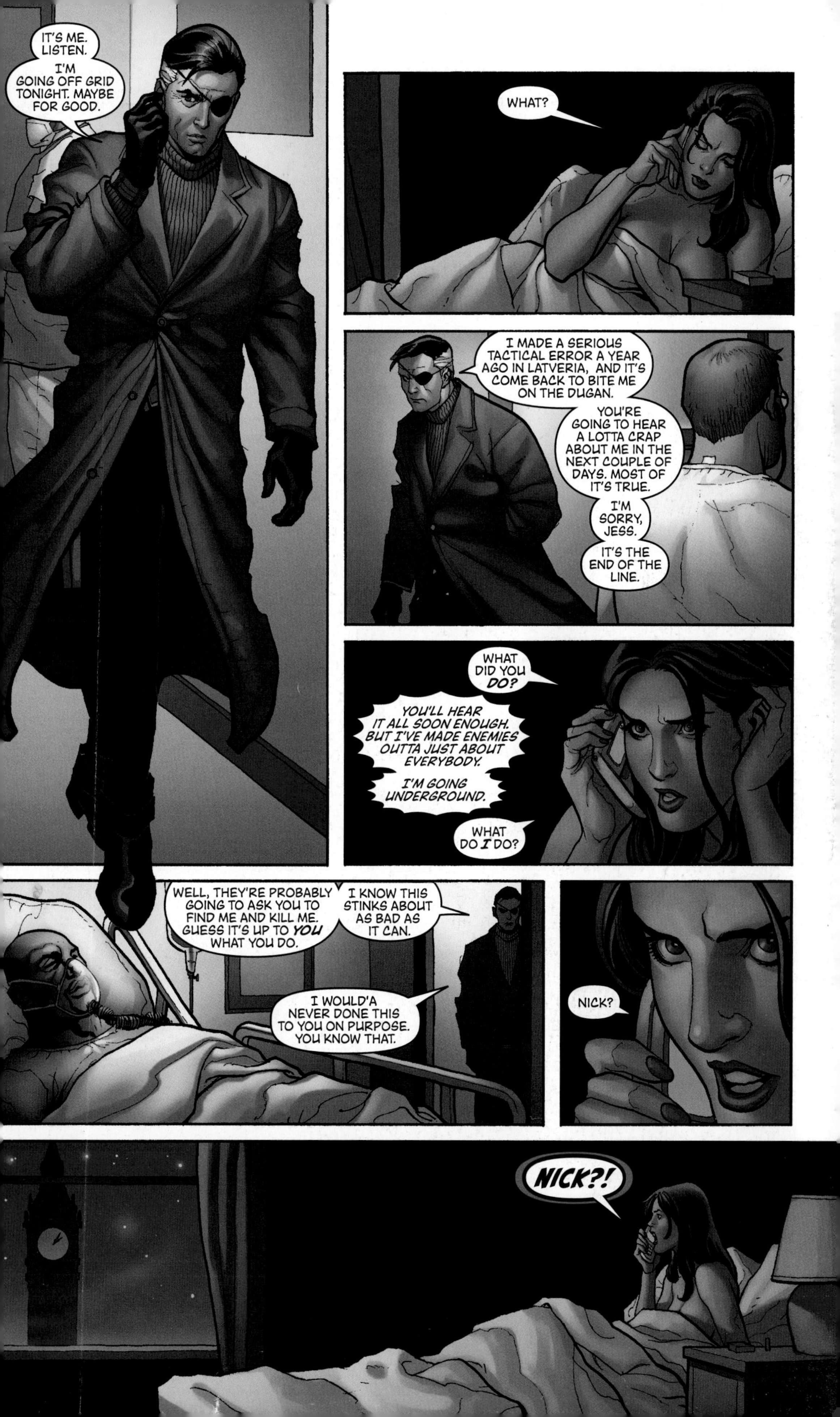
IT'S ME. LISTEN.
I'M GOING OFF GRID TONIGHT. MAYBE FOR GOOD.
WHAT?
I MADE A SERIOUS TACTICAL ERROR A YEAR AGO IN LATVERIA, AND IT'S COME BACK TO BITE ME ON THE DUGAN.
YOU'RE GOING TO HEAR A LOTTA CRAP ABOUT ME IN THE NEXT COUPLE OF DAYS. MOST OF IT'S TRUE.
I'M SORRY, JESS.
IT'S THE END OF THE LINE.
WHAT DID YOU *DO?*
YOU'LL HEAR IT ALL SOON ENOUGH. BUT I'VE MADE ENEMIES OUTTA JUST ABOUT EVERYBODY.
I'M GOING UNDERGROUND.
WHAT DO *I* DO?
WELL, THEY'RE PROBABLY GOING TO ASK YOU TO FIND ME AND KILL ME. GUESS IT'S UP TO *YOU* WHAT YOU DO.
I KNOW THIS STINKS ABOUT AS BAD AS IT CAN.
I WOULD'A NEVER DONE THIS TO YOU ON PURPOSE. YOU KNOW THAT.
NICK?
NICK?!

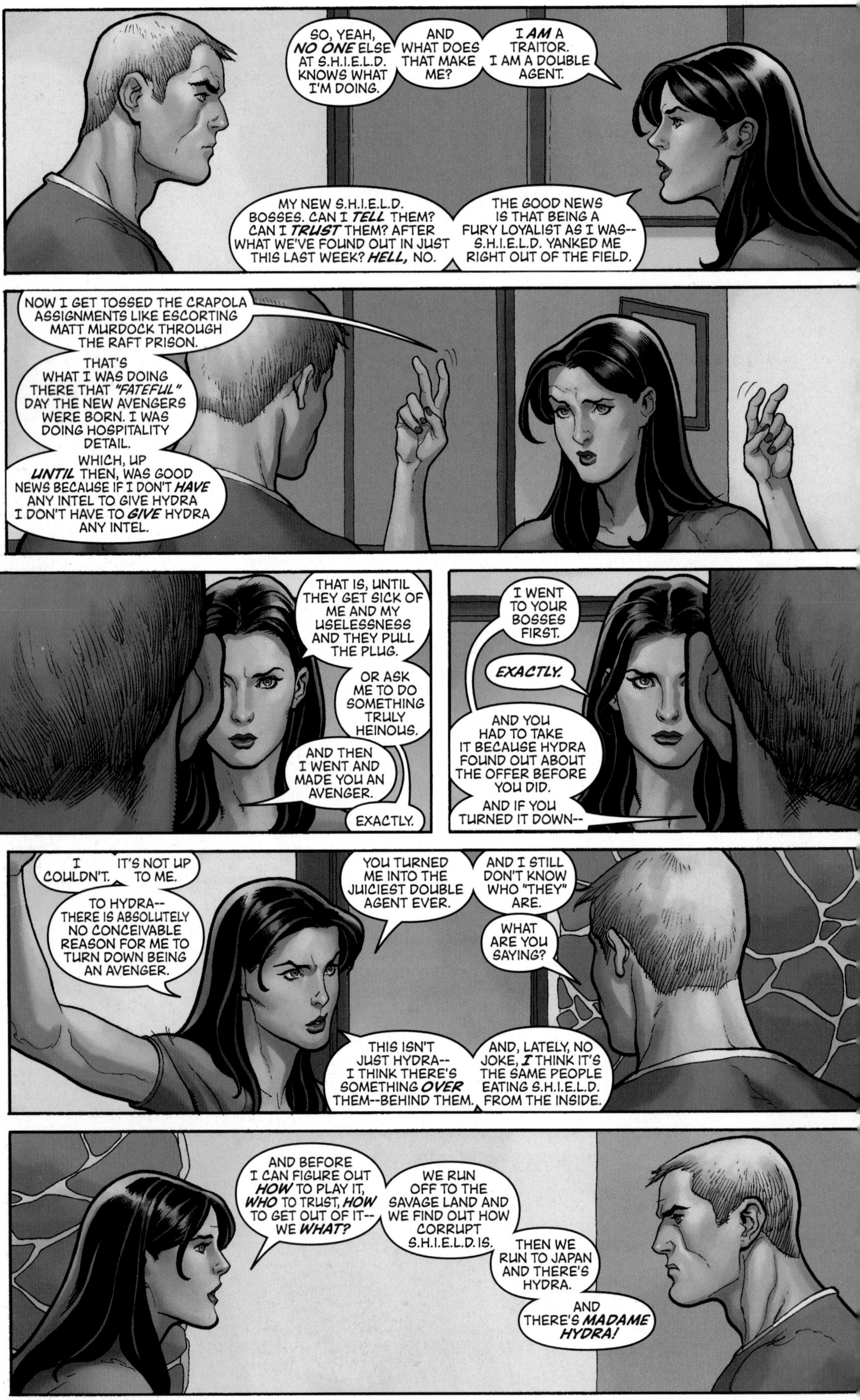

SO, YEAH, NO ONE ELSE AT S.H.I.E.L.D. KNOWS WHAT I'M DOING.
AND WHAT DOES THAT MAKE ME?
I AM A TRAITOR. I AM A DOUBLE AGENT.
MY NEW S.H.I.E.L.D. BOSSES. CAN I TELL THEM? CAN I TRUST THEM? AFTER WHAT WE'VE FOUND OUT IN JUST THIS LAST WEEK? HELL, NO.
THE GOOD NEWS IS THAT BEING A FURY LOYALIST AS I WAS-- S.H.I.E.L.D. YANKED ME RIGHT OUT OF THE FIELD.
NOW I GET TOSSED THE CRAPOLA ASSIGNMENTS LIKE ESCORTING MATT MURDOCK THROUGH THE RAFT PRISON.
THAT'S WHAT I WAS DOING THERE THAT "FATEFUL" DAY THE NEW AVENGERS WERE BORN. I WAS DOING HOSPITALITY DETAIL.
WHICH, UP UNTIL THEN, WAS GOOD NEWS BECAUSE IF I DON'T HAVE ANY INTEL TO GIVE HYDRA I DON'T HAVE TO GIVE HYDRA ANY INTEL.
THAT IS, UNTIL THEY GET SICK OF ME AND MY USELESSNESS AND THEY PULL THE PLUG.
OR ASK ME TO DO SOMETHING TRULY HEINOUS.
AND THEN I WENT AND MADE YOU AN AVENGER.
EXACTLY.
I WENT TO YOUR BOSSES FIRST.
EXACTLY.
AND YOU HAD TO TAKE IT BECAUSE HYDRA FOUND OUT ABOUT THE OFFER BEFORE YOU DID.
AND IF YOU TURNED IT DOWN--
I COULDN'T.
IT'S NOT UP TO ME.
TO HYDRA-- THERE IS ABSOLUTELY NO CONCEIVABLE REASON FOR ME TO TURN DOWN BEING AN AVENGER.
YOU TURNED ME INTO THE JUICIEST DOUBLE AGENT EVER.
AND I STILL DON'T KNOW WHO "THEY" ARE.
WHAT ARE YOU SAYING?
THIS ISN'T JUST HYDRA-- I THINK THERE'S SOMETHING OVER THEM--BEHIND THEM.
AND, LATELY, NO JOKE, I THINK IT'S THE SAME PEOPLE EATING S.H.I.E.L.D. FROM THE INSIDE.
AND BEFORE I CAN FIGURE OUT HOW TO PLAY IT, WHO TO TRUST, HOW TO GET OUT OF IT-- WE WHAT?
WE RUN OFF TO THE SAVAGE LAND AND WE FIND OUT HOW CORRUPT S.H.I.E.L.D. IS.
THEN WE RUN TO JAPAN AND THERE'S HYDRA.
AND THERE'S MADAME HYDRA!

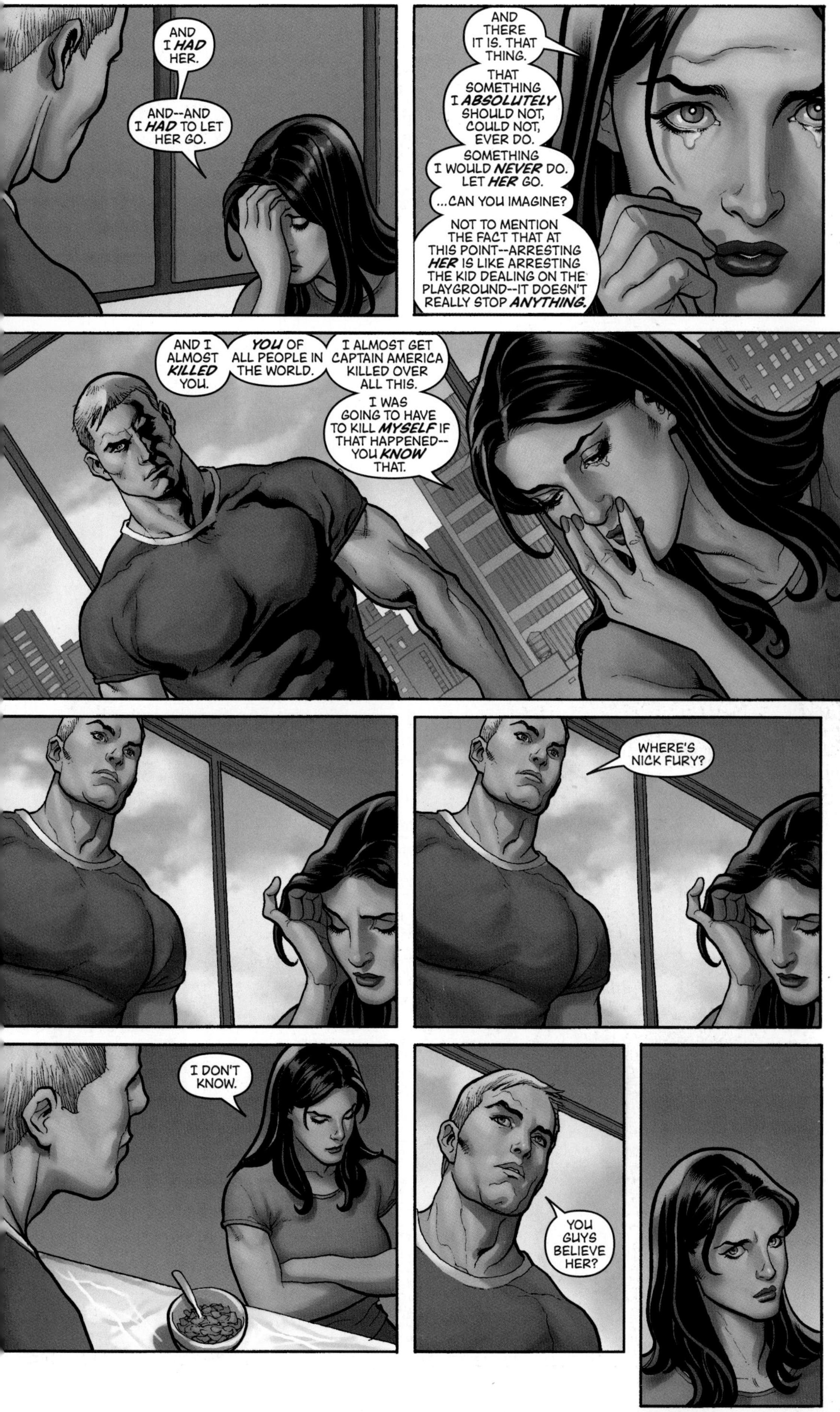
AND I *HAD* HER.
AND--AND I *HAD* TO LET HER GO.
AND THERE IT IS. THAT THING.
THAT SOMETHING I *ABSOLUTELY* SHOULD NOT, COULD NOT, EVER DO.
SOMETHING I WOULD *NEVER* DO. LET *HER* GO.
...CAN YOU IMAGINE?
NOT TO MENTION THE FACT THAT AT THIS POINT--ARRESTING *HER* IS LIKE ARRESTING THE KID DEALING ON THE PLAYGROUND--IT DOESN'T REALLY STOP *ANYTHING.*
AND I ALMOST *KILLED* YOU.
YOU OF ALL PEOPLE IN THE WORLD.
I ALMOST GET CAPTAIN AMERICA KILLED OVER ALL THIS.
I WAS GOING TO HAVE TO KILL *MYSELF* IF THAT HAPPENED--YOU *KNOW* THAT.
WHERE'S NICK FURY?
I DON'T KNOW.
YOU GUYS BELIEVE HER?

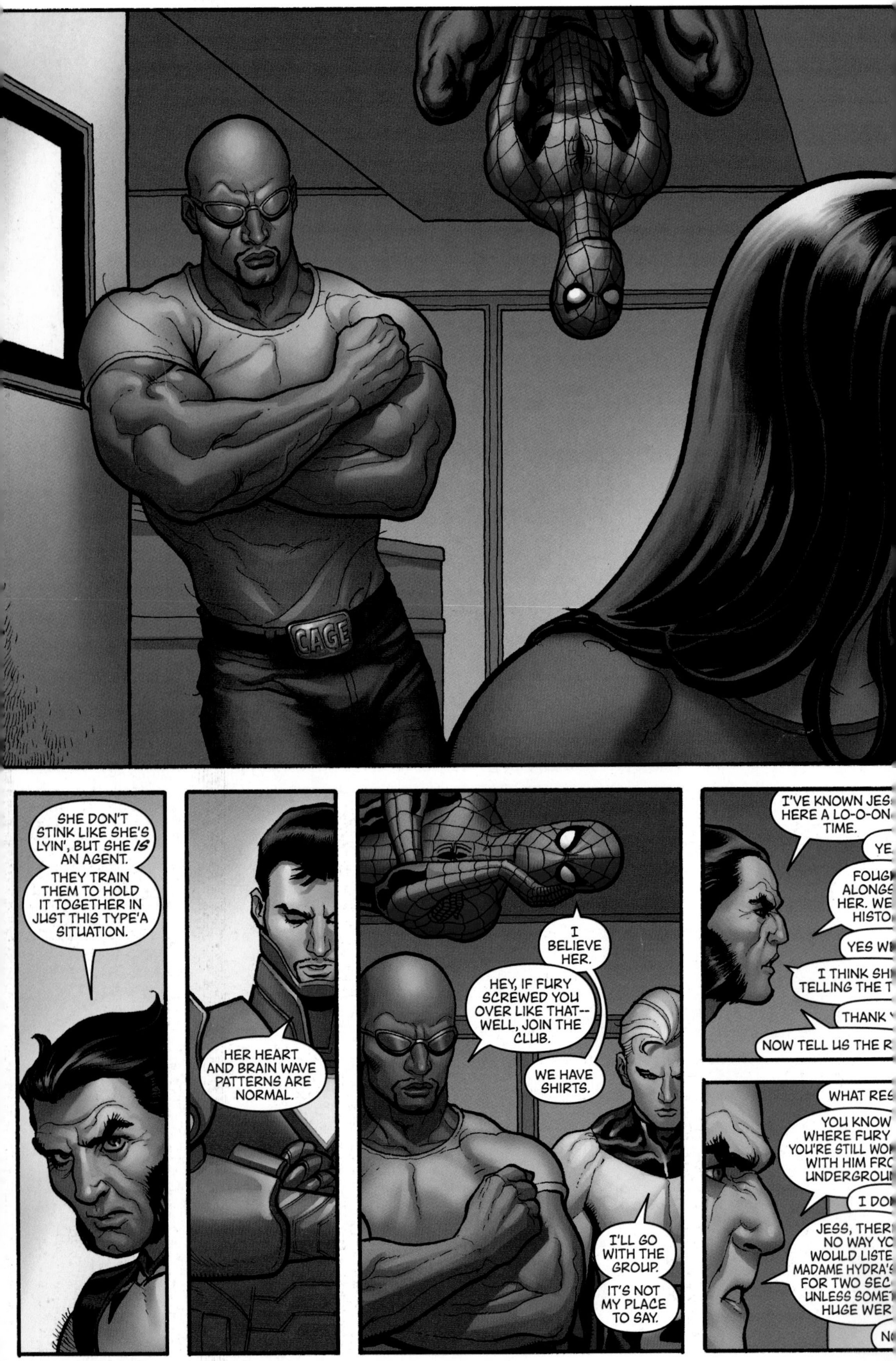

SHE DON'T STINK LIKE SHE'S LYIN', BUT SHE *IS* AN AGENT.
THEY TRAIN THEM TO HOLD IT TOGETHER IN JUST THIS TYPE'A SITUATION.
HER HEART AND BRAIN WAVE PATTERNS ARE NORMAL.
I BELIEVE HER.
HEY, IF FURY SCREWED YOU OVER LIKE THAT-- WELL, JOIN THE CLUB.
WE HAVE SHIRTS.
I'LL GO WITH THE GROUP.
IT'S NOT MY PLACE TO SAY.
I'VE KNOWN JES HERE A LO-O-ON TIME.
YE
FOUG ALONGS HER. WE HISTO
YES W
I THINK SH TELLING THE T
THANK
NOW TELL US THE R
WHAT RES
YOU KNOW WHERE FURY YOU'RE STILL WO WITH HIM FRO UNDERGROU
I DO
JESS, THER NO WAY YO WOULD LISTE MADAME HYDRA'S FOR TWO SEC UNLESS SOMET HUGE WER
N

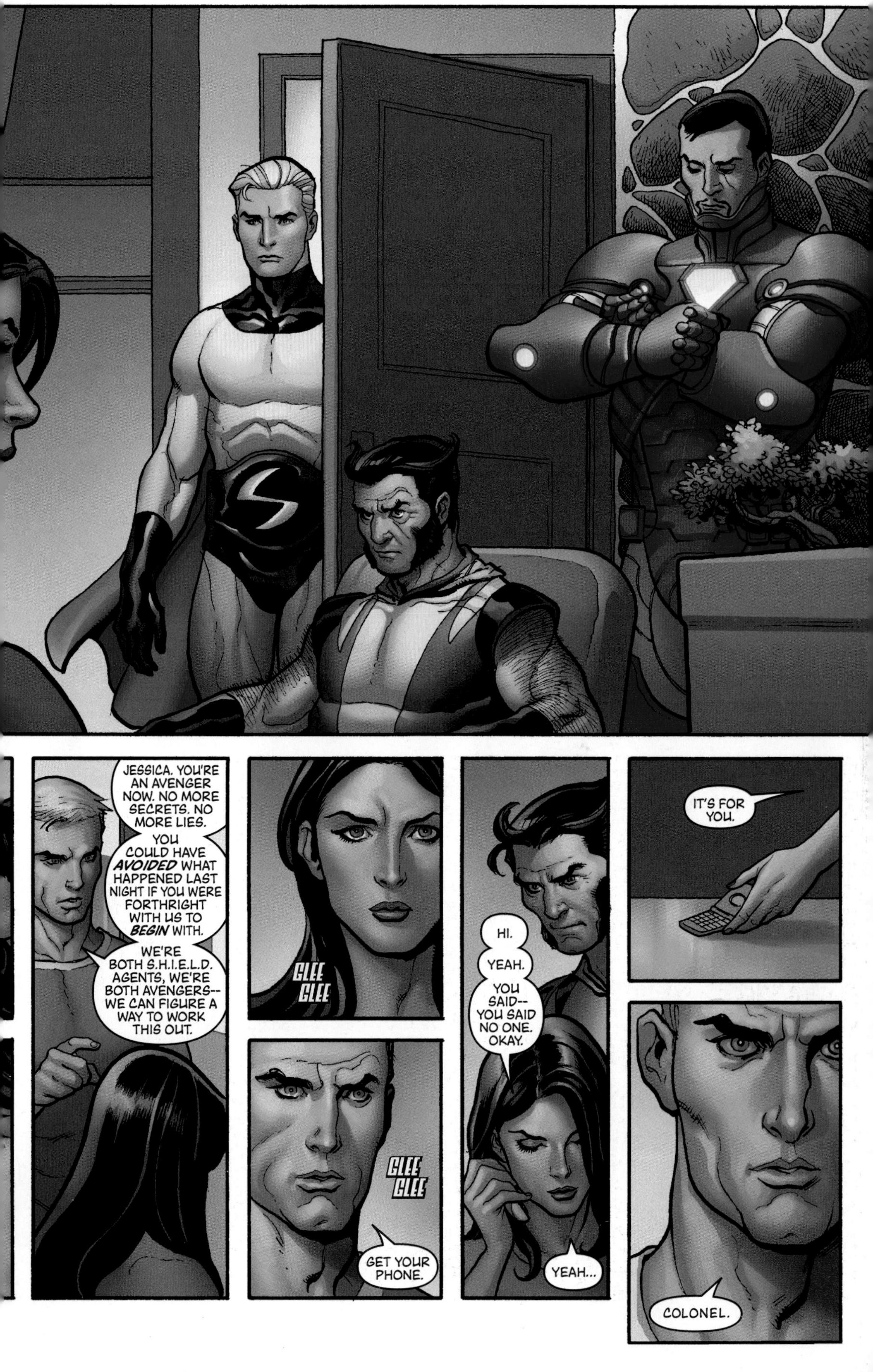
JESSICA. YOU'RE AN AVENGER NOW. NO MORE SECRETS. NO MORE LIES.
YOU COULD HAVE AVOIDED WHAT HAPPENED LAST NIGHT IF YOU WERE FORTHRIGHT WITH US TO BEGIN WITH.
WE'RE BOTH S.H.I.E.L.D. AGENTS, WE'RE BOTH AVENGERS-- WE CAN FIGURE A WAY TO WORK THIS OUT.
GLEE GLEE
GLEE GLEE
GET YOUR PHONE.
HI.
YEAH.
YOU SAID-- YOU SAID NO ONE. OKAY.
YEAH...
IT'S FOR YOU.
COLONEL.

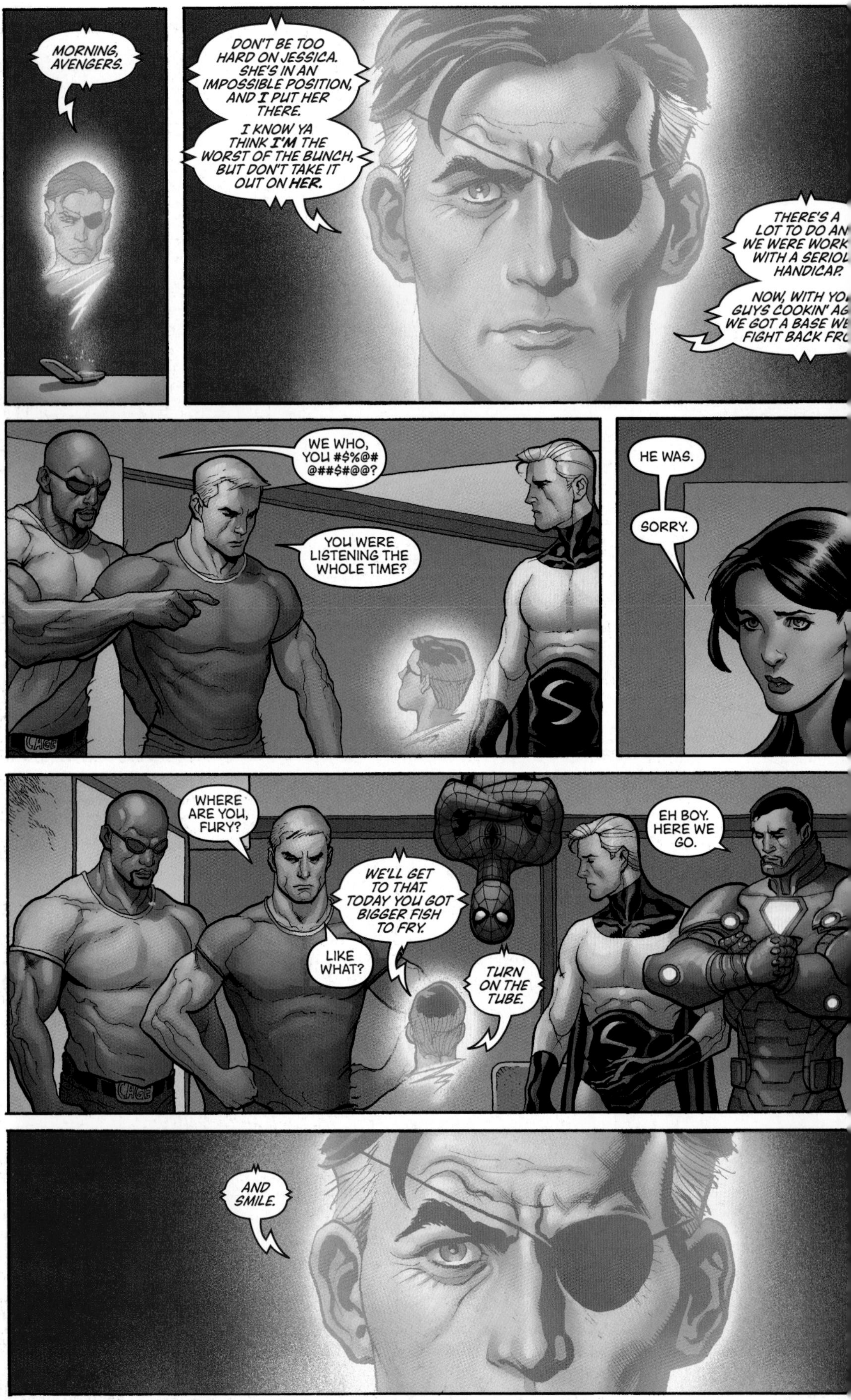
MORNING, AVENGERS.
DON'T BE TOO HARD ON JESSICA. SHE'S IN AN IMPOSSIBLE POSITION, AND I PUT HER THERE.
I KNOW YA THINK I'M THE WORST OF THE BUNCH, BUT DON'T TAKE IT OUT ON HER.
THERE'S A LOT TO DO AN WE WERE WORK WITH A SERIOU HANDICAP.
NOW, WITH YO GUYS COOKIN' AG WE GOT A BASE WE FIGHT BACK FR
WE WHO, YOU #$%@# @##$#@@?
YOU WERE LISTENING THE WHOLE TIME?
CAGE
HE WAS.
SORRY.
WHERE ARE YOU, FURY?
WE'LL GET TO THAT. TODAY YOU GOT BIGGER FISH TO FRY.
LIKE WHAT?
TURN ON THE TUBE.
EH BOY. HERE WE GO.
CAGE
AND SMILE.

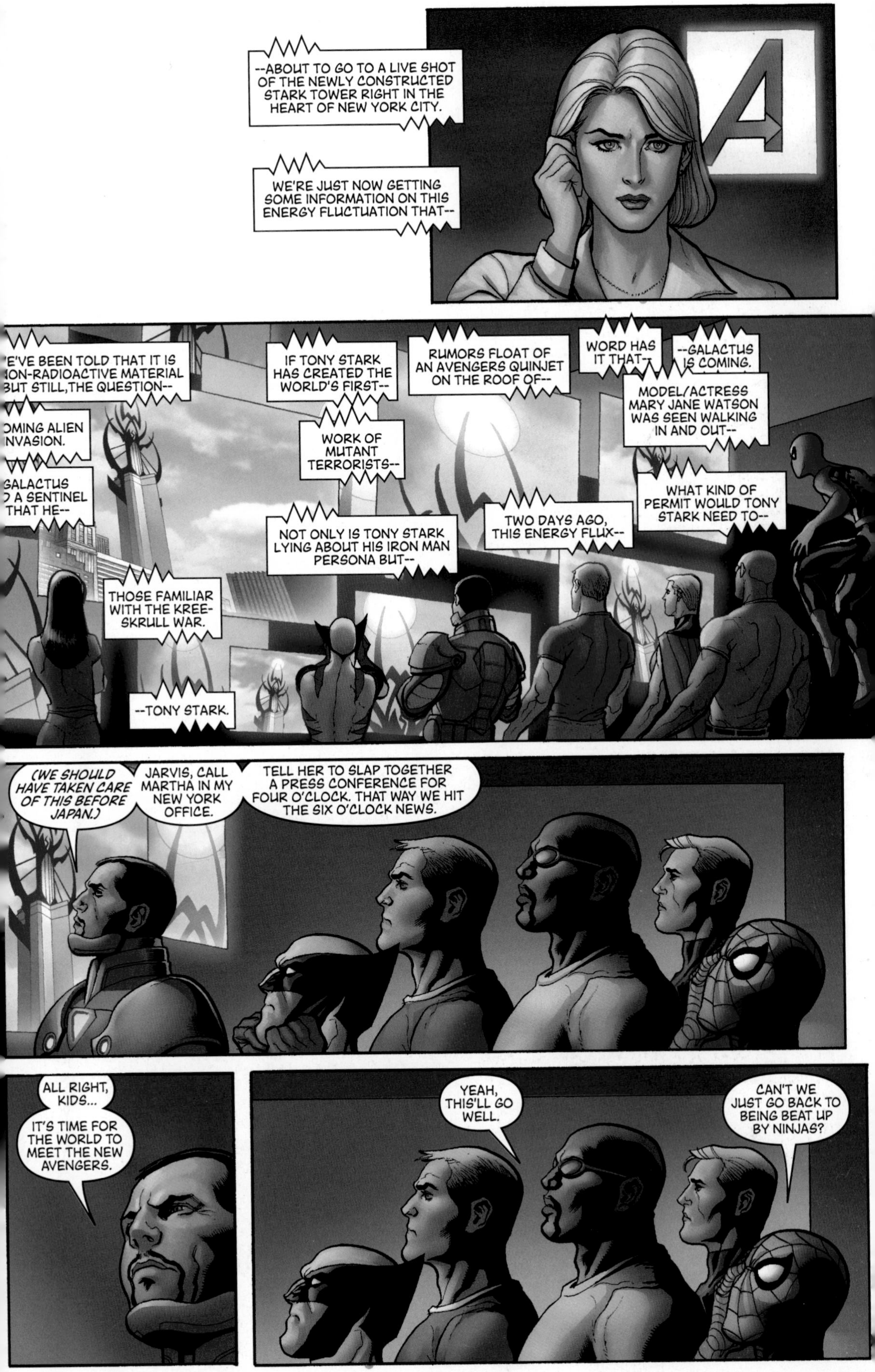

--ABOUT TO GO TO A LIVE SHOT OF THE NEWLY CONSTRUCTED STARK TOWER RIGHT IN THE HEART OF NEW YORK CITY.
WE'RE JUST NOW GETTING SOME INFORMATION ON THIS ENERGY FLUCTUATION THAT--
'E'VE BEEN TOLD THAT IT IS ION-RADIOACTIVE MATERIAL BUT STILL,THE QUESTION--
OMING ALIEN INVASION.
GALACTUS D A SENTINEL THAT HE--
IF TONY STARK HAS CREATED THE WORLD'S FIRST--
WORK OF MUTANT TERRORISTS--
NOT ONLY IS TONY STARK LYING ABOUT HIS IRON MAN PERSONA BUT--
THOSE FAMILIAR WITH THE KREE-SKRULL WAR.
--TONY STARK.
RUMORS FLOAT OF AN AVENGERS QUINJET ON THE ROOF OF--
WORD HAS IT THAT--
--GALACTUS IS COMING.
MODEL/ACTRESS MARY JANE WATSON WAS SEEN WALKING IN AND OUT--
TWO DAYS AGO, THIS ENERGY FLUX--
WHAT KIND OF PERMIT WOULD TONY STARK NEED TO--
(WE SHOULD HAVE TAKEN CARE OF THIS BEFORE JAPAN.)
JARVIS, CALL MARTHA IN MY NEW YORK OFFICE.
TELL HER TO SLAP TOGETHER A PRESS CONFERENCE FOR FOUR O'CLOCK. THAT WAY WE HIT THE SIX O'CLOCK NEWS.
ALL RIGHT, KIDS...
IT'S TIME FOR THE WORLD TO MEET THE NEW AVENGERS.
YEAH, THIS'LL GO WELL.
CAN'T WE JUST GO BACK TO BEING BEAT UP BY NINJAS?

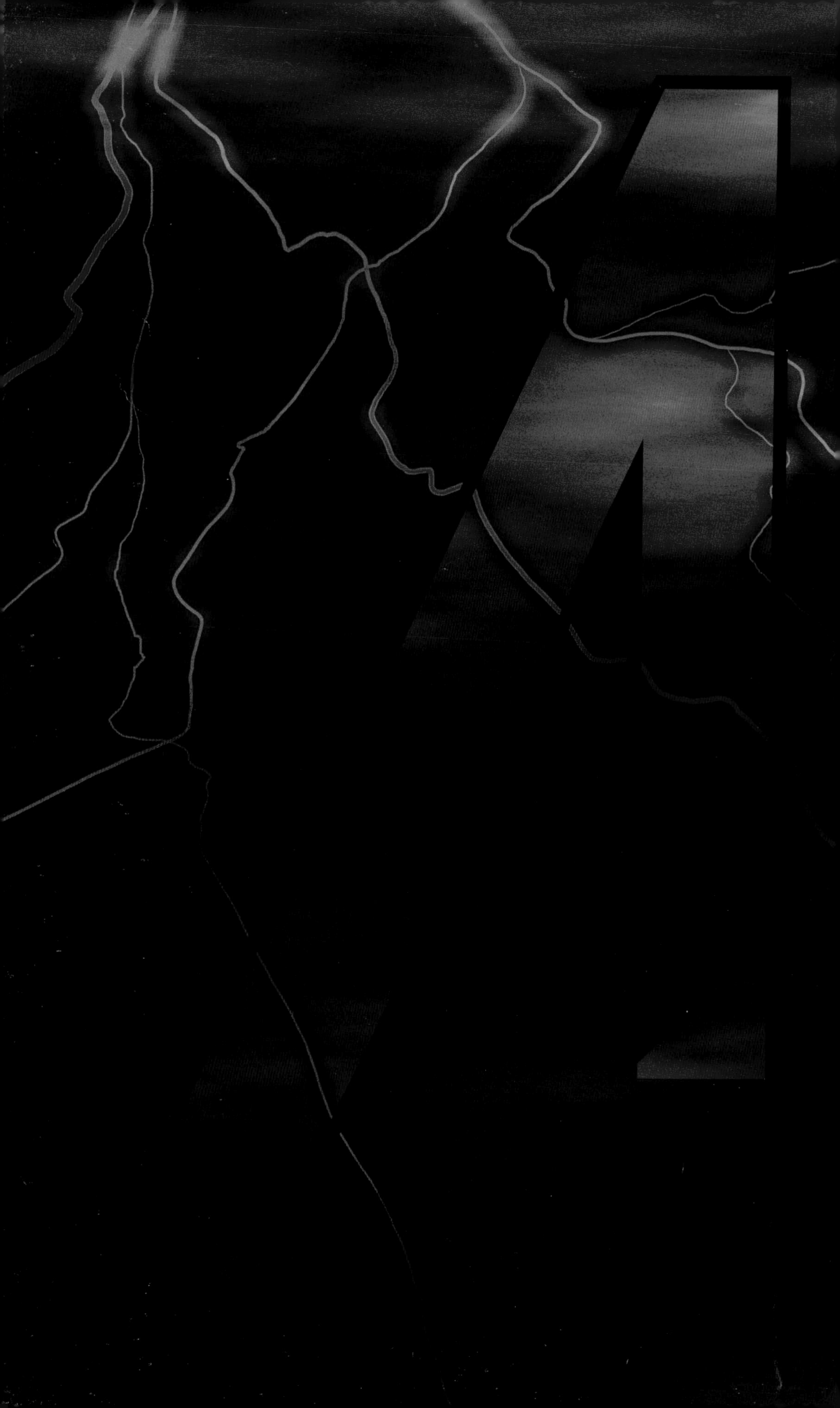

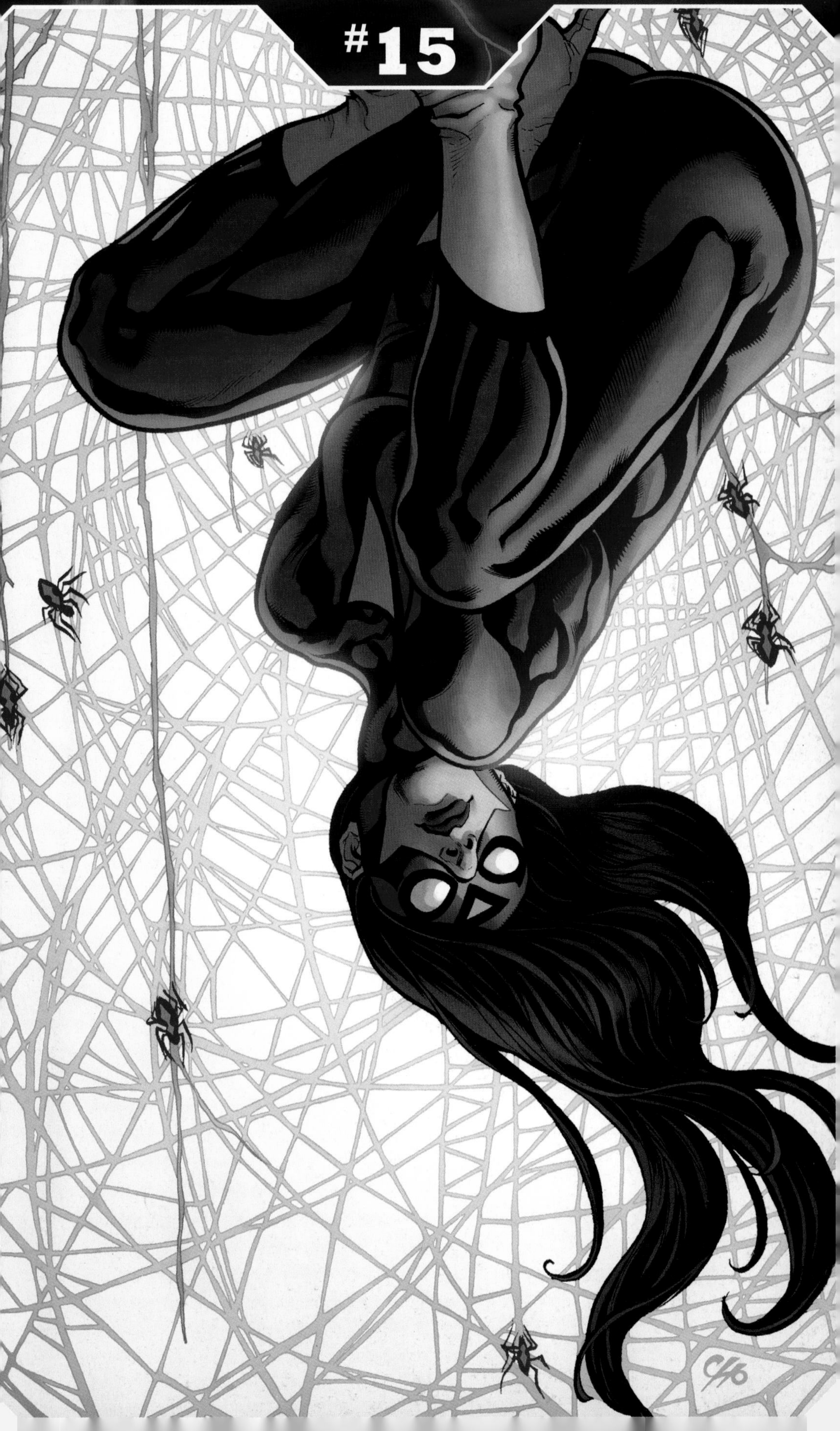
#15

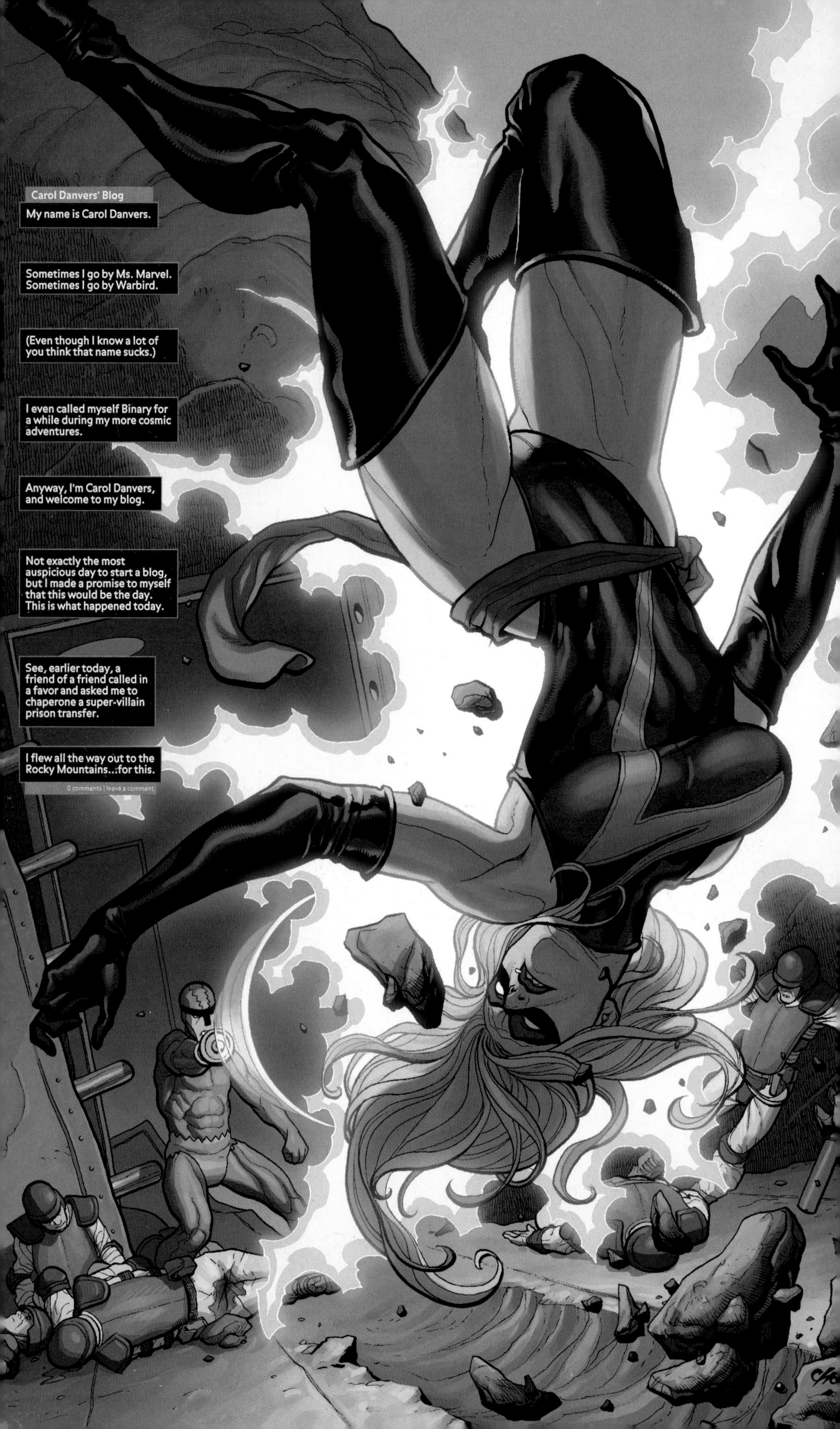
Carol Danvers' Blog
My name is Carol Danvers.
Sometimes I go by Ms. Marvel. Sometimes I go by Warbird.
(Even though I know a lot of you think that name sucks.)
I even called myself Binary for a while during my more cosmic adventures.
Anyway, I'm Carol Danvers, and welcome to my blog.
Not exactly the most auspicious day to start a blog, but I made a promise to myself that this would be the day. This is what happened today.
See, earlier today, a friend of a friend called in a favor and asked me to chaperone a super-villain prison transfer.
I flew all the way out to the Rocky Mountains...for this.
0 comments | leave a comment

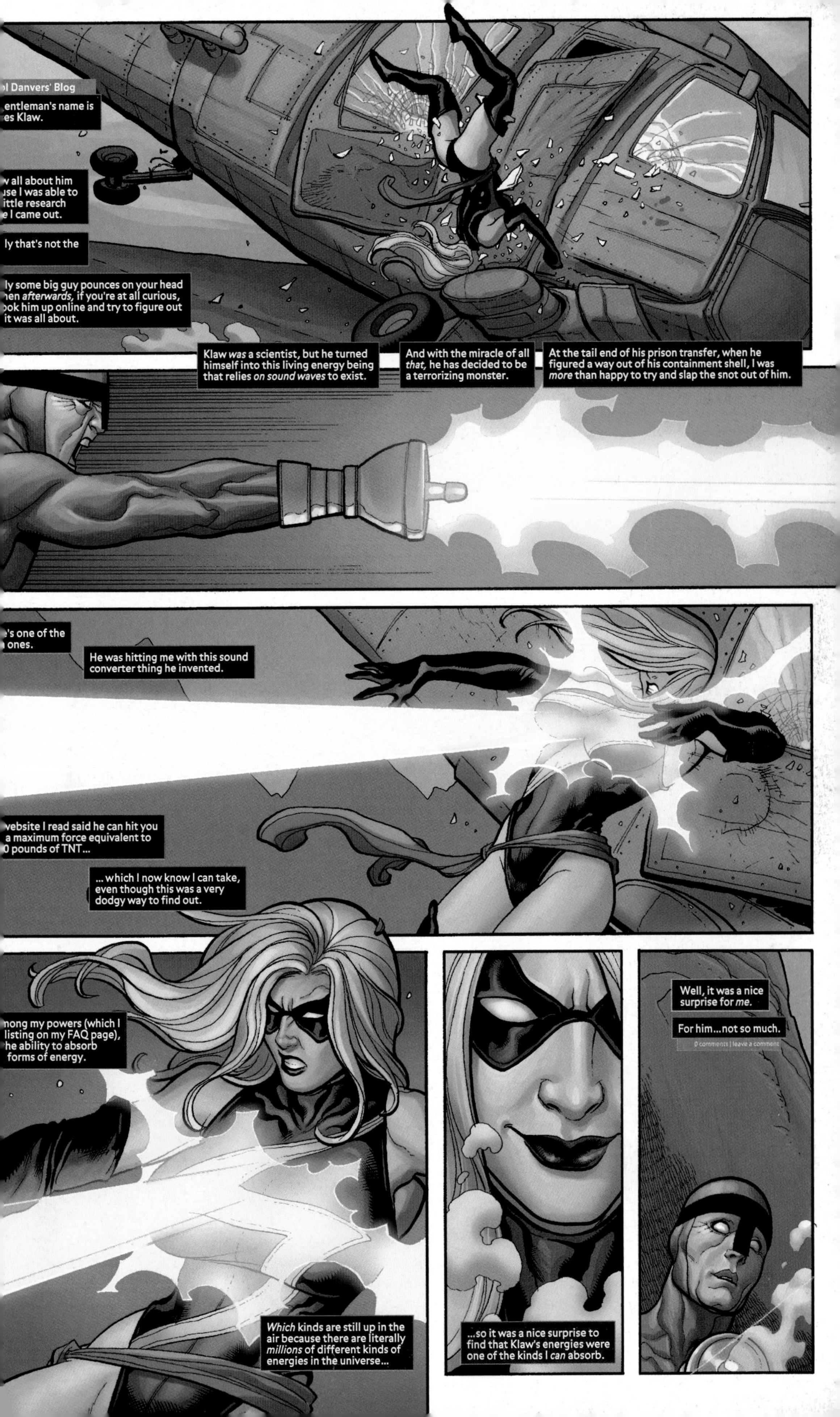

l Danvers' Blog
entleman's name is
es Klaw.
v all about him
use I was able to
ittle research
e I came out.
ly that's not the
ly some big guy pounces on your head
hen *afterwards,* if you're at all curious,
ook him up online and try to figure out
it was all about.
Klaw *was* a scientist, but he turned himself into this living energy being that relies *on sound waves* to exist.
And with the miracle of all *that,* he has decided to be a terrorizing monster.
At the tail end of his prison transfer, when he figured a way out of his containment shell, I was *more* than happy to try and slap the snot out of him.
's one of the
ones.
He was hitting me with this sound converter thing he invented.
website I read said he can hit you
a maximum force equivalent to
0 pounds of TNT...
...which I now know I can take, even though this was a very dodgy way to find out.
nong my powers (which I
listing on my FAQ page),
he ability to absorb
forms of energy.
Which kinds are still up in the air because there are literally *millions* of different kinds of energies in the universe...
...so it was a nice surprise to find that Klaw's energies were one of the kinds I *can* absorb.
Well, it was a nice surprise for *me.*
For him...not so much.
0 comments | leave a comment

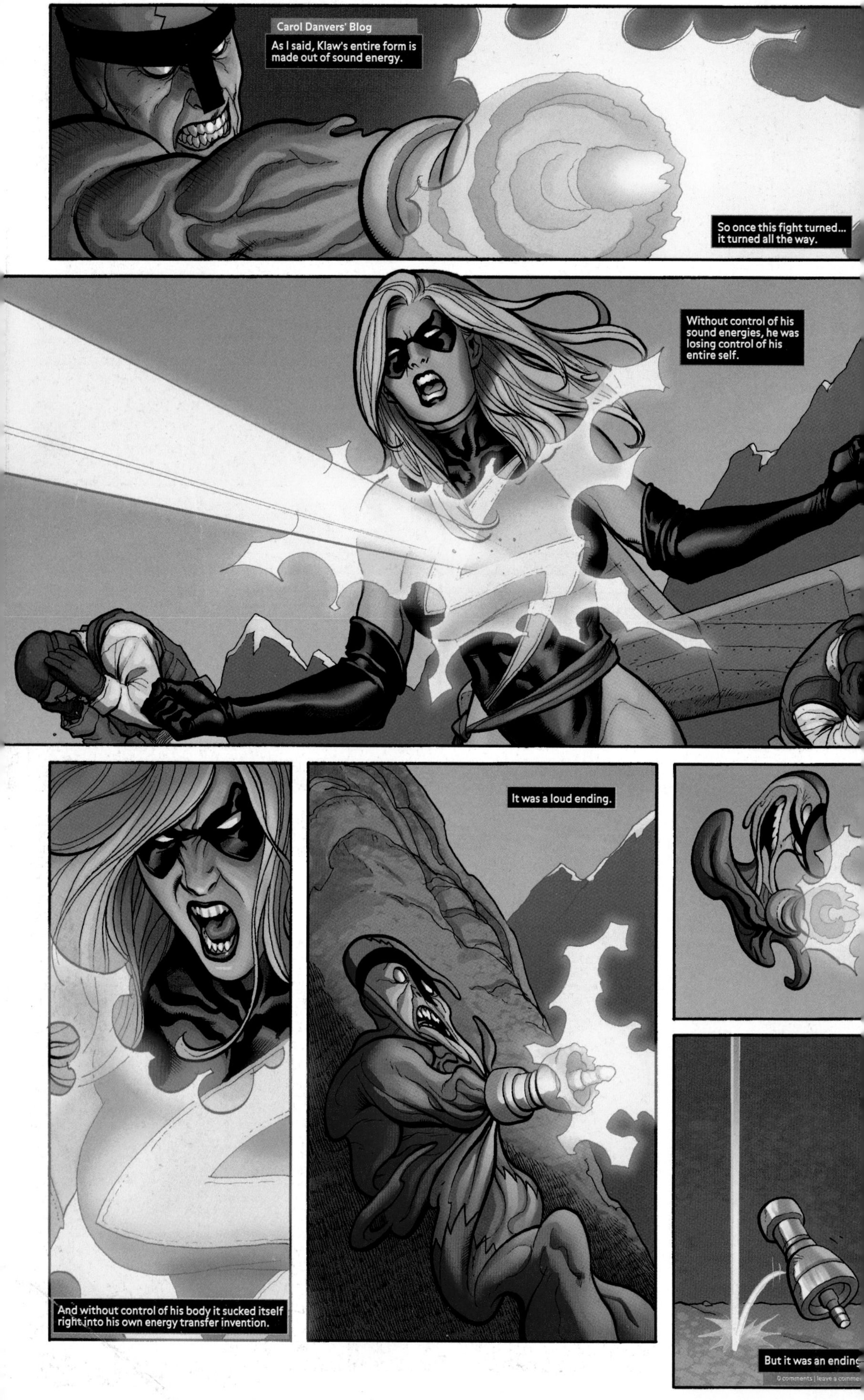
Carol Danvers' Blog
As I said, Klaw's entire form is made out of sound energy.
So once this fight turned... it turned all the way.
Without control of his sound energies, he was losing control of his entire self.
And without control of his body it sucked itself right into his own energy transfer invention.
It was a loud ending.
But it was an ending
0 comments | leave a comme

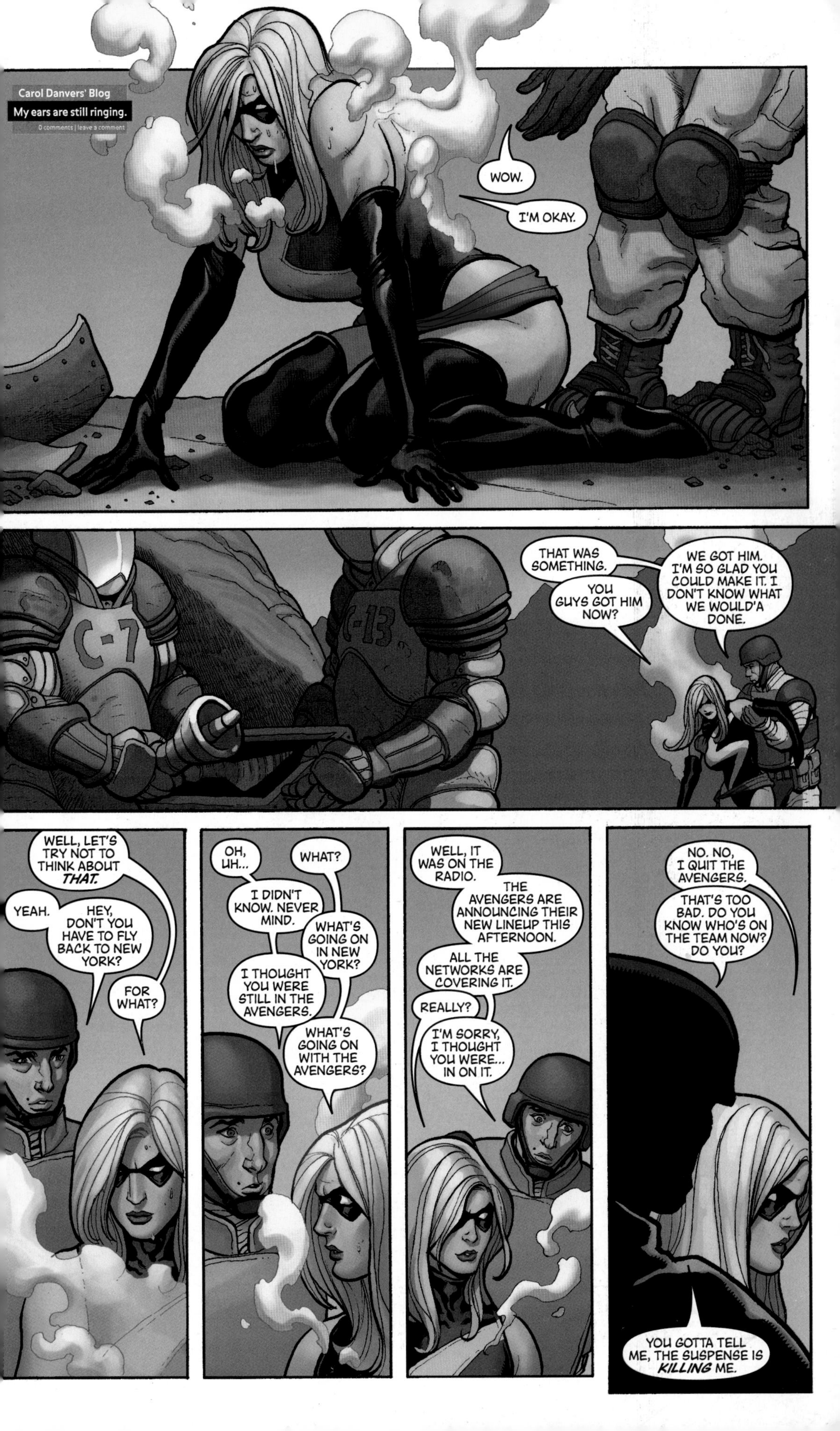

Carol Danvers' Blog
My ears are still ringing.
0 comments | leave a comment
WOW.
I'M OKAY.
THAT WAS SOMETHING.
YOU GUYS GOT HIM NOW?
WE GOT HIM. I'M SO GLAD YOU COULD MAKE IT. I DON'T KNOW WHAT WE WOULD'A DONE.
WELL, LET'S TRY NOT TO THINK ABOUT *THAT.*
YEAH.
HEY, DON'T YOU HAVE TO FLY BACK TO NEW YORK?
FOR WHAT?
OH, UH...
WHAT?
I DIDN'T KNOW. NEVER MIND.
WHAT'S GOING ON IN NEW YORK?
I THOUGHT YOU WERE STILL IN THE AVENGERS.
WHAT'S GOING ON WITH THE AVENGERS?
WELL, IT WAS ON THE RADIO.
THE AVENGERS ARE ANNOUNCING THEIR NEW LINEUP THIS AFTERNOON.
ALL THE NETWORKS ARE COVERING IT.
REALLY?
I'M SORRY, I THOUGHT YOU WERE... IN ON IT.
NO. NO, I QUIT THE AVENGERS.
THAT'S TOO BAD. DO YOU KNOW WHO'S ON THE TEAM NOW? DO YOU?
YOU GOTTA TELL ME, THE SUSPENSE IS *KILLING* ME.

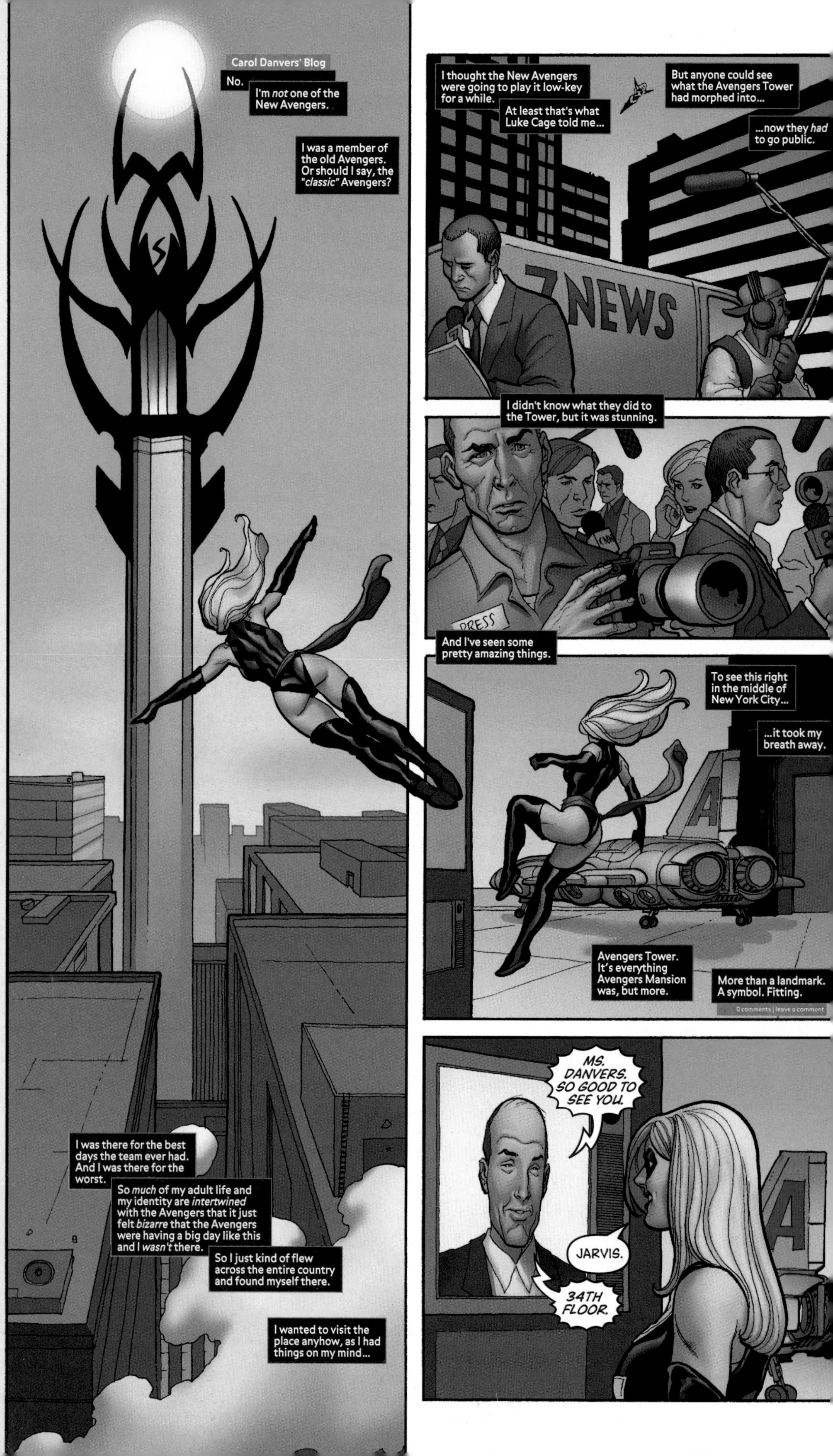

Carol Danvers' Blog
No.
I'm *not* one of the New Avengers.
I was a member of the old Avengers. Or should I say, the "*classic*" Avengers?
I was there for the best days the team ever had. And I was there for the worst.
So *much* of my adult life and my identity are *intertwined* with the Avengers that it just felt *bizarre* that the Avengers were having a big day like this and I *wasn't* there.
So I just kind of flew across the entire country and found myself there.
I wanted to visit the place anyhow, as I had things on my mind...
I thought the New Avengers were going to play it low-key for a while.
At least that's what Luke Cage told me...
But anyone could see what the Avengers Tower had morphed into...
...now they *had* to go public.
7NEWS
I didn't know what they did to the Tower, but it was stunning.
PRESS
And I've seen some pretty amazing things.
To see this right in the middle of New York City...
...it took my breath away.
Avengers Tower. It's everything Avengers Mansion was, but more.
More than a landmark. A symbol. Fitting.
0 comments | leave a comment
MS. DANVERS. SO GOOD TO SEE YOU.
JARVIS.
34TH FLOOR.

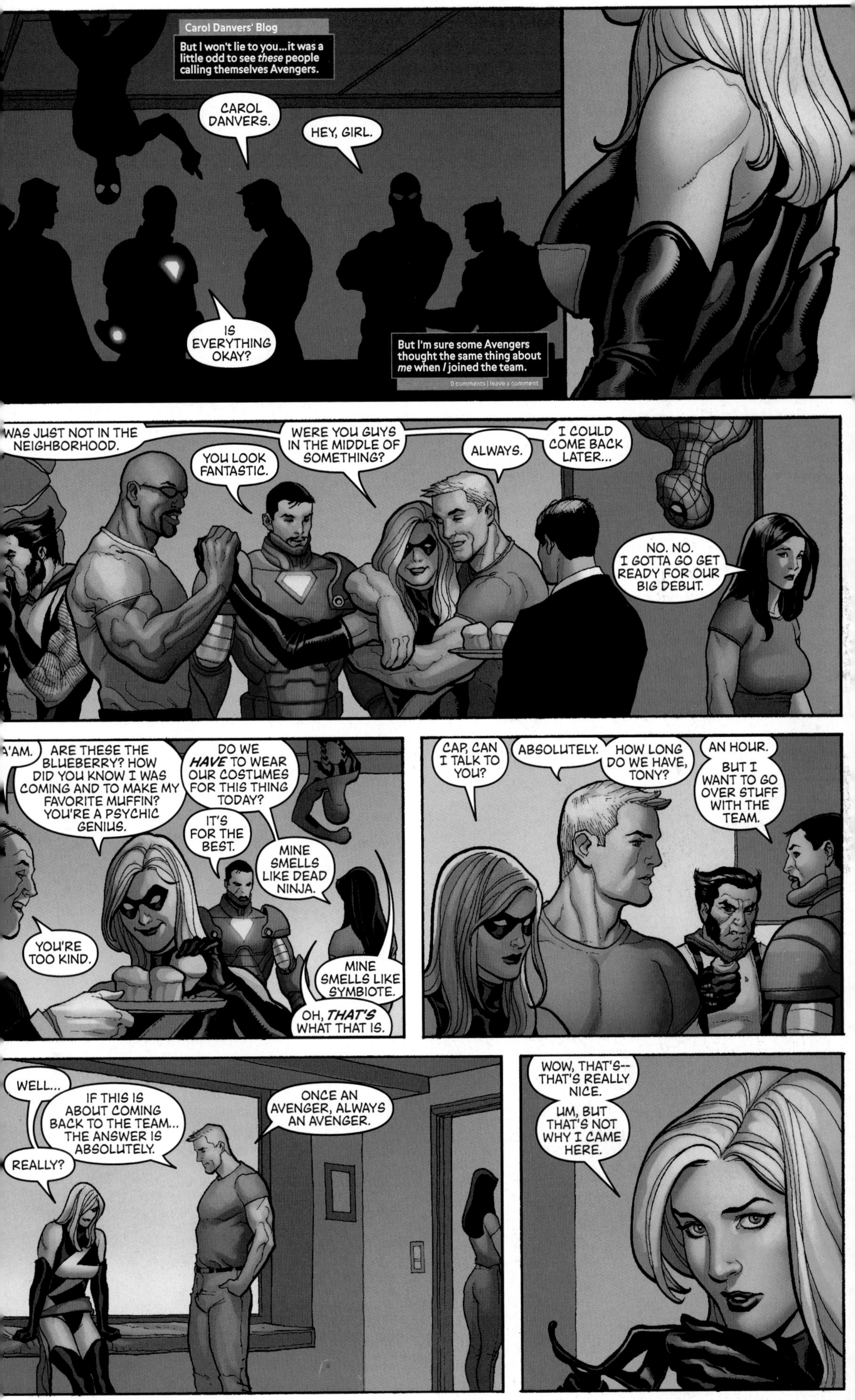
Carol Danvers' Blog
But I won't lie to you...it was a little odd to see *these* people calling themselves Avengers.
CAROL DANVERS.
HEY, GIRL.
IS EVERYTHING OKAY?
But I'm sure some Avengers thought the same thing about *me* when *I* joined the team.
0 comments | leave a comment
WAS JUST NOT IN THE NEIGHBORHOOD.
YOU LOOK FANTASTIC.
WERE YOU GUYS IN THE MIDDLE OF SOMETHING?
ALWAYS.
I COULD COME BACK LATER...
NO. NO. I GOTTA GO GET READY FOR OUR BIG DEBUT.
'AM.
ARE THESE THE BLUEBERRY? HOW DID YOU KNOW I WAS COMING AND TO MAKE MY FAVORITE MUFFIN? YOU'RE A PSYCHIC GENIUS.
YOU'RE TOO KIND.
DO WE *HAVE* TO WEAR OUR COSTUMES FOR THIS THING TODAY?
IT'S FOR THE BEST.
MINE SMELLS LIKE DEAD NINJA.
MINE SMELLS LIKE SYMBIOTE.
OH, *THAT'S* WHAT THAT IS.
CAP, CAN I TALK TO YOU?
ABSOLUTELY.
HOW LONG DO WE HAVE, TONY?
AN HOUR.
BUT I WANT TO GO OVER STUFF WITH THE TEAM.
WELL...
IF THIS IS ABOUT COMING BACK TO THE TEAM... THE ANSWER IS ABSOLUTELY.
REALLY?
ONCE AN AVENGER, ALWAYS AN AVENGER.
WOW, THAT'S-- THAT'S REALLY NICE.
UM, BUT THAT'S NOT WHY I CAME HERE.

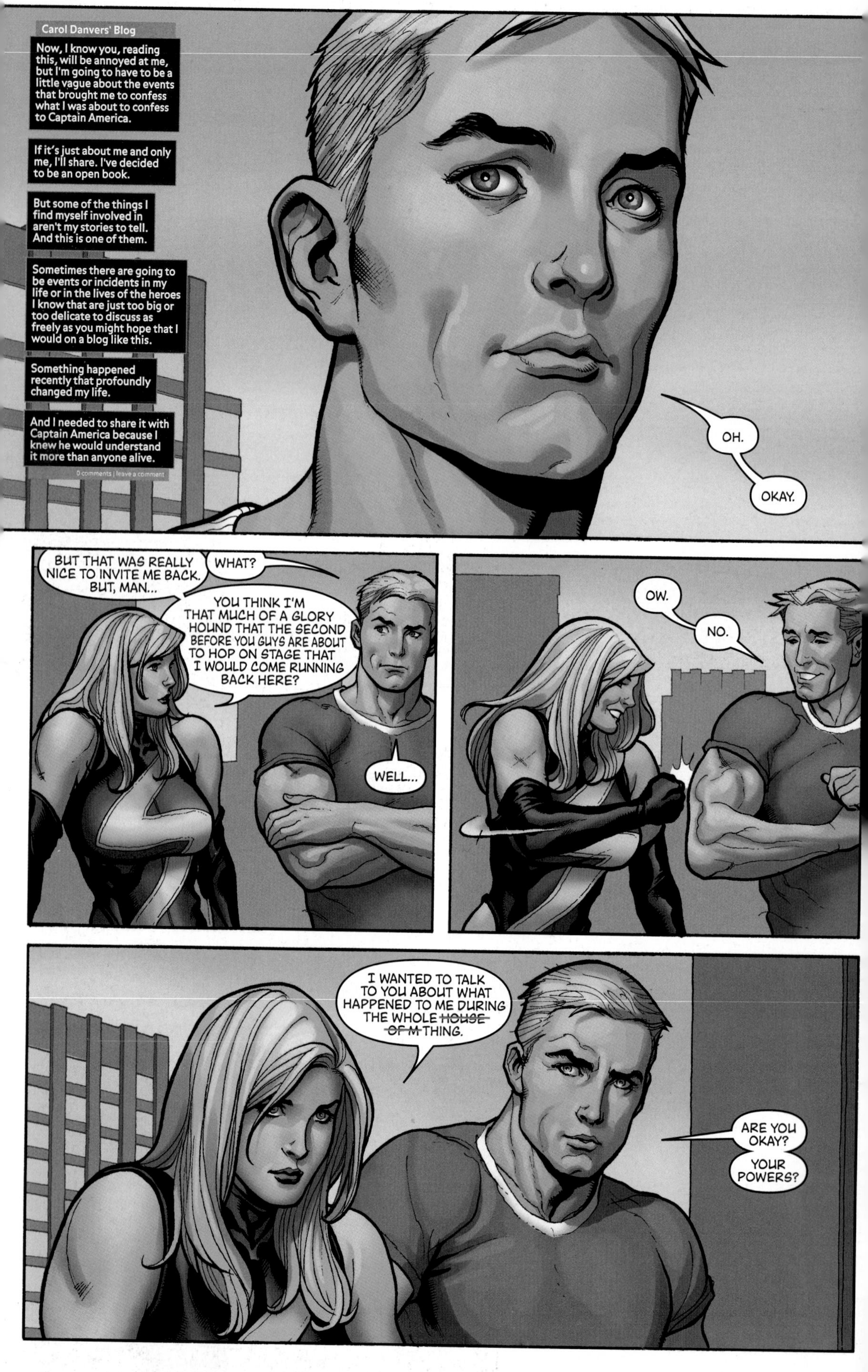
Carol Danvers' Blog
Now, I know you, reading this, will be annoyed at me, but I'm going to have to be a little vague about the events that brought me to confess what I was about to confess to Captain America.
If it's just about me and only me, I'll share. I've decided to be an open book.
But some of the things I find myself involved in aren't my stories to tell. And this is one of them.
Sometimes there are going to be events or incidents in my life or in the lives of the heroes I know that are just too big or too delicate to discuss as freely as you might hope that I would on a blog like this.
Something happened recently that profoundly changed my life.
And I needed to share it with Captain America because I knew he would understand it more than anyone alive.
0 comments | leave a comment
OH.
OKAY.
BUT THAT WAS REALLY NICE TO INVITE ME BACK. BUT, MAN...
WHAT?
YOU THINK I'M THAT MUCH OF A GLORY HOUND THAT THE SECOND BEFORE YOU GUYS ARE ABOUT TO HOP ON STAGE THAT I WOULD COME RUNNING BACK HERE?
WELL...
OW.
NO.
I WANTED TO TALK TO YOU ABOUT WHAT HAPPENED TO ME DURING THE WHOLE ~~HOUSE OF M~~ THING.
ARE YOU OKAY?
YOUR POWERS?

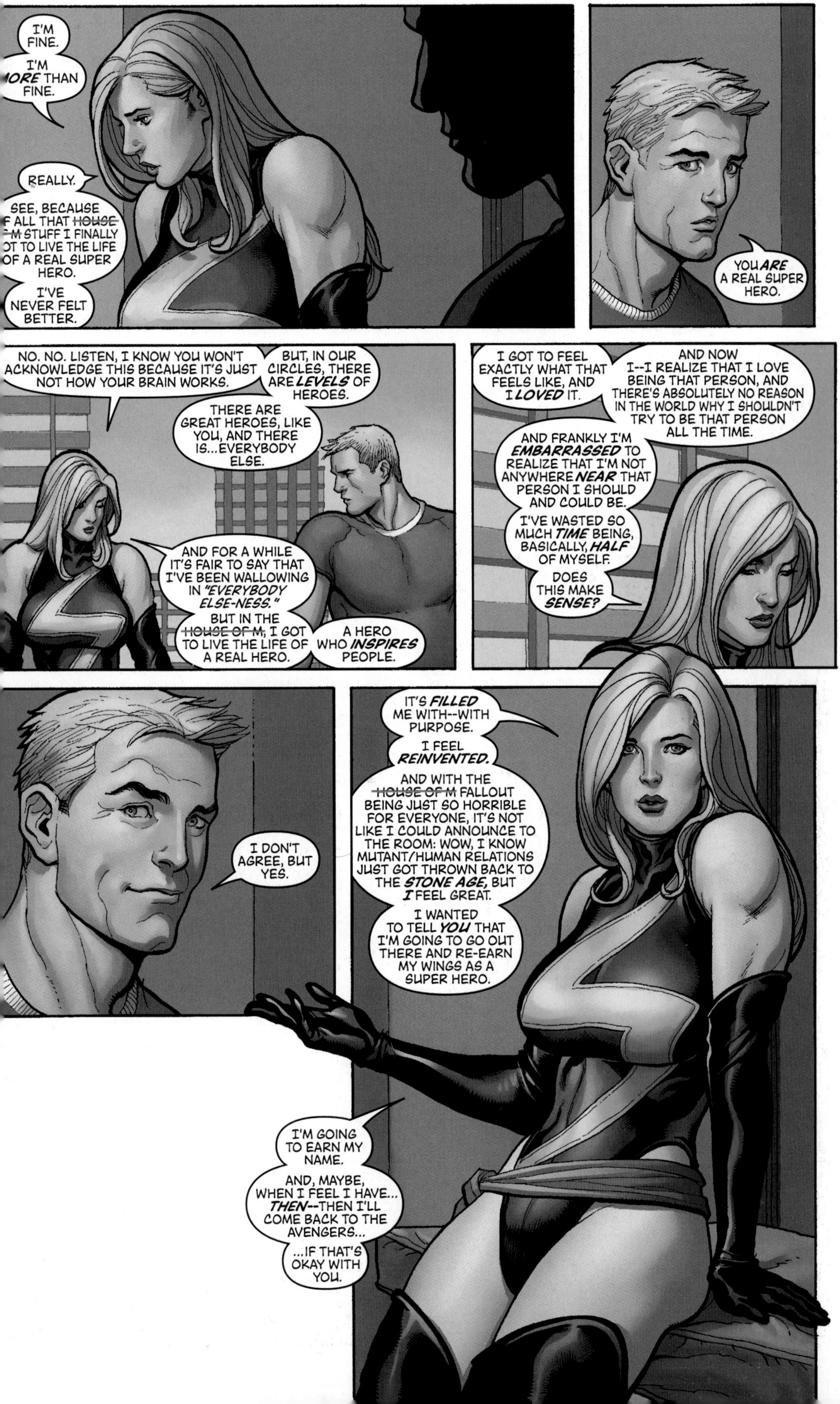

I'M FINE.
I'M ORE THAN FINE.
REALLY.
SEE, BECAUSE F ALL THAT HOUSE F M STUFF I FINALLY OT TO LIVE THE LIFE OF A REAL SUPER HERO.
I'VE NEVER FELT BETTER.
YOU ARE A REAL SUPER HERO.
NO. NO. LISTEN, I KNOW YOU WON'T ACKNOWLEDGE THIS BECAUSE IT'S JUST NOT HOW YOUR BRAIN WORKS.
BUT, IN OUR CIRCLES, THERE ARE LEVELS OF HEROES.
THERE ARE GREAT HEROES, LIKE YOU, AND THERE IS...EVERYBODY ELSE.
AND FOR A WHILE IT'S FAIR TO SAY THAT I'VE BEEN WALLOWING IN "EVERYBODY ELSE-NESS."
BUT IN THE HOUSE OF M, I GOT TO LIVE THE LIFE OF A REAL HERO.
A HERO WHO INSPIRES PEOPLE.
I GOT TO FEEL EXACTLY WHAT THAT FEELS LIKE, AND I LOVED IT.
AND NOW I--I REALIZE THAT I LOVE BEING THAT PERSON, AND THERE'S ABSOLUTELY NO REASON IN THE WORLD WHY I SHOULDN'T TRY TO BE THAT PERSON ALL THE TIME.
AND FRANKLY I'M EMBARRASSED TO REALIZE THAT I'M NOT ANYWHERE NEAR THAT PERSON I SHOULD AND COULD BE.
I'VE WASTED SO MUCH TIME BEING, BASICALLY, HALF OF MYSELF.
DOES THIS MAKE SENSE?
I DON'T AGREE, BUT YES.
IT'S FILLED ME WITH--WITH PURPOSE.
I FEEL REINVENTED.
AND WITH THE HOUSE OF M FALLOUT BEING JUST SO HORRIBLE FOR EVERYONE, IT'S NOT LIKE I COULD ANNOUNCE TO THE ROOM: WOW, I KNOW MUTANT/HUMAN RELATIONS JUST GOT THROWN BACK TO THE STONE AGE, BUT I FEEL GREAT.
I WANTED TO TELL YOU THAT I'M GOING TO GO OUT THERE AND RE-EARN MY WINGS AS A SUPER HERO.
I'M GOING TO EARN MY NAME.
AND, MAYBE, WHEN I FEEL I HAVE... THEN--THEN I'LL COME BACK TO THE AVENGERS...
...IF THAT'S OKAY WITH YOU.

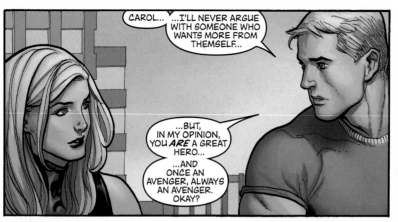

CAROL... ...I'LL NEVER ARGUE WITH SOMEONE WHO WANTS MORE FROM THEMSELF...

...BUT, IN MY OPINION, YOU *ARE* A GREAT HERO...

...AND ONCE AN AVENGER, ALWAYS AN AVENGER. OKAY?

OKAY.

AND YOU KNOW, IF YOU NEED ME FOR ANY--

YOU DON'T EVEN HAVE TO FINISH THE SENTENCE.

OKAY.

CAN I STAY AND HANG OUT FOR THE UNVEILING?

SURE.

COOL. THIS WAS ALWAYS MY *FAVORITE* DAY AS AN AVENGER.

UNVEILING THE NEW TEAM.

IT'S LIKE BEING BACK-STAGE AT A GREAT SHOW.

WELL... ...WE'LL SEE WHAT KIND OF SHOW IT IS.

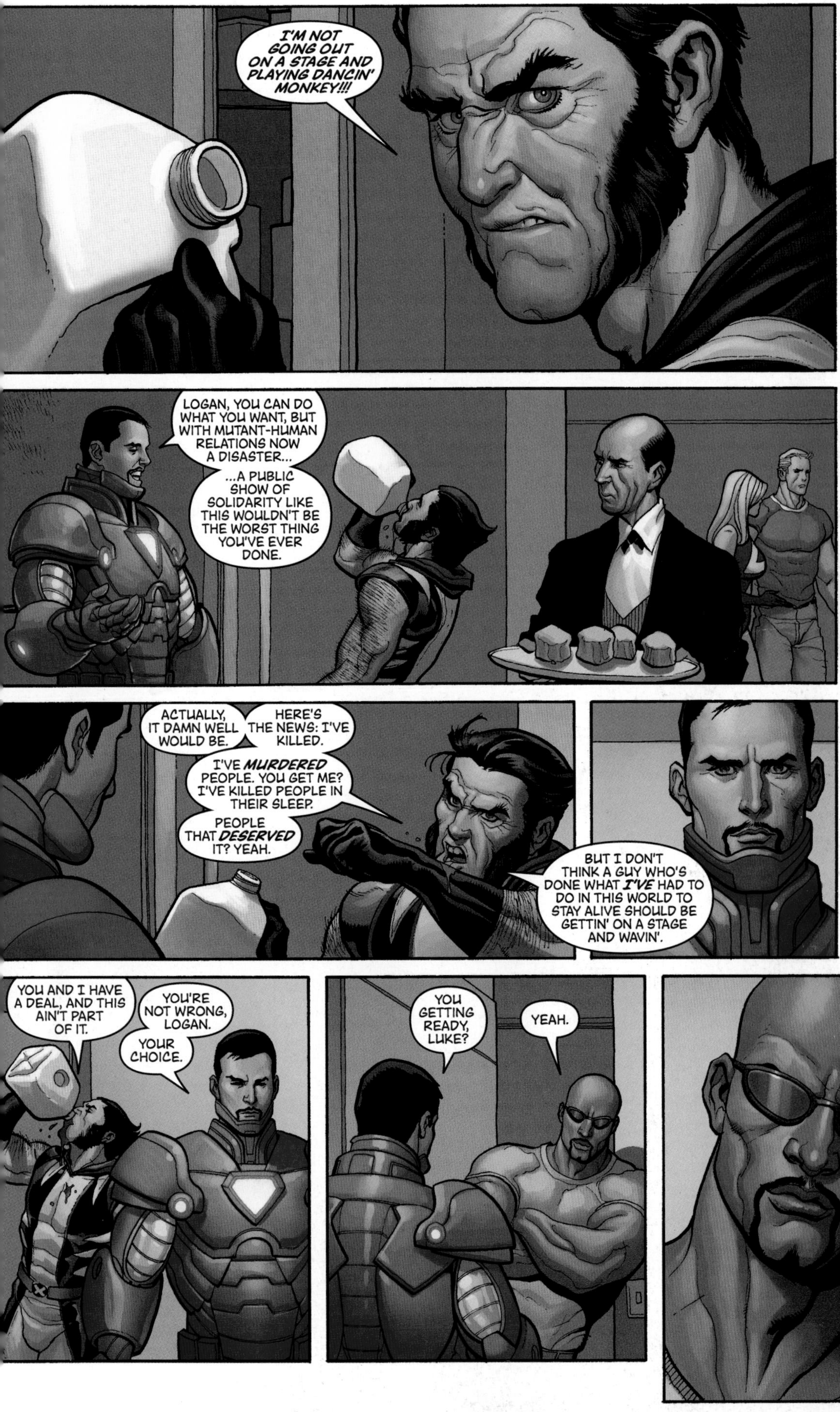
I'M NOT GOING OUT ON A STAGE AND PLAYING DANCIN' MONKEY!!!
LOGAN, YOU CAN DO WHAT YOU WANT, BUT WITH MUTANT-HUMAN RELATIONS NOW A DISASTER...
...A PUBLIC SHOW OF SOLIDARITY LIKE THIS WOULDN'T BE THE WORST THING YOU'VE EVER DONE.
ACTUALLY, IT DAMN WELL WOULD BE.
HERE'S THE NEWS: I'VE KILLED.
I'VE MURDERED PEOPLE. YOU GET ME? I'VE KILLED PEOPLE IN THEIR SLEEP.
PEOPLE THAT DESERVED IT? YEAH.
BUT I DON'T THINK A GUY WHO'S DONE WHAT I'VE HAD TO DO IN THIS WORLD TO STAY ALIVE SHOULD BE GETTIN' ON A STAGE AND WAVIN'.
YOU AND I HAVE A DEAL, AND THIS AIN'T PART OF IT.
YOU'RE NOT WRONG, LOGAN.
YOUR CHOICE.
YOU GETTING READY, LUKE?
YEAH.

OKAY, AVENGERS... THIS IS THE TOUGHEST AND, IN A LOT OF WAYS, THE MOST FUN PART OF THE JOB.
YOU'RE ABOUT TO BECOME MOVIE STARS, ROCK STARS, AND REALITY-SHOW STARS ALL WRAPPED UP IN ONE.
YOU'RE NOT HEROES ANYMORE, YOU'RE ICONS.
AND THIS IS WHERE I BECOME A HUGE LIABILITY TO THE TEAM.
SERIOUSLY, I, UH, I DON'T GET GOOD PRESS. AT ALL.
WE'VE ALL GOTTEN OUR FAIR SHARE OF BAD PRESS.
UH... NOT LIKE ME.
COME ON, YOU'VE SEEN THE DAILY BUGLE HEADLINES.
SPIDER-MAN: MENACE.
SPIDER-MAN: MURDERER.
EVERY DAY SINCE I WAS A JUNIOR IN HIGH SCHOOL.
GREEN DAY MADE A SONG OUT OF IT.
IT'S NOT A BAD SONG.
OKAY--WELL, PETE, THIS ISN'T WHERE YOU BECOME A LIABILITY TO US, THIS IS WHERE WE BECOME A--A WHAT'S THE OPPOSITE OF LIABILITY?
GOOD THING?
A GOOD THING FOR YOU.
THIS IS WHERE YOU'RE GOING TO SEE HOW THE MACHINE WORKS FOR YOU.
HOW SO?
GO PUT YOUR MASK ON AND HIDE YOUR WIFE AND AUNT.
HE'LL BE HERE IN 27 MINUTES.
HE WHO?

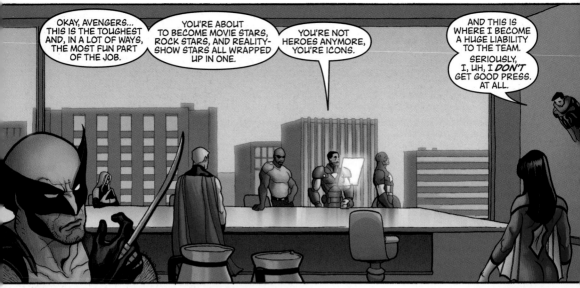

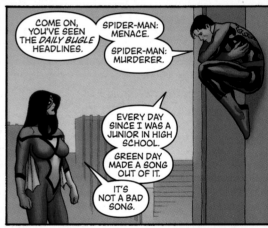

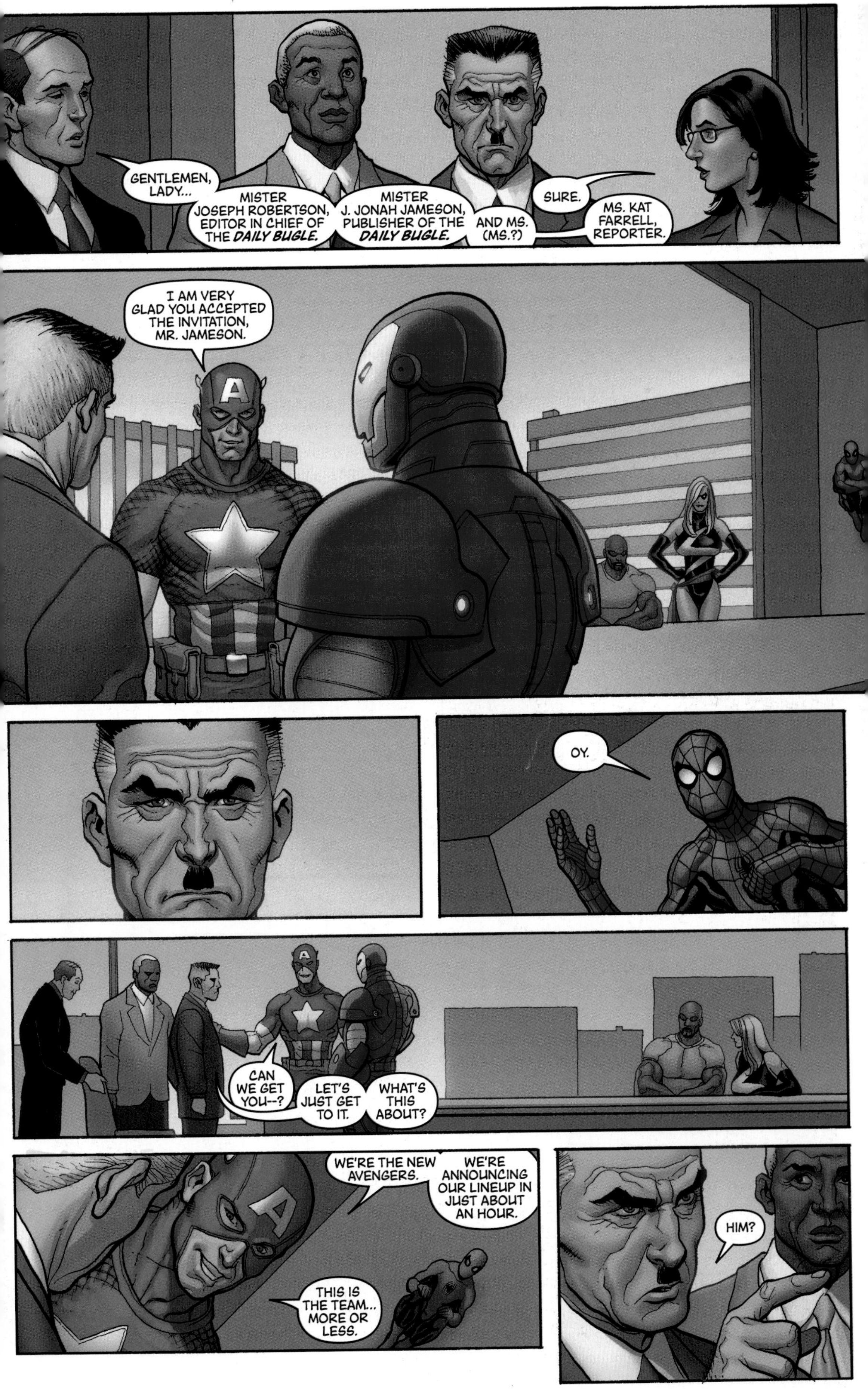

GENTLEMEN, LADY...
MISTER JOSEPH ROBERTSON, EDITOR IN CHIEF OF THE *DAILY BUGLE.*
MISTER J. JONAH JAMESON, PUBLISHER OF THE *DAILY BUGLE.*
AND MS. (MS.?)
SURE.
MS. KAT FARRELL, REPORTER.
I AM VERY GLAD YOU ACCEPTED THE INVITATION, MR. JAMESON.
OY.
CAN WE GET YOU--?
LET'S JUST GET TO IT.
WHAT'S THIS ABOUT?
WE'RE THE NEW AVENGERS.
WE'RE ANNOUNCING OUR LINEUP IN JUST ABOUT AN HOUR.
THIS IS THE TEAM... MORE OR LESS.
HIM?

YES. AND WE KNOW YOU AND HE HAVE A HISTORY.

I KNOW YOU HAVE YOUR OPINIONS ABOUT HIM, BUT I WANTED TO TELL YOU, FROM *ME*, THAT THE MAN IN THAT UNIFORM IS A TRUE AMERICAN HERO.

THIS IS A FACT. I'VE SEEN HIM IN ACTION WITH MY OWN EYES.

HE'S BEEN THROUGH MORE THAN ALL OF US PUT TOGETHER, AND STILL HE PERSEVERES.

I REPORT THE *NEWS*.

AND YOU EDITORIALIZE.

AND THAT'S YOUR RIGHT.

IT'S YOUR PAPER AND IT'S YOUR POINT OF VIEW.

AND YOU HAVE TO FILL THOSE PAGES.

DAILY BUGLE
NEW YORK'S FINEST DAILY NEWSPAPER
SPIDER-MAN: MURDERER

DAILY BUGLE
NEW YORK'S FINEST DAILY NEWSPAPER
SPIDER-MAN: MENACE

DAILY BUGLE
NEW YORK'S FINEST DAILY NEWSPAPER
SPIDER-MAN CLONE IS A MENACE

DAILY BUGLE
WEBBED WOND TERRORIZES CI

EXCLUSIVE COVERAGE.

EXCLUSIVE ACCESS.

IF I LAY OFF HIM....

SAY YES OR I QUIT.

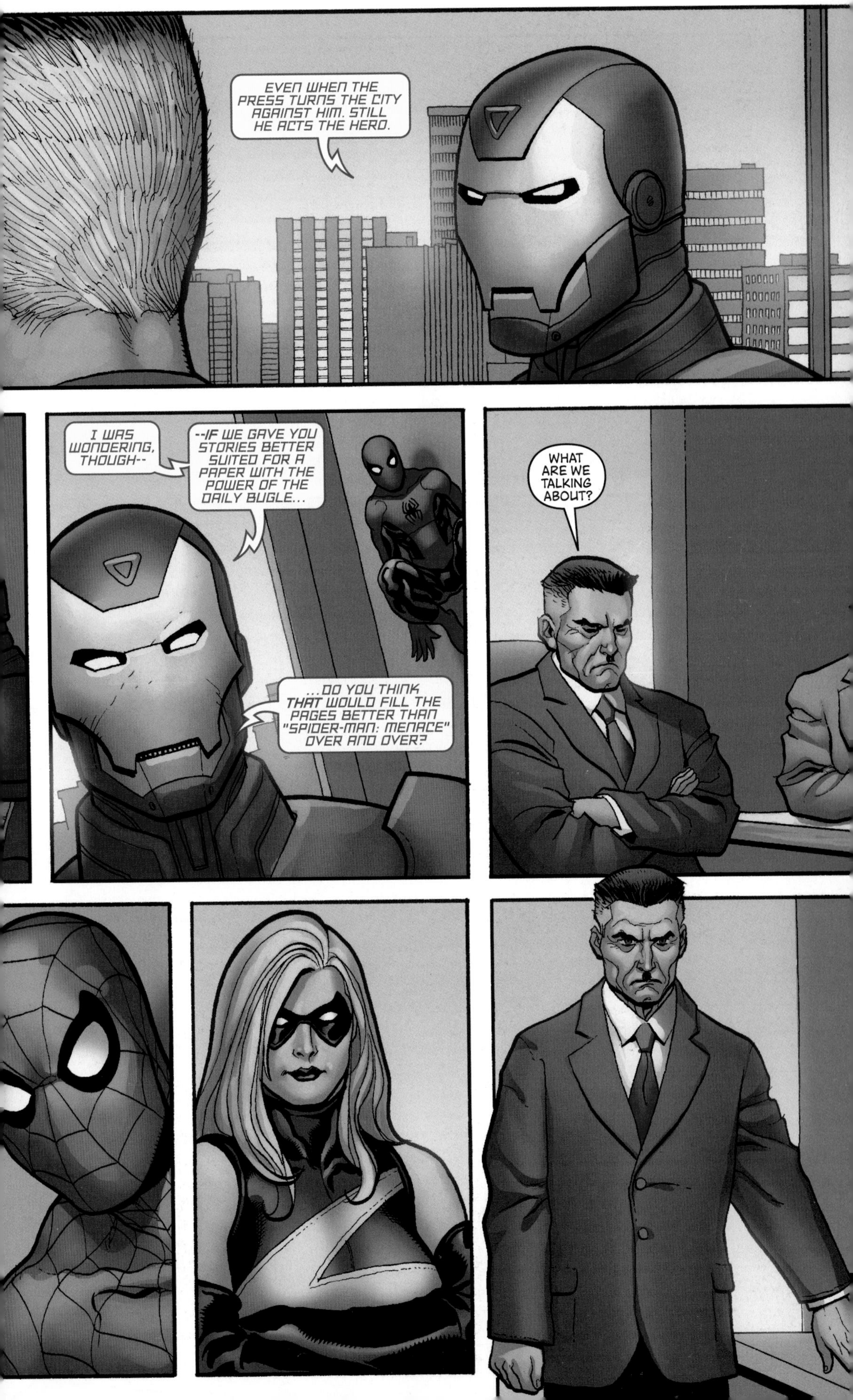
EVEN WHEN THE PRESS TURNS THE CITY AGAINST HIM. STILL HE ACTS THE HERO.
I WAS WONDERING, THOUGH--
--IF WE GAVE YOU STORIES BETTER SUITED FOR A PAPER WITH THE POWER OF THE DAILY BUGLE...
...DO YOU THINK THAT WOULD FILL THE PAGES BETTER THAN "SPIDER-MAN: MENACE" OVER AND OVER?
WHAT ARE WE TALKING ABOUT?

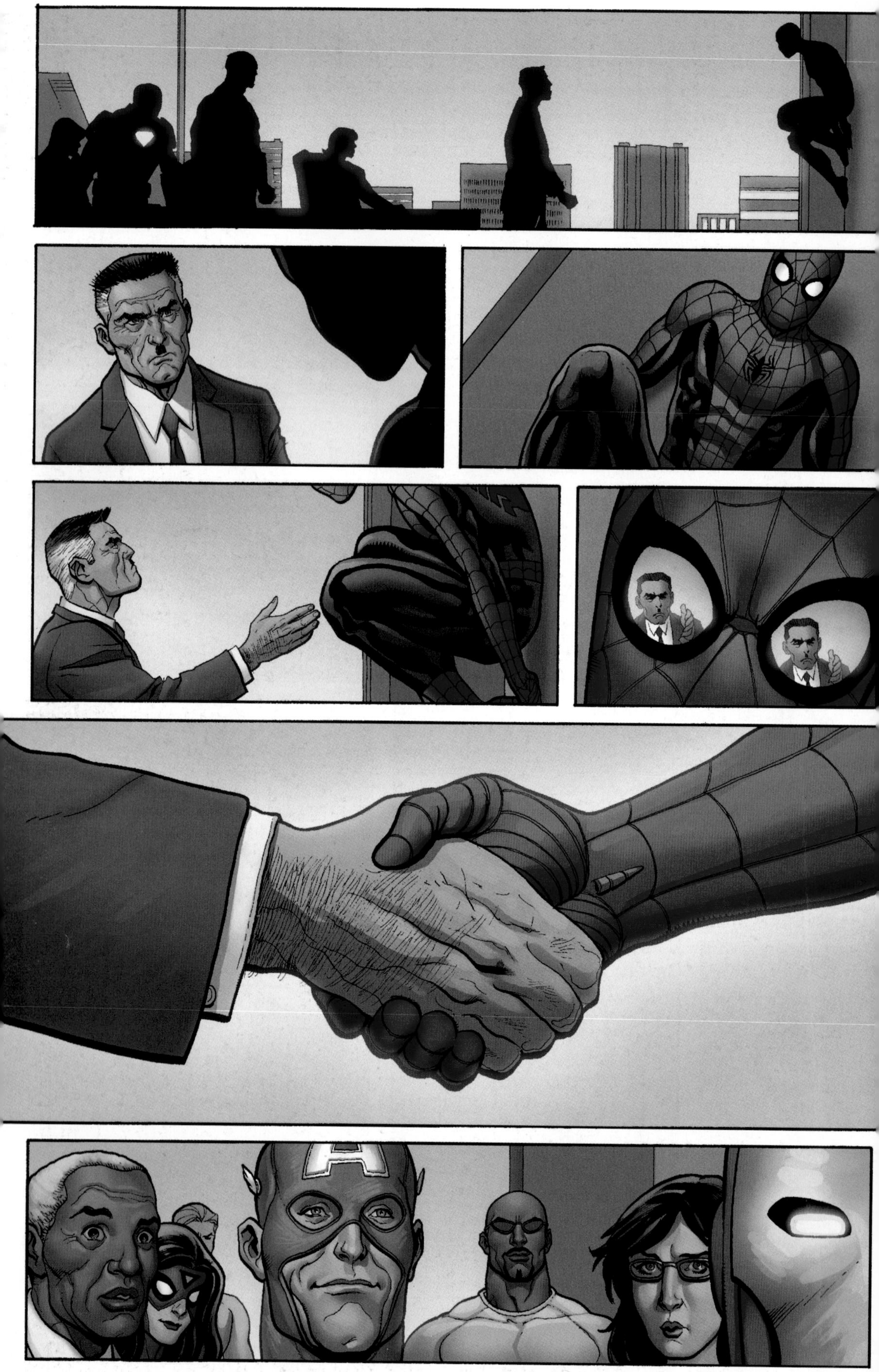

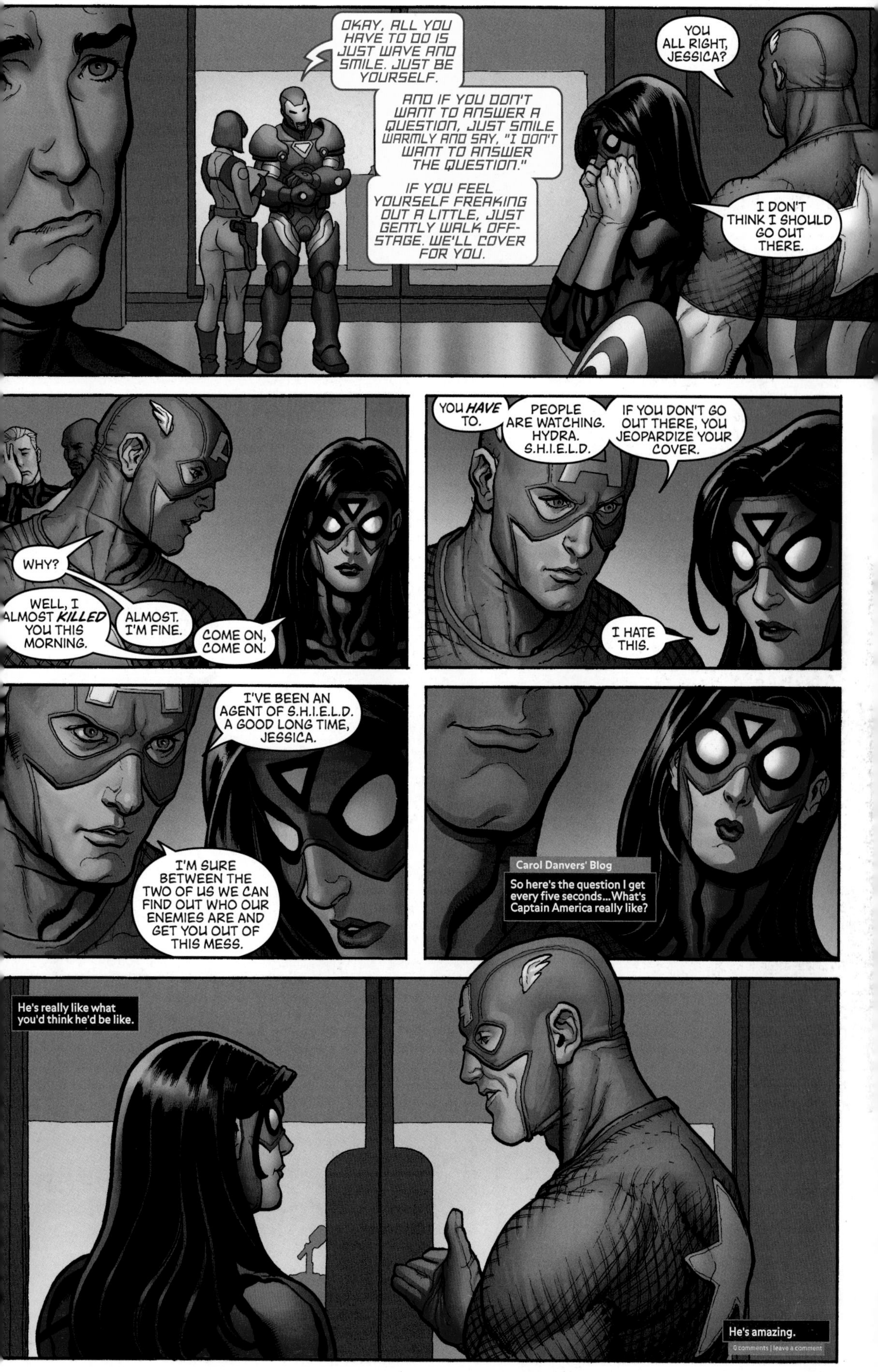
OKAY, ALL YOU HAVE TO DO IS JUST WAVE AND SMILE. JUST BE YOURSELF.
AND IF YOU DON'T WANT TO ANSWER A QUESTION, JUST SMILE WARMLY AND SAY, "I DON'T WANT TO ANSWER THE QUESTION."
IF YOU FEEL YOURSELF FREAKING OUT A LITTLE, JUST GENTLY WALK OFF-STAGE. WE'LL COVER FOR YOU.
YOU ALL RIGHT, JESSICA?
I DON'T THINK I SHOULD GO OUT THERE.
WHY?
WELL, I ALMOST KILLED YOU THIS MORNING.
ALMOST. I'M FINE.
COME ON, COME ON.
YOU HAVE TO.
PEOPLE ARE WATCHING. HYDRA. S.H.I.E.L.D.
IF YOU DON'T GO OUT THERE, YOU JEOPARDIZE YOUR COVER.
I HATE THIS.
I'VE BEEN AN AGENT OF S.H.I.E.L.D. A GOOD LONG TIME, JESSICA.
I'M SURE BETWEEN THE TWO OF US WE CAN FIND OUT WHO OUR ENEMIES ARE AND GET YOU OUT OF THIS MESS.
Carol Danvers' Blog
So here's the question I get every five seconds... What's Captain America really like?
He's really like what you'd think he'd be like.
He's amazing.
0 comments | leave a comment

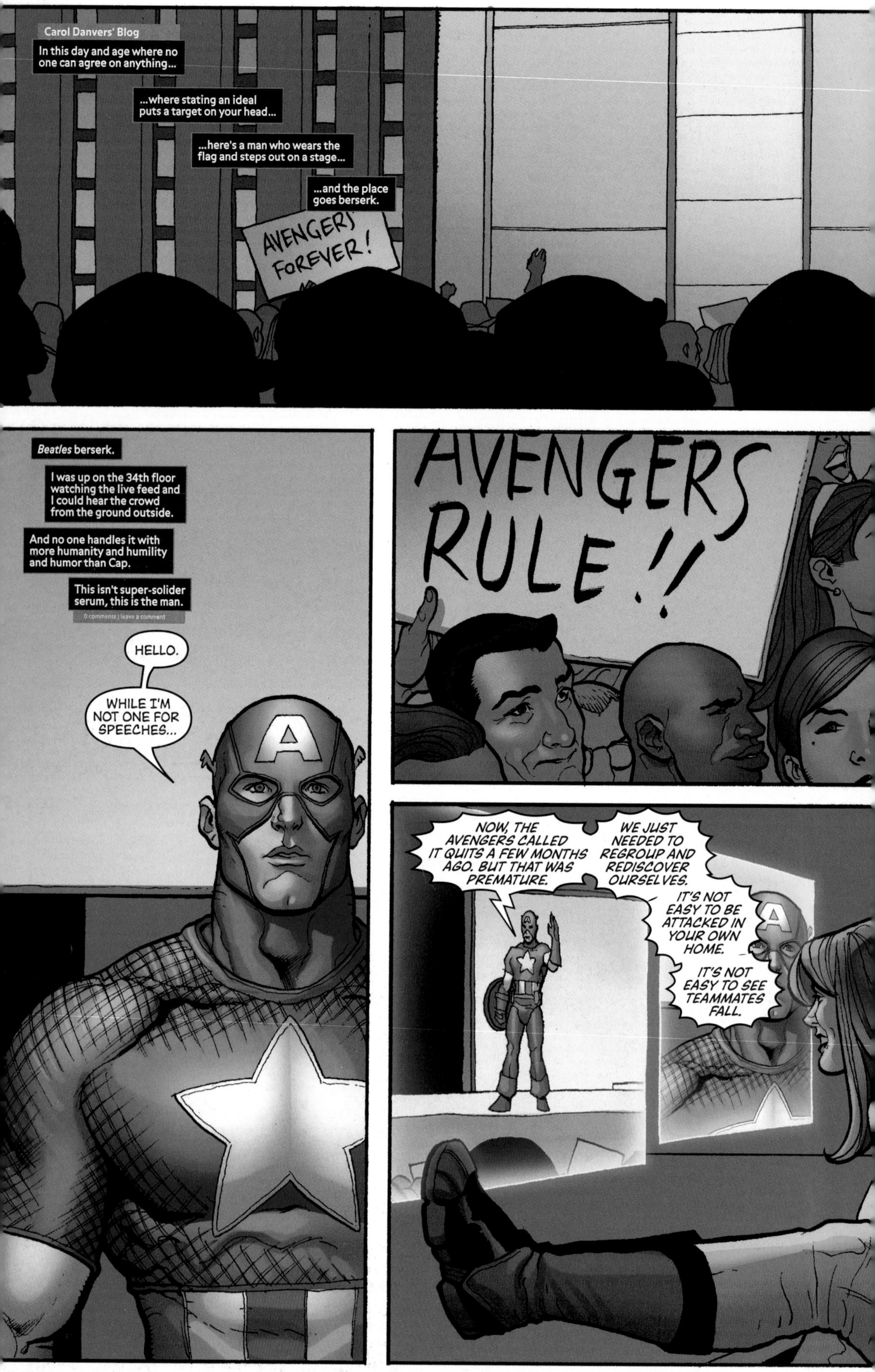

Carol Danvers' Blog
In this day and age where no one can agree on anything...
...where stating an ideal puts a target on your head...
...here's a man who wears the flag and steps out on a stage...
...and the place goes berserk.
AVENGERS FOREVER!
Beatles berserk.
I was up on the 34th floor watching the live feed and I could hear the crowd from the ground outside.
And no one handles it with more humanity and humility and humor than Cap.
This isn't super-solider serum, this is the man.
0 comments | leave a comment
HELLO.
WHILE I'M NOT ONE FOR SPEECHES...
AVENGERS RULE!!
NOW, THE AVENGERS CALLED IT QUITS A FEW MONTHS AGO. BUT THAT WAS PREMATURE.
WE JUST NEEDED TO REGROUP AND REDISCOVER OURSELVES.
IT'S NOT EASY TO BE ATTACKED IN YOUR OWN HOME.
IT'S NOT EASY TO SEE TEAMMATES FALL.

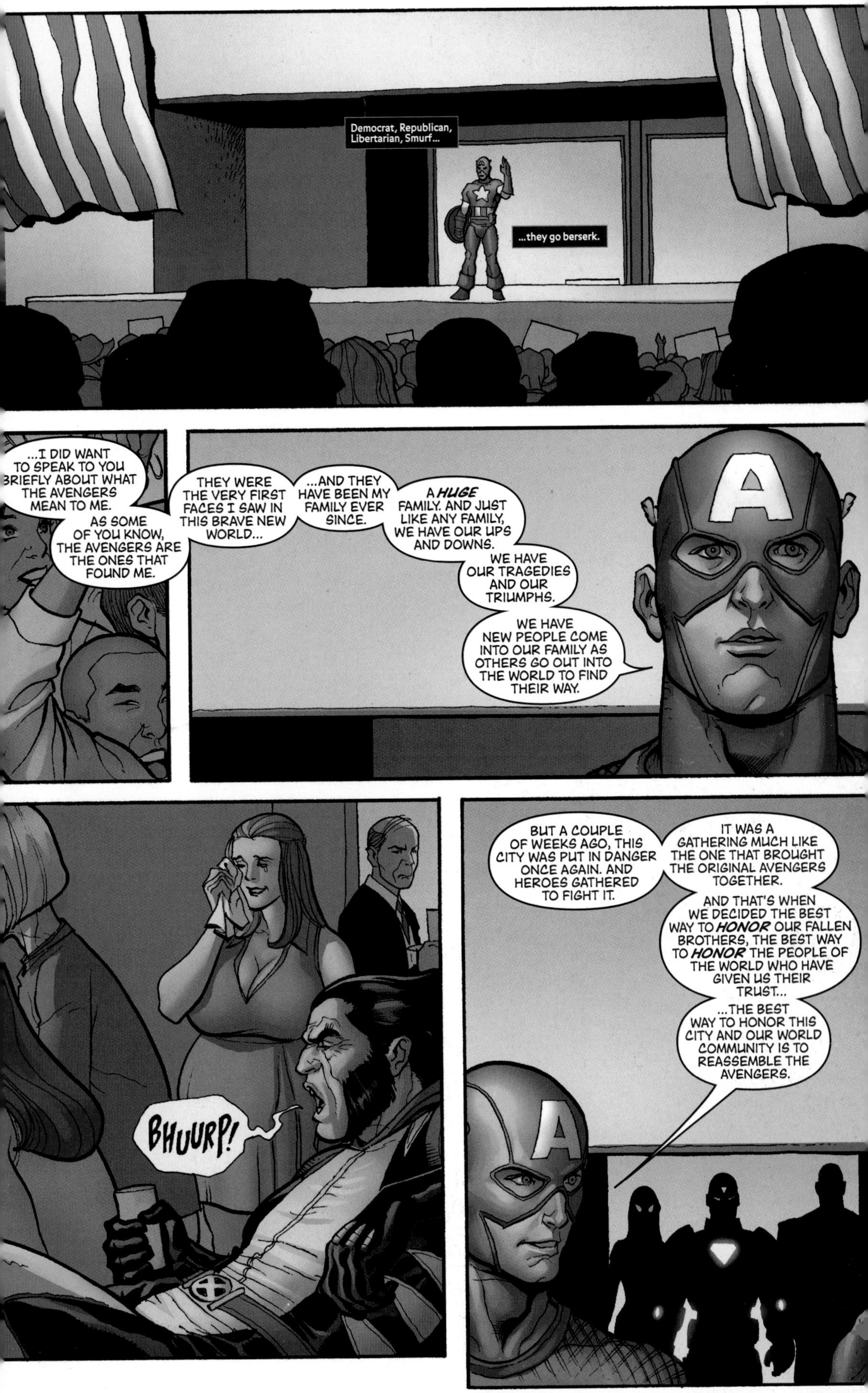
Democrat, Republican, Libertarian, Smurf...
...they go berserk.
...I DID WANT TO SPEAK TO YOU BRIEFLY ABOUT WHAT THE AVENGERS MEAN TO ME.
AS SOME OF YOU KNOW, THE AVENGERS ARE THE ONES THAT FOUND ME.
THEY WERE THE VERY FIRST FACES I SAW IN THIS BRAVE NEW WORLD...
...AND THEY HAVE BEEN MY FAMILY EVER SINCE.
A *HUGE* FAMILY. AND JUST LIKE ANY FAMILY, WE HAVE OUR UPS AND DOWNS.
WE HAVE OUR TRAGEDIES AND OUR TRIUMPHS.
WE HAVE NEW PEOPLE COME INTO OUR FAMILY AS OTHERS GO OUT INTO THE WORLD TO FIND THEIR WAY.
BHUURP!
BUT A COUPLE OF WEEKS AGO, THIS CITY WAS PUT IN DANGER ONCE AGAIN. AND HEROES GATHERED TO FIGHT IT.
IT WAS A GATHERING MUCH LIKE THE ONE THAT BROUGHT THE ORIGINAL AVENGERS TOGETHER.
AND THAT'S WHEN WE DECIDED THE BEST WAY TO *HONOR* OUR FALLEN BROTHERS, THE BEST WAY TO *HONOR* THE PEOPLE OF THE WORLD WHO HAVE GIVEN US THEIR TRUST...
...THE BEST WAY TO HONOR THIS CITY AND OUR WORLD COMMUNITY IS TO REASSEMBLE THE AVENGERS.

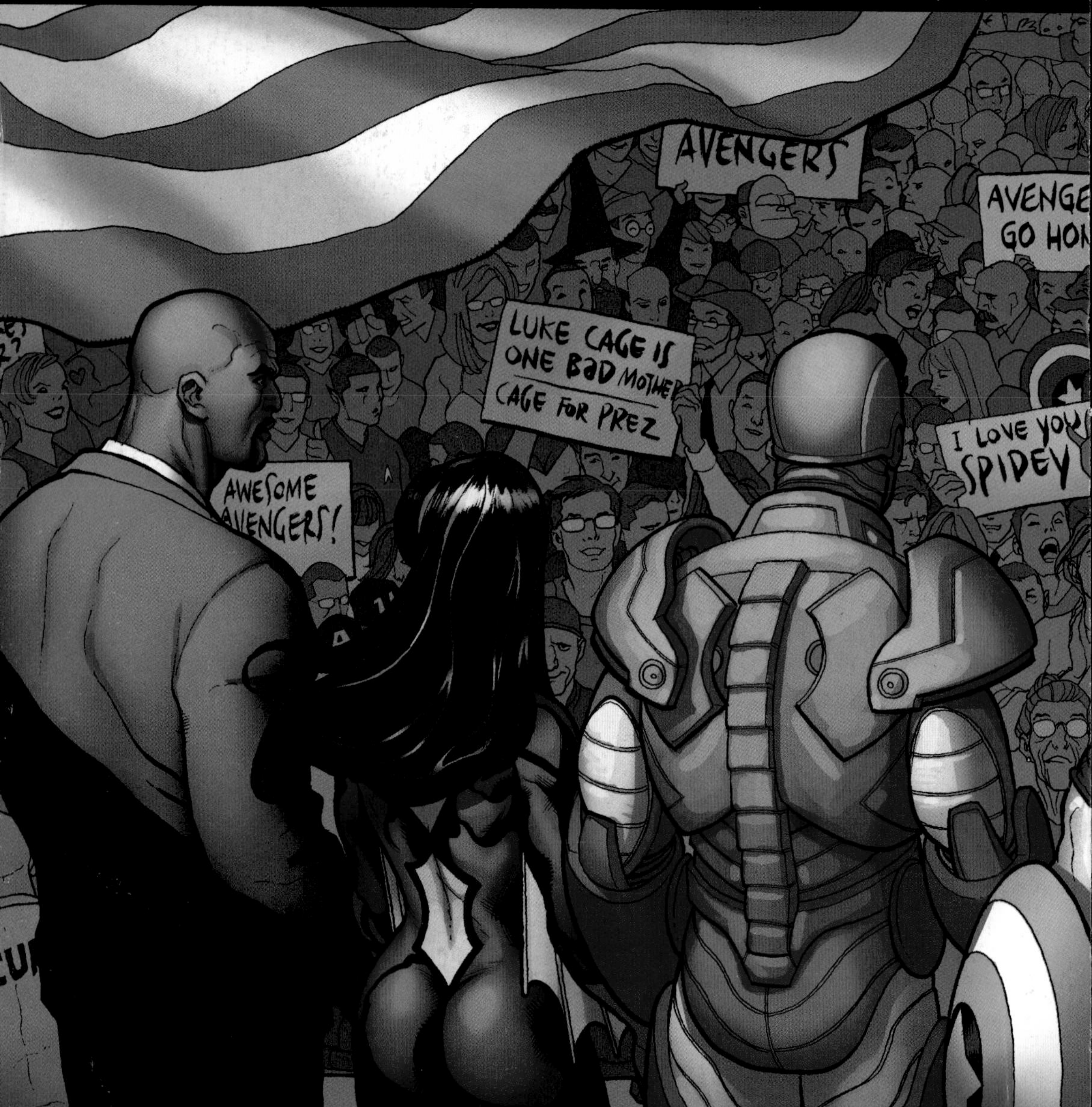
AVENGERS
LUKE CAGE IS ONE BAD MOTHER
CAGE FOR PREZ
AWESOME AVENGERS!
I LOVE YOU
SPIDEY

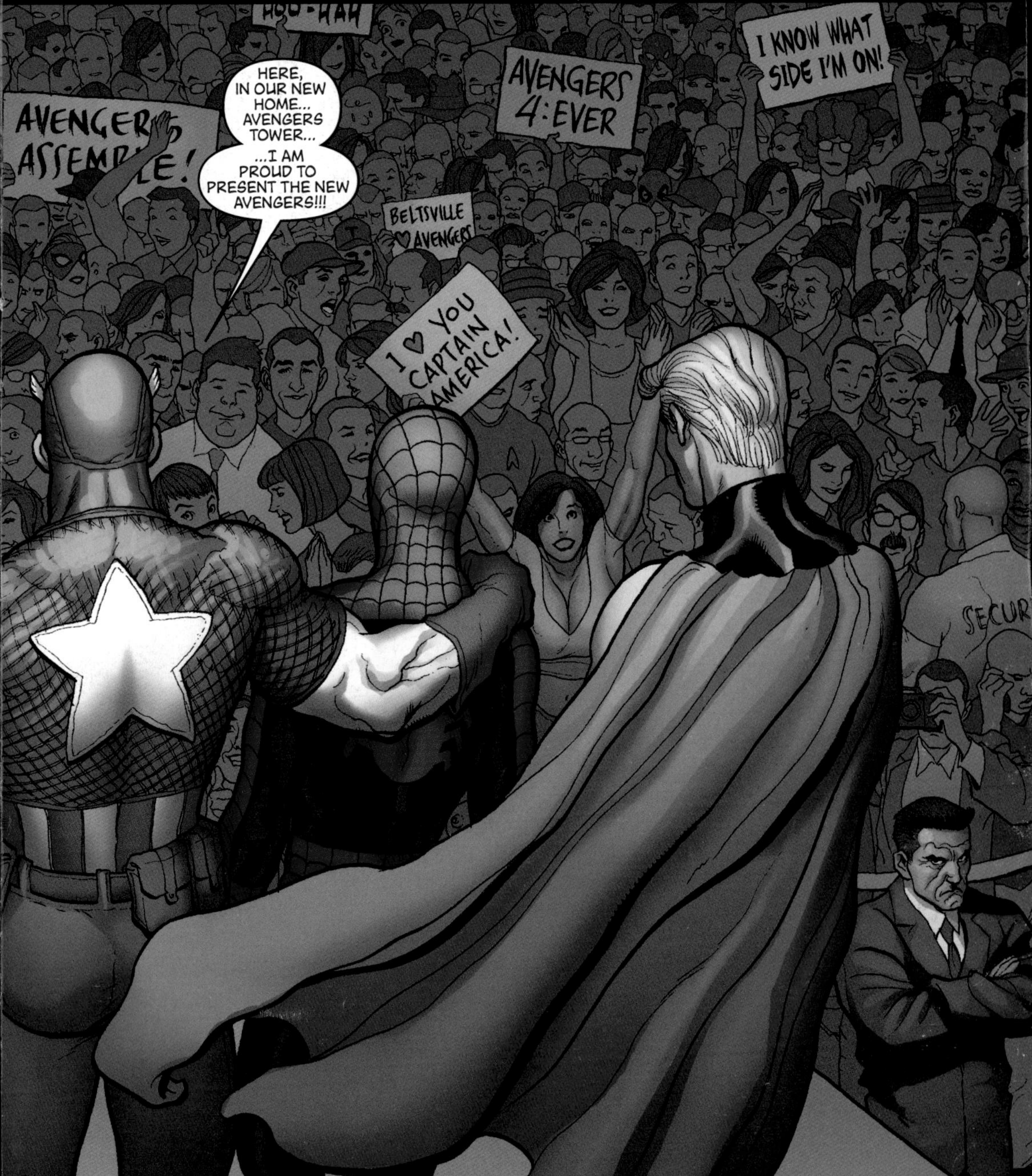
HERE, IN OUR NEW HOME... AVENGERS TOWER...
...I AM PROUD TO PRESENT THE NEW AVENGERS!!!
AVENGERS 4:EVER
I KNOW WHAT SIDE I'M ON!
BELTSVILLE ♥ AVENGERS
I ♥ YOU CAPTAIN AMERICA!
Carol Danvers' Blog
It *was* a great day. As good as it looked on TV.
I'm glad I stayed...
0 comments | leave a comment

Carol Danvers' Blog

...I should have left before it got ugly.

0 comments | leave a comment

NO!

"A WANTED MURDERER, AN ALLEGED EX-MEMBER OF A GLOBAL TERRORIST ORGANIZATION, AND A CONVICTED HEROIN DEALER ARE JUST A FEW OF THE NEW RECRUITS WHO ARE POSED TO BURY THE ONCE GOOD NAME OF THE AVENGERS ONCE AND FOR ALL."

WHO'S A TERRORIST?

ME.

WHO'S A CONVICTED HEROIN--?

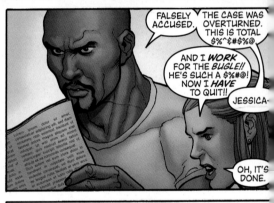

FALSELY ACCUSED.

THE CASE WAS OVERTURNED. THIS IS TOTAL $%^¢#$%@.

AND I *WORK* FOR THE *BUGLE*!! HE'S SUCH A $%#@! NOW I *HAVE* TO QUIT!!

JESSICA--

OH, IT'S DONE.

I CAN'T *BELIEVE* JAMESON WALKED RIGHT INTO MY HOME, LOOKED ME RIGHT IN THE EYE AND TOLD ME WE HAD A DEAL, AND THEN WENT AND *DID* THIS. I CAN'T BELIEVE IT.

SEE... I CAN.

"AND TO IMAGINE THAT THESE MASKED VIGILANTES HAD THE GALL TO INVITE ME...

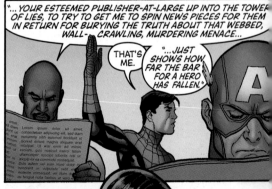

"... YOUR ESTEEMED PUBLISHER-AT-LARGE UP INTO THE TOWER OF LIES, TO TRY TO GET ME TO SPIN NEWS PIECES FOR THEM IN RETURN FOR BURYING THE TRUTH ABOUT THAT WEBBED, WALL-- CRAWLING, MURDERING MENACE...

THAT'S ME.

"...JUST SHOWS HOW FAR THE BAR FOR A HERO HAS FALLEN."

BELTSVILLE

I'M GOING OUT.

I'LL COME WITH.

NAH, I'VE HAD A DAY OF IT. I NEED ALONE TIME.

I'LL DRINK YOU UNDER THE TABLE SOME OTHER TIME.

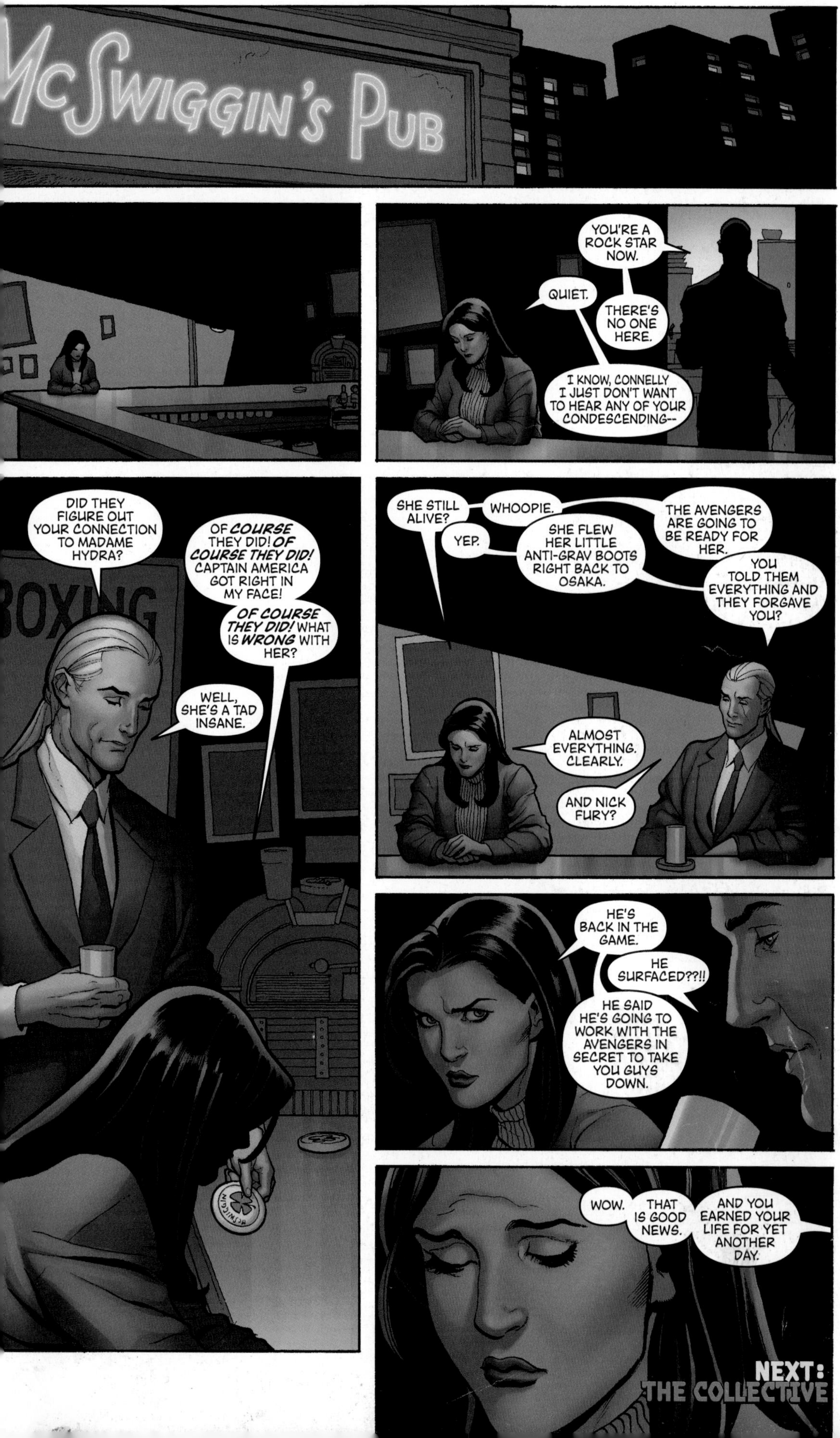
McSWIGGIN'S PUB
YOU'RE A ROCK STAR NOW.
QUIET.
THERE'S NO ONE HERE.
I KNOW, CONNELLY I JUST DON'T WANT TO HEAR ANY OF YOUR CONDESCENDING--
BOXING
DID THEY FIGURE OUT YOUR CONNECTION TO MADAME HYDRA?
OF *COURSE* THEY DID! *OF COURSE THEY DID!* CAPTAIN AMERICA GOT RIGHT IN MY FACE!
OF COURSE THEY DID! WHAT IS *WRONG* WITH HER?
WELL, SHE'S A TAD INSANE.
McSWIGGIN
SHE STILL ALIVE?
YEP.
WHOOPIE.
SHE FLEW HER LITTLE ANTI-GRAV BOOTS RIGHT BACK TO OSAKA.
THE AVENGERS ARE GOING TO BE READY FOR HER.
YOU TOLD THEM EVERYTHING AND THEY FORGAVE YOU?
ALMOST EVERYTHING. CLEARLY.
AND NICK FURY?
HE'S BACK IN THE GAME.
HE SURFACED??!!
HE SAID HE'S GOING TO WORK WITH THE AVENGERS IN SECRET TO TAKE YOU GUYS DOWN.
WOW.
THAT IS GOOD NEWS.
AND YOU EARNED YOUR LIFE FOR YET ANOTHER DAY.
NEXT: THE COLLECTIVE

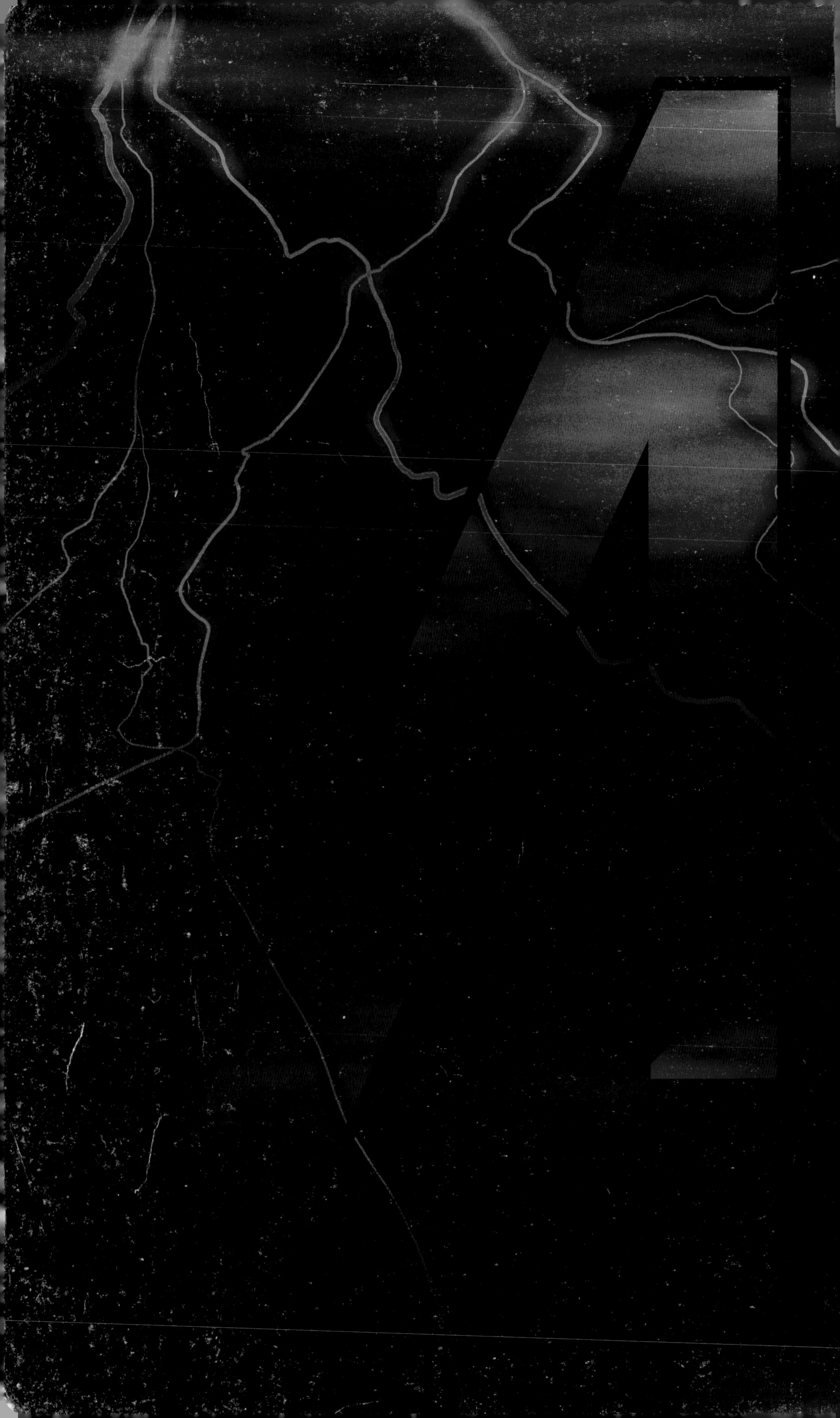